It is said that composer Johannes Sebastian Bach's final words were, "Don't cry for me for I go where music is born." In Ancient Greece, Orpheus, endowed with superhuman musical skills, was able to navigate the underworld and charm even Hades with his songs. Throughout the centuries, music is associated with powers beyond our own, in the realm of the afterlife. Laurie Majka brings together music and the communications of her beloved in her fascinating book *Signs Surround You*. She offers a modern-day account of how a musician, the man she loves, brings her a connection to the Other Side and convinces her that, indeed, our loved ones can communicate with us even after death. Her story carries mythic importance, for it resonates with the tales over the centuries that bring together the makers of music with the mysteries of a world beyond this one.

~Dr. Raymond Moody, bestselling author of Life after Life, co – founder of The University of Heaven theuniversityofheaven.com

Signs Surround You invites you into Laurie Majka's surprising relationship with lead guitarist Mark Abrahamian of the band Starship. The page turner shares a magnetic love story, which draws you into the world of rock and roll, with stunning lyrics and intimate conversations that open the heart and lift the spirit. *Signs Surround You* is a book that celebrates the power of love and its ability to endure even after death. Be inspired by one woman's remarkable account of meeting her Soul Mate and then losing him and what she learned about communication beyond the veil. You will be convinced that, indeed, **love never dies**.

~Lisa Smartt, author of *Words at the Threshold & Cante Bardo*

In *Signs Surround You,* Laurie Majka shares intimate stories about her relationship with her Soul Mate, Mark, both before and after his death. These stories prove that our loved ones can continue to communicate with us after they die, and knowing this, you will be left with a sense of hope that love knows no boundaries, even death.

~Elisa Medhus, MD author of *My Son and the Afterlife* and *My Life After Death, a memoir from Heaven*

Signs Surround You

SIGNS
SURROUND
YOU

Love Never Dies

Signs Surround You

SIGNS SURROUND YOU

Love Never Dies

Laurie Majka

S

Storm Publishing

Copyright © 2020 Laurie Majka

All rights reserved. No part of this book may be reproduced in any form or by any electronic or mechanical means, including information storage and retrieval systems, without permission in writing from the publisher, except by reviewers, who may quote brief passages in a review.

ISBN 978-1-7343932-2-4

Library of Congress Control Number 2019920059

Permissions to reprint Lyrics Copyright Granted by:

Alfred Music; Hal Leonard LLC; Round Hill Carlin, LLC

For full permissions see Resources section

Editing by Marilyn Abrahamian

Cover design and images by Ryan Majka

Proof reading by Lisa Smartt and Chuck Teater

Credits for illustrations and photos by Laurie Majka

Storm Publishing

Cave Creek, Arizona

Printed in the United States of America

Second Edition August 2020

For Permissions: SignsSurroundYou@gmail.com

Visit https://www.LaurieMajka.com

Dedicated to Mark Abrahamian

****

Thank you for being such a powerful force in my life
and for putting me on a path that allowed me to
make changes I never thought possible.
I will love you through eternity
and look forward to seeing you again on
the Other Side...

Table of Contents

Introduction i

Part One Our Story...1

Chapter 1 White Flag...3

Chapter 2 Hearts 5

Chapter 3 The Heart of the Matter 9

Chapter 4 Meet You All the Way 13

Chapter 5 Miracles 23

Chapter 6 Guitar Man 35

Chapter 7 Help Me 41

Chapter 8 Fool If You Think It's Over 51

Chapter 9 I've Been Searchin' So Long....................... 61

Chapter 10 Seasons Change..69

Chapter 11 The Voice... 75

Chapter 12 Right Back Where We Started From 83

Chapter 13 Lessons in Love 87

Chapter 14 If You Leave Me Now 91

Chapter 15 Shattered Dreams.....................................93

Chapter 16 Should've Known Better............................99

Chapter 17 Harden My Heart...................................... 103

Chapter 18 Feelin' Stronger Every Day 107

Chapter 19 Obsession...113

Chapter 20 It's My Life 119

Chapter 21 I Wanna Go Back 129

Chapter 22 Always 133

Chapter 23 You're Still Here.. 135

Chapter 24 Fire and Rain... 139

Chapter 25 Woman in Love 143

Part Two Signs Surround You 147

Introduction 149

Chapter 1 My Musical Signs 151

Chapter 2 Manipulating Electronics 167

Chapter 3 Signs Designed to Reach You With a Message 171

Chapter 4 Facilitated by the Other Side 173

Chapter 5 Dreams With New Information.............................179

Chapter 6 Energy Healing 187

Chapter 7 Mark's Point of View from the Other Side 193

Chapter 8 Receiving Information Intuitively.............................203

Chapter 9 Animals and Insects as Messengers.................................. 205

Chapter 10 Feathers... 211

Chapter 11 Multiple Signs Woven Together............................215

Chapter 12 Signs I Received While Writing This Book 231

Chapter 13 The Story of This Book....................................... 239

A New Beginning... 243

Appendix 251

Resources 259

Acknowledgments.. 263

About the Author 266

Introduction

This is a book about signs – spiritual signs. Signs from loved ones who have passed on to "the Other Side." I have written it in two parts. Part one is the story of Mark and me – "Our Story" – the WHY behind the signs: why he would want to reach out to me from beyond, why some of the signs were so significant to me, and why I was able to connect with them. Part two was compiled from the notes I wrote about signs I was receiving over the two-year period after Mark's death. I have also included the more significant signs that happened while writing this book, although there were many more than I have shared here.

When I started getting these amazing signs, I didn't want to forget them. I bought a special notebook, so I could immediately write them down and not lose any of the details. I had no other intention than to document them for myself. On the two-year anniversary of Mark's death, I wrote about the sign he had sent me that day – only to discover I had reached the end of my notebook. It was as if it were planned that way all along – an end to my two-year journey.

It wasn't until I had a visitation that everything was set in motion to write this book: I had a dream where Mark said to me, "I'm most proud of *Our Story*." That very afternoon a chapter "wrote itself" in my mind and I felt compelled to capture it on paper. Then a steady flow began to stream out, collecting in sentences, paragraphs, and chapters – I never felt like I was writing it by myself. I have a unique style of writing I developed over time through my blog and Daily Soul Whispers. I use ellipses, dashes, and capital letters in non-traditional ways intentionally and I have carried my personal writing style into this book.

Mark and I intensely connected through music. He was a very accomplished musician and I have had a life-long love affair with songs, their lyrics and meanings. As a result, this book is heavily imbued with music. Each chapter is named for a song that expresses the mood of what was happening during that time. I have provided a Spotify link to for you

Signs Surround You

to connect with the songs representing each chapter. Spotify is a streaming audio platform that allows you access to millions of songs. There is a free version. I am choosing this service because the song writers receive a royalty when music is accessed on this site. I had to pay a copyright fee for every song lyrics that appear in this book and I don't want to violate that agreement by sending you to a place that doesn't compensate the artists.

I designed this book to be accompanied by the music, kind of like a sound track to this book. You may choose to listen to the song first, then read the chapter, or absorb the chapter then reflect on it while listening to the song. Or my favorite way, to softly play the song as a background enhancement *while* reading the chapter; I turn the repeat song feature on so the song plays in a loop. You can use this link to access: The Signs Surround You – Spotify playlist:

https://open.spotify.com/playlist/OCAEYQ3p2Et2zliyS4s1nt?si=8u7CEBjTRhWFSEHcRKLppw

Time clouds one's memory, and I would have expected my recollection of details to not be particularly accurate. Fortunately, I had saved much of the correspondence between Mark and me, allowing me to check and cross-reference many details. I was always surprised with my level of accuracy – some things that were said I even remembered verbatim.

The signs have been very healing for me and for others connected to Mark. Some of the signs led to bigger things, like my paintings and the Daily Soul Whispers I send out by email, as a feature of my blog *Soul Heart Art* – inspired thoughts which now reach hundreds of thousands of people a month.

Maybe you are reading this book because you are curious about signs: Do they exist and how do we know for sure if they are *really* signs? Or maybe you have already explored this concept and you just want, need, or are seeking more. Maybe you have suffered a loss and are looking for a way to connect with your loved one, but you don't know where to start.

Signs surround me, and signs surround you. They are different for everyone. What resonates with me won't necessarily resonate with you, but you can use this book as a confirmation that signs are *very* real and are designed to get your attention. You may notice that certain signs are

Signs Surround You

common and occur for many people – such as butterflies, dragonflies, feathers, pennies, dimes, music, manipulation of energy sources, and dreams. Other signs may be very specific to you, the way beaver sightings are for me – who else sees beavers everywhere?

Our passed-away loved ones never leave us! They are at peace and they want to remain connected to us. If you have sent them thoughts, they have heard them; if you have sent them prayers, they have received them; if you have sent them love, they have felt it. Love never dies: we are all made of energy, which can neither be created nor destroyed. I hope this book not only brings you comfort in knowing that you are not alone, but also serves as a step towards being able to prove it to yourself...xo Laurie

Signs Surround You

Part One

Our Story

Signs Surround You

Signs Surround You

Chapter 1

White Flag

~song by Dido

https://open.spotify.com/track/3adnLFXKO5rC1IhUNSeg3N?si=QYk7zWxhSjKKnOlaJH_Bkw

The flames of love still burned just as brightly as they had seven years before when I first met him. And in that time, not a single day had passed where I didn't think of him. Which was crazy! Crazy, because today was the second anniversary of his death, a day that I dreaded because it put a huge spotlight on the loss – the loss whose pain still ebbed and flowed with the days.

When I first lost him, I remember thinking how quickly time passes and before I'd know it, I would be not marking days or months but marking years. And I wondered if the pain would always be this raw – this close to the surface.

Today surprised me, as I sat in my overstuffed, velvety blue chair, looking at pictures and memories. I thumbed through my blue accordion file folder overflowing with pages and pages of our email correspondence, occasionally picking one page at random and reliving the memory of those times. I stared at the photo he had taken of himself with his new hair cut as he sat in his vintage El Camino; his eyes looked like they had white stars shining from them, and it felt like he was staring back at me. Then it occurred to me that not only was his death the worst thing that had ever happened to me, but in a sense it was also the best thing that had ever happened to me. Life has a way of doing that – taking you all the way down to the deepest abyss, only to shove you back up to the surface, gasping for more. More love – more life – more self-discovery...

Signs Surround You

Signs Surround You

Chapter 2

Hearts

"Do you ever think of me

And how we loved one another?"

~song by *Marty Balin*

https://open.spotify.com/track/150LOyOSOISsZ9IcwPf6iT?si=9doVBlrWQ-ihHi4sHAqndA

The month leading up to his death had been fairly eventful and full of thoughts about him – mostly because the five-year anniversary of our meeting each other was quickly approaching. It was now August 2012, three full years since we had even seen each other. Two years since that hateful day of text messages, where he texted me out of the blue:

~~"I'm happy, healthy and in love. Be good." ~~

And I responded back:

~~"I am really happy for u Mark!! I saw posts alluding to u being in love. Jason and I got back together a month ago...he made huge changes over the last two years n so did I. I am so in love with him now, and for the first time I feel like I have everything I always wanted...we r renewing our vows Labor Day on a beach on Lake Superior – he never signed divorce papers that I filed in Feb 09. I could not have all I do now unless I had left him completely. In many ways u were my first real spiritual love. It all works out. Live in your truth." ~~

Like the infamous "woman scorned," I said it to kick him right back – right in the stomach, where his words had kicked me. Because that's how I felt when he told me he was IN LOVE. He could've said it any other way, but he was all about the words and he always chose them wisely. It was done on purpose – said that way because, this particular

Signs Surround You

day, he was in town and he wanted to make sure I was NOT going to come and see him. Mission accomplished!

So how did I respond? I said the one thing I knew I could say that would shove my situation right in his face. Jason and I had been together for 20 years when Mark came into my life. Mark had been the catalyst that brought my marriage to its knees. Now Jason and I were getting back together, and this was the first that Mark was hearing of it. Oh, he pretended it was great news:

~*"That is great news about you and your lifelong love. It all works out. Live in your truth!"*~

But I knew it took him by surprise, probably even took his breath away. I think it had been his fear all along – that if he rearranged his life around me, I might still go back to Jason at some point. It was an amusing thought, because in my mind there was never a choice between Jason and Mark – they really couldn't be compared. They were in two different categories and might as well have been from two different planets. The correspondence between Mark and me had already ruptured, but this was to be the last time Mark and I would *ever* correspond...

About two days before the five-year anniversary date of our meeting – August 12, 2012 – I had decided that on the anniversary I would send him an email message. I no longer had any idea of his situation – if he was still with someone, or not with someone. But that didn't matter. I had some things I had been stewing about for a long time – thoughts and realizations about impressions I knew Mark had of certain situations. These thoughts were still swirling around in my head, never leaving me alone, begging me to resolve them and put them to rest.

I wanted to resolve them – *needed* to resolve them – but I was having second thoughts about sending an email. It was the fear talking, the fear that I would pour my heart out and Mark would never respond. And the fear that he *would* respond – and how that might open up a crack that had since healed in my heart, opening me up to him once again. That was the risk.

After weighing the options, all the pros and cons, trying to decide what to do – I decided I would create the email first, *then* decide what to do. I spent several hours that Sunday morning composing it – writing,

Signs Surround You

rewriting, making it say exactly what I wanted it to say in the *way* I wanted to say it – hoping that my carefully crafted words would, at the very least, elicit a response from him. In addition to the wrongs I was trying to set right, I also shared some of my deep, intimate thoughts about how I had never stopped thinking about him since the day we met.

The email said a lot – it probably said too much. And it had all been said before in some other place and time. But this was MY heart. It was MY truth – and I felt compelled to create it. I also included a song I wanted him to listen to. The song was *"Hearts"* by *Marty Balin*. It was a good song, one that said everything I wished I could've said to him in person. Ironically, it was a song composed by the same man whose song "*Miracles*" had started this whole crazy thing five years earlier. Funny how fate can make a full circle around you...

After I finally finished the email and had read it and reread it a dozen times, I still wasn't ready to click the "send" button. I decided to reach out to the one person who probably understood me best – my "twin sister," Kelly. She's not a twin in the ordinary sense. We don't even look that much alike, although we both have blue eyes. We don't have the same parents – and that makes us not even sisters. But we called ourselves "twins separated at birth." We literally felt that we were each one-half of the same person. Kelly knew me so well, knew what made me tick. And most importantly at the time – she knew all about Mark.

We met in the parking lot at the carnival where we were to pick up our kids. Sitting there in my car, we discussed the email – breaking it down, dissecting and analyzing every word of it. I even played her the song "Hearts." It's kind of awkward "showing" a song to someone. The song always seems to last ten times longer than when you listen to it by yourself. And you wonder if the person is really catching all the lines of the lyrics, pulling the story together.

It didn't matter. All Kelly had to hear was the first line: *"...I just called to say how lost I feel without you"* – and she said, "No way! You can't send that!" I don't even know if she bothered listening to another word – even though I insisted on playing the song in its entirety.

Kelly was not exactly thrilled with me. She warned that this had the potential to "start things" again. And she was right – there was ALWAYS that risk. She actually talked me out of it, putting even more

Signs Surround You

fear in me than I already had. I really did love Jason and didn't want to screw things up. We hadn't been back together very long, and it was going rather smoothly. Kelly's advice to me was to call Mark, talk to him live and say all the things I wanted to say. But she knew I would be more moderate in a phone conversation than I had been in the email, and a phone call would not leave a paper trail that Jason might discover and get the wrong idea.

A phone call...?? THAT sounded impossible to me! My immediate reaction was "No fucking way am I calling him!" What if he didn't answer? What if he *did* answer? What if he wouldn't take my call – or if I had to leave a message and he never called back? What if, what if, what if...I didn't think my ego was strong enough to handle that kind of rejection. Nope, I couldn't do it. So, I didn't. I didn't send it. Instead, I decided I needed a second opinion.

Signs Surround You

Chapter 3

The Heart of the Matter

~song by Don Henley

https://open.spotify.com/track/7jZ4UZAmg006Qx3rVuF7Jl?si=GF5p7o9lTRabpLmYlf1-pg

I had been into mediums for a long time. I love the remarkable perspective that someone has who can communicate with deceased loved ones on the Other Side. It's like they have a leg up on the world.

I went to the website of a respected medium, Allison DuBois, who I knew was going to be almost impossible to get an appointment with. I looked at her reference page, which I had never done before, and noted that her cousin was listed. Apparently, he had inherited the same ability – the ability to speak with the dead. They were from the same family, the same lineage, and maybe he would be as good as she was. I assumed he would be more accessible and thought it a sign that his name too was Mark.

Intuitively, I knew that if I contacted him and gave him a day that was open for me later in the week, it would "work out." Within an hour after I sent him an email, I had a response and an appointment for two days later. I had been able to do that for a long time – to see ahead how a situation would play out. I should have been used to it, but it still always surprised me when I watched it play out.

I was excited for the reading. I needed answers and I was going to get my answers. The day of the reading I had a visit scheduled with Dawn, one of my best friends and a true Soul Sister. We met for lunch near the hospital where her dad was staying.

As I knew I wouldn't make it home in time for the medium's call, I needed to find a quiet place to sit and take the call in my car. As

Signs Surround You

synchronicity would have it, the location was two blocks away from the very place where I had last seen Mark in person...

Two years earlier...

I pulled my car into the parking lot across the street from the stage. My view was partially obscured by some bushes, but that was a good thing – I didn't want Mark to see me anyway. What would he think?

I knew from snippets that I had seen on Facebook and from our text correspondence earlier that day that he was in a new relationship – that he was "in love." In any case, Jason and I had gotten back together after a two-year separation, and I really wanted my family back. Besides, I drove right by this very spot several days a week – so it wasn't like I had *really* gone out of my way to be here today.

They were setting up for a *Starship* show that was to take place later that night in the library's parking lot. The band consisted of THE Mickey Thomas, the voice behind the songs "*Jane*," "*We Built This City*," and "*Sara*," to name a few. Mickey was a class act with a great voice, and still going strong doing 170+ shows a year at the age of 60-something. Then there was Daryl Verdusco, the drummer – with Mickey for 20+ years and a standard in the show. Stephanie Calvert was the singer, the new voice of Grace Slick, who had long since stopped performing with the band. Jeff Adams was the bassist, and Phil Bennett on keyboards – both had been with the band for over a decade. Phil was Mark's brother's grade-school friend and Phil brought Mark in, recommending him when the vacancy was there.

Then there was Mark. Mark Abrahamian, lead guitarist. From my vantage point, I could clearly see him. He always played on the left side of the stage and my car was positioned perfectly. To *my* eyes, he was all I ever saw.

Mark was definitely "doing his thing." The guitar was the *true* love of his life – it was never me. He once said to me, "Could you be with someone who lives, eats and breathes guitar? "I didn't answer his question but retorted, "Could you be with someone who lives, eats and breathes their kids?" There really was no question about that for me. But the "living with" – the everyday-life part

Signs Surround You

– was always in question. I was never sure if our lifestyles would jive with each other.

Today, however, I wasn't thinking about any of those things. I was intently watching. I loved watching him play. I had all the windows rolled down so I could easily hear the music. They were on their first song of the sound check, and I couldn't believe my luck in arriving right as they were taking the stage. But with Mark and me, there truly was no "luck" – just a long string of faith and "coincidences" and meant-to-be happenings that always seemed to transcend space and time and this world.

The lines from the song surged through the air. It wasn't as loud as being near the stage, but I could still feel the music – and still feel *him*. I always felt him. We always felt each other. Sometimes *that* was the problem – feeling each other even when one was trying to forget the other.

I stayed for the three partial songs. When I saw him step off the stage, I took the cue and started to drive away – driving right past him, hoping both that he would see me and not see me. It was the last time I would see him. The last time...

So there I was, two years later, wanting to create the proper energy for my phone reading with the medium. I positioned my car in the very spot where the stage had once been. Energy is a real thing and time is an illusion, so if there is no time and everything is happening "now," as mystics claim, then Mark's energy was still there. Right? Right! At least it couldn't hurt anything. Anyway, no worries – I was to talk to the talented "Mark the Medium." In presenting his evidential information, he had led me to believe he possessed some serious skills.

After Mark the Medium shared his insights, I asked him a few questions about Mark. I explained about the anniversary date that had just passed and about wanting – but being afraid – to send him the message I had so carefully crafted. Mark the Medium said that he "saw" me taking the note and burning it. Unbelievable! Just that morning on my walk I had the crazy thought of burning my email. It was a sign from the Universe, to be sure. When I shared that thought with Mark the Medium, he said, "The Universe is confirming your answer."

Signs Surround You

It was cemented at that very moment – the decision NOT to send the anniversary email to Mark. And it was to be a decision I would look back on again and again and again...

Chapter 4

Meet You All the Way

"Not quite a year since she went away

Rosanna, yeah

Now she's gone and I have to say…"

~song "Rosanna" by Toto

https://open.spotify.com/track/37BTh5gO5cxBlRYMbw8g2T?si=AJ91MZw_RECN3mtgGi7ewA

It had been a while since I last saw him, and that's how I wanted to remember him. Not from the drive-by – that was too impersonal – but from our last in-person, physical interaction.

I had finally moved out of my life with Jason and into a life of my own making. A few months prior to that, I had bought a foreclosure house and gutted it to its core, then in six weeks rebuilt it and moved in – the project mirrored my life. It was a *labor* of love and, fittingly, it was now Labor Day weekend, 2009. My parents, Chuck and Ivy, came to visit and stay for the weekend – the ribbon-cutting weekend. The grand reopening of my new life.

I was surprised when Mark called me. We had been on and off for two years and recently had settled into a nice friendship. Mark had once declared, "Can't we be friends who think each other is fucking HOT!" Well, yes and no. We could be friends – at a distance. But it was always more than friends in our hearts.

He called me on Saturday morning. I was pleased to hear his voice and surprised to hear that he was coming to town. The band travelled constantly, and I had long since stopped following and tracking Mark's whereabouts. Mostly, I didn't want to know where he was. There was a

Signs Surround You

time when I always knew, always wanted to know. But later, there were times when I knew he was close and knew he didn't want to see me. It was better not to know – the draw was too strong. If I knew, I would want to see him, so I shut the door to knowing. I could be strong – it was the stubborn Taurus in me – and once I made up my mind, I had a will of steel. That's why I always took a long time deciding – knowing that if I chose, I wouldn't go back.

But this time, Mark called *me*. He wanted me to know he was going to be in town and that he was to perform the next day, and he asked me to come to the show. It was going to be in my old stomping grounds, in the town where I once lived - and walking distance from my friend Dawn's house. And it was in the very park where my wedding photos had been taken – that irony was not lost on me.

The problem was my dad. AND the fact that I had been dating someone else for six months – someone I had grown to care for. Someone that Jason (my soon-to-be ex, if he would ever sign the divorce papers) insisted I not see until I moved out of our house into my own house. Just the day before, I had finally been able to see Mark T. – the boyfriend – for the first time since making that promise. Mark T... "Mark #2." We met after Mark and I had ended things.

So things were once again complicated. In my relationship with Mark, things were always complicated. Mark knew about Mark T. – it was no secret, nothing to hide. I had always been an open book with Mark. That was part of the problem – he always knew everything, which makes it hard to forget everything. But there he was, asking me to go to his show. I wanted to go...really, I did...

The boyfriend wasn't even the immediate problem – it was my dad. Actually, Dad was partly responsible, for fueling my love of music in the first place. But that wasn't the problem either: Dad suffers from progressive muscle atrophy – a slow-progressing form of Lou Gehrig's disease that affected his lower body and made walking difficult. He was too proud to use a cane and too proud to say he couldn't do something. But I knew this would be a lot for him. Even if we could park close to the venue, it might prove too much. I told Mark we would talk it over and I would let him know.

Signs Surround You

Two hours later he called *me* back. That was typical Mark – if he decided he wanted something, he would keep at me, knowing it wasn't ever very hard to wear me down. But this time, I wasn't only considering myself. Mark had never met my parents, never spent any time with my dad, and really couldn't understand how walking like that would affect him for days after.

Dad had already given up so many things he loved. He had been a racing cyclist, then he cut back to riding a lot, then infrequently, and now he was a spectator at best. He had also given up flying. Prior to that, he had been building his own airplane from a kit but sold the partially built kit in favor of a fully built airplane so he could more quickly get back in the air. But the muscle atrophy had taken its toll there too and no longer allowed him to climb up and down, in and out of the plane. He was grounded now – literally. Walking any distance was the next thing to go, and I knew we were getting close to that. It was almost too much to ask.

I knew Dad would *want* to go. He loved live music, he loved *Starship* – he loved *me,* and knew I didn't often see Mark. I didn't let him decide; I decided for us all – for Dad and Mom and me and Mark. I told Mark, "No." He didn't like the answer but said he understood. My parents had driven eight hours to come visit me and leaving them behind was out of the question, and he knew it – didn't even suggest it.

But now, three hours later, he was calling me *again* – this time pulling out all the stops by telling me *Starship* was playing with *Toto.* Oh, my God – I had been dying to see him play with *Toto* for years! He really knew how to get to me. I think he wanted to surprise me with the *Toto* thing but realized my attendance was looking slimmer, so he blurted it out and then was silent – just like the perfect salesman, which wasn't even like him.

In the end, I decided my dad was a big boy and could decide for himself. After all, he loved the band *Toto* too. "*Rosanna,*" "*Hold the Line,*" "*Africa*" – visions of music danced in his head. It didn't take long for us to formulate a plan. We would drop Dad off as close as possible and Mom would walk him to the concert area nice and slow. I would park at Dawn's house and walk there with her. She would already have friends and family parked on a big tarp ready to greet my parents. Concert etiquette lets people stake their claim on a spot by setting up a large tarp in advance of

Signs Surround You

a concert. That way you can get a great spot without having to be there hours in advance. So it was all set up – nice and neat.

I called Mark back to tell him. He was pretty excited at the news, but no doubt not surprised. I don't think he ever doubted that he could convince me to go – with the added bonus of my parents being there. I was really excited to have them see Mark play live. He was an accomplished guitarist and they had been hearing me hype him for years. I had seen Mark play many times over the past few years, but this show would be special. Two for one – twice: *Starship* **and** *Toto*, my mom **and** dad. I couldn't wait!

The only other thing to do was invite Mark T. How could I not? Mark T. had planned on getting together with my parents again anyway, before they went back to Kansas. How perfect. Kill two birds with one stone – fit in my boyfriend and see the love of my life, all in one event. To top it all off, my friend Dawn and her husband Dale were the ones who had set Mark T. and me up on our first (blind) date. It was Dawn's attempt to help me get over Mark – kind of a rebound date, a nice transition out of my old life with Jason and a bandage over my time with Mark. And surprisingly, it turned into a relationship.

The evening would turn out to be the biggest "What if?" of my entire relationship with Mark. But fate had sealed the deal – Mark T. was invited. And in one way, that turned out to be a blessing because he took care of my parents at the needed time.

I hadn't anticipated how crowded the show was going to be. It was looking impossible to even find a place to stop and drop my parents off. They hadn't been in this park since my wedding day, 18 years earlier, but they were familiar with the area, even though it had been years since we all lived there.

My stress level was high. I was feeling bad, knowing how far my dad was going to have to walk – and also feeling bad that I had invited Mark T. What was I thinking? Mark T. knew all about Mark. "Stand in your truth" ...sometimes I had a way of being too truthful. Maybe I was trying to make up for lost time in the relationship I had had with Jason – because with him, I totally lacked in standing in my truth. I had been a *"Don't rock the boat'"* kind of gal. A *"Don't say what you really think or feel because that will change things'"* person. Even a *"Don't talk to your partner – save those truths for your friends"* kind of a girl.

Signs Surround You

But that girl was gone! I was an open book now, once saying to Mark T., "I feel like I have three people in my heart." He said, "Three?" I said, "Yes – you, Jason and Mark." He was taken aback by the last one. Sure, he knew about Mark, the catalyst, the very reason I was even here with him now. But he was still surprised – like the light had suddenly turned on: Ohhhhhh, wow – didn't figure on that. He thought he was only working on me overcoming Jason, the soon-to-be ex. But adding Mark to the mix I'm sure was a bit intimidating.

To everyone's relief and delight, Dad made it and we all settled onto the tarp area. This was a big show – I would guess over 5,000 people, maybe 10,000. So hard to tell. This was the only *Starship* show I had ever attended where I didn't (1) see Mark before the show started and (2) sit in practically the front row. This time, I was lucky to even get to the show before it started!

We were gathered into a group of about 15 people on that hot summer night. Dawn had staked her claim to the spot with her tarp hours earlier. Amazing to think that until yesterday I didn't even know Mark and *Starship* were playing here. Dawn did – she had been my partner in crime all along, attending all but the first two *Starship* concerts in person with me. She had been my friend, my confidante, my shoulder to cry on. And there had been plenty to cry about, with Mark over the past two years.

But there would be no tears today. Today I was happy – elated, really. I loved seeing Mark in his element. And being able to share the show with my parents was a special treat all by itself. Dawn and her parents and a splattering of friends, along with me, my parents and Mark T., made the group of us a cozy bunch.

The show started in normal *Starship* fashion. It had been the same lineup for as long as I had been going. The biggest difference was that I was a mile away from the stage, far enough back that it was easier to watch the show on the giant monitor than to watch the stage with my naked eyes.

Speaking of "naked" – I was feeling pretty exposed with Mark T. being there. Watching Mark on stage during a live concert, I was never able to contain any of my feelings. I cheered and clapped and whistled so loudly I made myself and everyone around me deaf, and tonight was no exception.

Signs Surround You

The band called a show like this a "singer's show." They weren't playing with the whole *Toto* band, just one of the singers – Bobby Kimball. The show would always start with *Starship* opening with *"Laying It on the Line"* followed by *"No Way Out," "Jane," "Sara," "Nothin's Gonna Stop Us Now," "Stranger", "Set the Night to Music," "White Rabbit,"* and *"Miracles."* Then they would introduce Bobby Kimball and he would join the band to sing a few *Toto* hits, starting with *"Africa."* I remember that when I first met Mark, he had about a week to learn all five songs for their first *"Starship* and Friends" show with Bobby Kimball – that's how long I had wanted to hear Mark play with *Toto*.

The song *"Rosanna"* started in the usual way. But at the end of the song, with Mark wailing on the guitar and the drummer then doing a "big finish" – Mark suddenly stepped forward again and began this incredible two-minute guitar solo. You could see that the band was just as surprised as the audience that this was happening. My jaw dropped. I had seen Mark play at many shows, but he never did the solo thing. A couple of others in the band took a solo during every show. Daryl, the drummer, did a cool drum solo. The keyboardist, Phil, did a cool solo too – and it was long enough that the rest of the band would leave the stage. Mark would even go smoke a cigarette and return when it ended.

But Mark never did a solo, at least not in any of the shows I had ever seen. He was a pretty modest guy. Confidently modest. He didn't feel the need to show off his skills in every show – it wasn't his style. What happened that night took me by surprise – but a moment after he began playing, I knew why he had insisted I come to THIS show. He had to have planned it out for a while!

(See: https://www.youtube.com/watch?v=-TOKmDXvzpE Solo begins at 6:40 and continues to 8:20.)

Mark was a professional guitar player and you would think that since he spent so many days on the road playing, he wouldn't want to play in his off time. But the guitar was his passion. It was as if there weren't enough hours in the day for him to play. When he was home, he was either eating, sleeping, building amps, helping people on forums – or playing around with his guitar. Off the road, Mark was a real homebody. Most of his "social life" consisted of the internet forums he contributed to, from discussions about music and amps to fixing cars.

Signs Surround You

But today, he was not Mark the homebody. He was Mark Abrahamian the Rock Star. Or, as he called it, "Rockstah." To me, he was a guitar god, and I was in awe of his skills. He truly had magic fingers.

After an astounding two minutes, the solo was finished – followed by an eruption of appreciation from the crowd. I don't think I ever whistled as hard in my life. I knew it had all been for me, and so did the rest of my group. They whispered it in waves during the whole performance, including Mark T., who – to his credit – didn't seem one bit jealous.

The show ended in its usual fashion with an encore of *"We Built This City"*...

"Who rides the wrecking ball into our guitars?" Not tonight!

As the show ended, I of course knew I was going to go find Mark...but now that felt weird. My mom would have wanted to go, and if the walk hadn't been so far I would've taken both my parents to meet Mark. But I didn't want to take Mark T. – that would've been way too awkward. And after that awesome solo, I wouldn't have thrown a surprise like that on Mark.

If I took my parents, it was going to be both of them or neither. But how could I take my mom with me...? I knew I would want to kiss Mark – that I *would* kiss him. My parents are pretty progressive and there's only a 20-year age difference between us. But even though my mom knew how I had felt about Mark– *still* felt about Mark – I wouldn't have wanted her to see me kiss him, knowing my boyfriend was also there. That settled it – I was going alone.

Right about then the fireworks started. I love fireworks and stayed to watch them with my parents and friends – a missed opportunity to kiss Mark under the fireworks. But I didn't kiss Mark T. under the fireworks...

As soon as it ended, Mark T. worked with my friends Dawn and Dale to take my parents, mainly my dad, back to the drop spot, and Mom would drive him to Dawn's house. Dad was just strong enough to go the distance. Knowing he was in good hands, I made a mad dash to find Mark.

Mark often didn't bring his phone to the shows but left it at the hotel room, and this was one such time. He never got my texts telling him I had arrived, or that I was watching the fireworks with my group. When

Signs Surround You

I finally reached him, he was pacing the backstage area scanning the crowd for me. Since he hadn't gotten any of the texts, he was surprised that I was arriving alone, but so happy to see me. A few days later, he told me that he had actually practiced meeting my dad in the mirror. I explained to him that Dad wouldn't have been able to walk all the way to meet him and then make it back to my friend's house. I know now Mark didn't really understand that...

We didn't have much time together, maybe five minutes before the band informed him that the one and only vehicle would be leaving in a few minutes for the hotel. Normally, when I attended a show I would grab Mark and haul him to my car where we would drive to his hotel and spend hours talking and making out. But this time I couldn't offer to take Mark with me. We kissed each other for the last few precious minutes together, before the band started honking and making their way towards the exit. Every part of me wanted to whisk Mark away, to take him to Dawn and Dale's beautiful house half a mile away – to meet Dawn and Dale, who had loyally attended numerous concerts with me and had never formally met Mark. And Mark would have been able to lay his rehearsed introduction on my dad!

One thing, and one thing only, stopped me – Mark T. It had been a rash decision to invite him to the concert. In hindsight – what a mistake. It had been awkward for Mark T. to see my reactions to Mark playing with the band, and awkward for him to see the one who was still in my heart play a two-minute guitar solo clearly meant for me. That one decision would haunt me for a couple years. I contemplated what would have happened if Mark T. had never gone to the show: I know Mark would then have gone with me to Dawn and Dale's house. I know I would also have taken him to see my refurbished foreclosure house, there in its beautiful ribbon-cutting-ceremony glory.

I was so proud of that house! I had put so much work into it. A lot of the demolition and renovation on it was done with my own two hands. I was the general contractor on the job and decided on every detail – from the design, to the roof shingles, to the outlet covers. With so many details to manage, it was phenomenal how it all came together – and it was the one thing I most wanted Mark to see. He never saw it. At least not while he was on this Earth plane. And I never did hear all the details around the surprise guitar solo – and why Mark decided to do it. He and I never got

Signs Surround You

a chance to discuss it. But I still have all the original text messages he sent me that night on my old phone. I now use that phone as my alarm clock.

It carries the gift of Mark's words safely locked inside, for me to revisit and relive:

~~Sunday September 6, 2009 11:25pm: *I'm so glad I got to see you – u r beautiful – I love you* ~~

~~Monday September 7, 2009 7:14am: *Ya know, in case I didn't indicate it, I'm most glad that u got to hear me play my guitar solo. U were in my thoughts during every single note of it ;)* ~~

~~Monday September 7, 2009 7:18am: *As far as the show goes, that is! More glad I got to see and talk with you, of course...and the kiss :-D* ~~

~~Monday September 7, 2009 11:21am: *U r special. I played it all for you. :) I wish u were closer to the stage if u weren't...don't even know where u were!* ~~

Those words meant everything. How special it was for me to have someone make such a gesture. One short month later, Mark would meet a woman he would later move in with and become engaged to...

It's funny how time gives us perspective, like it did four years later. I was in Japan on business and in my hotel room – listening to music, thinking about Mark, wondering if he travels with me now that he resides on the Other Side. I got into the shower and let the music play. "*Rosanna*" came on, and for some reason, even though I had heard the song many times since the guitar-solo concert – I had an epiphany. The words hit me and I knew: "*...Meet you all the way.*" I saw everything with crystal-clear clarity! How could I not have seen it before – it was so obvious to me now!

At the time of concert on the previous Labor Day, Mark and I had been on and off for a while. He wanted me to "figure things out with Jason." A short while later, when he finally pulled away for real, I began "figuring them out." After a series of counseling sessions with Jason, I decided I needed to move on. I found the foreclosure house, bought it and then filed for divorce.

So there I was, on the night of the concert one year later, "totally figured out" as far as the subject of Jason was concerned. I hadn't done it

Signs Surround You

for Mark, although he was the catalyst. I had done it for me. I was now divorcing Jason, had moved out of our house and was living in my own house.

Mark and I still talked enough for him to know all these things. He knew I planned to move out Labor Day weekend and move into my new place. How "coincidental" that Mark's band would play just ten miles from my new house on the very weekend I became *truly* free and clear – except for Mark T. Mark knew about him too, of course – knew that Mark T. and I were dating. Mark T. was a great guy, a great person, and I'm sure that the circumstances clouded my ability to SEE the full picture of what Mark had tried to do with his surprise solo.

There in the shower, four years later, I saw it ALL. The song – the words – the solo – the timing – his wanting to meet my parents. He wanted us BACK! How could I not have seen it! I had already realized, several years before, the damage that not introducing Mark to my parents had done. It had finally dawned on me that by not taking them to meet him, he assumed I didn't *want* to introduce him to them. Several days after the concert, he mentioned the mirror thing – practicing in front of it to meet my dad. I immediately apologized – even though I had not known at the concert that it had been his expectation.

I tried to get Mark to understand how bad off my dad was with his legs. I don't think he ever really understood or believed me, since he had never been around anyone like that. It bothered me later when I thought about the damage that must have been caused by the assumptions he had made. I felt certain that was what made him pull away from me – because there was a definite pullback a couple weeks after the concert. He had gone from "I love you" to no contact. And I was so wrapped up in my own life that I didn't recognize what had happened until about December, when I reached out to him and he politely "blew me off." Time would tell that he had begun dating another woman...

Signs Surround You

Chapter 5

Miracles

"From that very first look in your eyes

I could see you and I had but one heart

Only our bodies were apart"

~song by Jefferson Starship

https://open.spotify.com/track/5dFvprlP5JS7gxeaMhMOWS?si=UigVffmzTOmwJTSTLeaYqQ

To truly understand the significance of my connection with Mark, I have to take you back – back to the beginning, before text messages and sound checks and guitar solos, before parents and foreclosure houses and divorce papers...

August 11, 2007 started out as a sunny summer day, with a giant pink, bouncy, princess castle sitting in my yard. It was the day of my daughter Rachel's ninth birthday party. Normally, we would have been two states away in Iowa for a family reunion. But not this year. I had seen a flyer advertising "Addison Days," our town's annual celebration. The town would be hosting the bands *.38 Special* and *Starship*.

I only owned about 20 CDs at the time, even though I loved music and concerts. I especially loved *Starship* and *.38 Special*, and each band's CDs held a spot in my collection. *Starship* was particularly special. The band had undergone several changes over the years. They got their start in San Francisco in 1965 (the year before Mark was born) as *Jefferson Airplane*, morphing into *Jefferson Starship* and later, as a spin-off, became just plain *"Starship"* – although there was nothing plain about *Starship* in my eyes. I had always loved their song *"Miracles."*

Signs Surround You

One night in my college days, I was driving on a dark two-lane highway in the middle of Iowa, when *"Miracles"* began playing on the radio. I don't know if it was because I was in a romantic relationship at the time or because I was driving under a beautiful dark sky filled with stars, but the song struck me hard. And from that moment on, it was cemented in my Heart and Soul as my all-time favorite song. For twenty years, that song had held its title. And now here they were – the band *Starship* coming to our very town! My cherished hope was to hear them play MY song...

So instead of going to Iowa for a family reunion, we stayed home that weekend and threw my daughter's birthday party. That evening my kids, my mom, a few friends and I went to see the first leg of the Fest's concerts. *Head East* would open followed by *.38 Special.* When we got to the show, my son Ryan took me aside and showed me that he had brought a guitar pick with him. How shrewd of him – he brought it with him in the hopes that he could get a real live guitar player to sign it.

Ryan had mentioned a few times wanting to play the electric guitar – and because I believed that learning to play an instrument was an excellent use of his free time, I agreed to it. We had a guitar store not far from our house, but every time I drove by it was closed. One day I got detained waiting for a delivery, and when I was finally free to leave, I drove by the guitar store and found it open. It was unusual that I even had the time to stop in the store that day, as it was a workday and I had clients to see, but I made the time. Later that night, my husband Jason and I took our son there, and $150 later we walked out with a guitar and a lesson scheduled for later in the week.

Ryan had only been playing the guitar for about a month by the time the concert came around. Now, this wasn't like a regular concert at a venue where you buy a ticket and guards hold you at a distance – but you also couldn't just walk up to the band and get your guitar pick signed! So we went to a stand where they were selling t-shirts for the band and talked to a nice man working the booth. When we explained to him what we wanted, we discovered he was the concert promoter who had set up the whole show! He just happened to be filling in for someone who was on a break.

Signs Surround You

Fifteen minutes later, we were meeting the band *Head East*, who had just performed. The lead guitarist came out and signed my son's guitar pick. Ryan was elated. We visited for a few minutes, thanked him, and he went backstage. While standing there chatting with the concert promoter for a few more minutes, my daughter Rachel announced that it was her "birthday-party day." The next thing we knew we were all standing backstage with backstage passes around our necks. The band *Head East*'s guitarist spotted us and came over with the whole band. On hearing it was my daughter's birthday, the drummer presented her with the set of drumsticks he had used in the show. My kids were really on a roll with getting their minds blown!

We all then settled in to watch *.38 Special* perform. It was a great show, and as Donnie Van Zant, the lead singer, walked offstage, he threw me his sweaty white towel. I guess I was flattered! The promoter then told us to come back tomorrow and bring the backstage passes, so we could use them to see *Starship* backstage. Wow! We all parted ways to a chorus of "See you tomorrow."

Since we would be meeting the band members, I decided to go online and check them out. The band was officially called "*Starship* featuring Mickey Thomas." Mickey had joined *Jefferson Starship* in 1979 as the co-lead singer replacing Marty Balin, the band's original lead singer and originator of the song "*Miracles*." Mickey was a wonderful replacement, penning the song "*Layin' It on the Line*" and singing "*No Way Out*," "*Jane*," "*Sara*," "*Nothin's Gonna Stop Us Now*," "*Count on Me*," "*Somebody to Love*," "*Find Your Way Back*," and "*We Built This City*." Some of those songs were thoroughly ingrained into the memories of my high school years. *Starship* was on the radio constantly during the '80s.

Current band members joined the band starting in the late'90s, with Darryl on drums as the first to join, then Phil on keyboards and Jeff on bass guitar. The newest member of the band, Stephanie, became the female vocalist, stepping into the legacy of former female lead vocalist Grace Slick. Half a dozen years before Stephanie came along, the one I was most interested in joined – Mark Abrahamian on guitar. Ryan would surely be anticipating another signed guitar pick.

Signs Surround You

I gazed at the online photo of Mark. He had a very masculine, exotic look. His face was long and oval with a strong jawline and a prominent Adam's apple. He had expressive, chocolate-brown eyes that were both sexy and confident. His hair, in this younger picture of him, was brown and wavy and long – flowing into a lighter brown and hitting him about mid upper arm. He was 5'8" with a slimmer build. Wearing a black leather vest with nothing underneath, the picture showed him holding his guitar in muscular arms. He had a buff chest, absent of hair, leading down to six-pack abs. I yelled downstairs to the family, "The lead guitarist is HOT."

I read his bio and learned that the song *"Eruption"* by *Van Halen* had prompted Mark to spend his eighth-grade summer locked in his room, learning to play it. Some years later, prior to joining the band, he had been a guitar teacher for several years. When I read that, I thought to myself, "Hmmm...interesting. How cool it would be for Ryan to get a lesson from him."

Now I had the names to match the faces and was ready to meet the band. I asked Jason to go with us to the concert, but he was completely disinterested and also had to be up early the next morning. So it was me, my nine-year-old daughter Rachel and my ten-year-old son Ryan.

We parked on the back streets and prepared to walk into the venue using our backstage passes. But everything was configured differently from the night before and we couldn't find our way in. Just as I was about to give up, a woman who had been backstage with us the night before approached and told us to follow her in the back way.

As we made our way toward the stage, two men sat together taking up the sidewalk. I would later discover that the men were band members Jeff and Mark and that Mark had just said a prayer in his head moments earlier, asking God to "Please send me a beautiful woman." Mark later told me this was just before I walked by. Not recognizing either of the men, in spite of all my internet research, we walked around them and headed toward the side of the stage.

There was almost no one in the backstage area and our concert promoter was nowhere to be found. I felt so out of place. Everything had changed since yesterday. The cordoned-off space between the stage and

Signs Surround You

the crowd was much bigger than it had been the night before and we were much more visible. I saw several people I knew in the crowd throwing us looks of "How did you get back there?"

We had noticed the day before that some people would stand right in front of the stage to watch the show. So shortly after the concert started, the kids followed my lead and we stood in front of the stage. We watched a couple of songs from that fantastic vantage point, until a security guard approached us and said he didn't have us on "Mickey's list." I explained that the concert promoter had given us the passes and that we were to meet the band and have our CD and guitar pick signed. He didn't know the promoter but agreed to let us move back off to the side, where we had been before, to finish watching the show I remember being glad Jason hadn't come, feeling certain that if he had, the security guard wouldn't have let us stay because there would've been too many people. And me being a woman there by myself without a guy may have also been to our advantage.

When the show ended, the security guard escorted us to the place where the band would exit the stage and told us, "Do your business but don't hold up the band too long." So as Mickey came down the stairs, I asked him to sign my CD *Starship's Greatest Hits*, which he cordially did. I then presented Stephanie with fresh-cut flowers from my garden and said hi to everyone – except Mark, who had slipped by us as we were talking to Mickey.

The kids and I stood around awkwardly, not quite knowing if we should wait to see if Mark would come back out of the band area, or if we shouldn't push our luck and should just leave. I decided that we had come this far and asked Jeff if he would go get Mark.

A few minutes later Mark appeared with a beer in his hand and a smile on his face. I introduced myself and the kids and explained that Ryan had just started playing guitar and would like to have his pick signed. Mark did one better and handed Ryan the guitar pick he had used during the show. He then looked at Ryan's pick with a puzzled expression, as if wondering how he was going to sign something so small, and in the end just put his initials on it.

We entered into an informative discussion about guitars and what Ryan could do to help him learn. Mark recommended a tool by *Line 6* that

Signs Surround You

we could find on their website. We continued to talk guitars until someone came over to steal Mark away to meet some other people. When he left, we again stood there awkwardly, not sure what to do. Just as I made the decision that we should leave, Mark reappeared at our side, apologizing for the disruption and wanting to continue the conversation.

As we were ending off, Mark said, "I can tell you have read about me online, but if you have any more questions, you know how to reach me." And with that simple comment the ball was set in motion...

When we got home, the kids excitedly shared their concert adventures with their dad, who had already gone to bed. Ryan just had to turn on the light to show off his guitar pick – that kind of news couldn't be contained until the next day. After the kids left, there in the darkness, I said to my husband, "I'm going to keep in contact with Mark so that next summer when the band comes back to our area, I will see about getting a guitar lesson for Ryan with a real live Rock Star."

That same night Ryan and I formulated a question to ask Mark – a reason to reach out and contact him. Ryan had noticed that Mark's guitar pick had been worn very specifically on both sides with nicks and gouges. We sent the following email:

~~To: Mark Abrahamian

From: Laurie Majka

Tuesday, August 14, 2007, 11:38 p.m.

Subject: Line 6 tip

Hi Mark,

We met you on Sunday at the Addison, Illinois concert. Wow!! The show was really fantastic. By the way, I really like your hair this length.

We checked out the Line 6 website – thanks for the great info! Ryan, my son, was curious about the pick you gave him. All the picks from other guitarists seem to be played on one side – yours seem to be played on both sides. Is it a difference in technique or do they just get flipped during the show? Also, Ryan's guitar instructor has him playing with the tip, but you utilize the entire side of the pick. Can you explain?

Signs Surround You

I hope you enjoy your week off!

Laurie Majka~~

~~To: Laurie Majka

From: Mark Abrahamian

Wednesday, August 15, 2007, 9:43 a.m.

Subject: Re: Line 6 tip

Hi Laurie!

great to meet you! glad you liked the show! and thanks, I like the shorter hair too ;)

so you went and read about the guitar port, did ya? it's a cool tool indeed! I too have noticed how guitar players wear picks differently. as we are all unique in our own ways, picks get worn differently. For me, I do alternate pic, down up down up etc, as well as I tend to think of a brushing or sweeping motion at a 45-degree angle. and you can see it on my pick!

at times I apply more of the pick or less of the pick if I want more of an attack, fatter tone, or if I'm playing fast with the very tip of the pick, so as to not get stuck on the strings, if that makes sense. it would be easy to demonstrate this in person. hope this makes sense in text. we have been working our tails off, so yeah I'm enjoying the 4 1/2 days off. are you going to be at the Homewood show on the 24th? perhaps you have plans. if not I would love to see you there! Hope all is well on your end Laurie and take care. email me anytime!

Mark~~

In the spirit of keeping the volley going, I answered back. I was so curious about his lifestyle. I imagined they all lived on a bus and toured the country together, like one big family. It didn't work that way, I was to learn.

The band performed 150+ shows a year – which is a lot of time "on the road." They were busiest from April to October, the time of year

Signs Surround You

when many towns, like mine, have their spring, summer and fall festivals. *Starship* would play at festivals and concert halls, mostly in the U.S., but they also traveled all over the world. Since our concert had been on August 12, Mark would have been smack dab in the middle of his busiest season.

The crew got along with each other fine. Some of them were even really good buddies. But they did not travel on a bus together as I had imagined, because they lived all over the country – California, North Carolina, Las Vegas, and Austin, where Mark lived. He had moved from the San Francisco Bay Area about seven years before to live with his girlfriend. Mark told me he had a girlfriend but that they were "talking about not being together anymore." I told Mark I was happily married. That wasn't entirely true but was said to make sure there wasn't any expectation on his part. And so it went – we began telling each other our life stories, all via email.

Mark loved being in the band *Starship*. It had always been his dream to play the guitar for a living. I truly admired someone who followed his dreams at all costs – and there were definitely costs associated with this kind of gig. To start with, since the band members were spread across the country, everyone would fly to the show – and as far as Mark was concerned, he was "paid to travel." A typical show would last one and a half hours or so, two hours if you figured in the sound check. The rest was all travel time. Tedious, grueling, frustrating travel time.

As for the pay, Mark and his band mates were paid a set dollar amount per show. In addition, the cost of airfare, hotel room, and rental car when shows were a drive from a major airport were all taken care of. The band would usually meet at the airport and all drive together. The downside was that someone was spending their time waiting – and things like cab rides to and from the airport, parking at the airport, and airport food were not taken care of. After a concert, there would sometimes be food for the band in the band hangout area behind the stage, but mostly they were on their own for food, and those expenses added up. One thing the band never had to pay for at shows was alcohol – everyone wanted to buy them a drink!

Signs Surround You

Mickey might get paid a lot for doing a show, but he was left with all the expenses, including airfare for the six band members plus the sound guys. Also, equipment and stages had to be assembled and taken down and shipped quickly across the country for a show the next night that might be hundreds of miles away. Show expenses added up, and this meant Mark and the rest of the band were relegated to cheap airfare.

With all the miles they logged, they had status on all the major airlines, but Mark would often have to make two or three connections to his destination because those were the less expensive flights. It wasn't unusual for him to spend an entire day traveling, just to get to a show. Most shows started after 7 p.m., with sound check sometime in the afternoon, to make sure the music would "rock". So, as Mark explained – he was "paid to travel."

The correspondence between Mark and me continued to be entirely by email. Two days after I met him, Jason left on a hunting trip for a couple weeks in Alaska, and I was consumed with projects I had hoped to finish while he was gone. But Mark was becoming quite the distraction. I found myself running back and forth, up and down the 13 stairs to my office area, where the computer was tethered to the internet connection – checking for email replies from Mark. He had gotten under my skin and I was really enjoying our back and forth volley. In his first reply email, he had already invited me to attend his *Starship* show in a few days, and I was looking forward to seeing him again.

After the first several days of emailing, Mark wrote, "It might be too much to say, but you've been on my mind all day." Already crossing lines. About a week in, we decided it was time to have a live phone conversation. I had been looking forward to it all day and was very nervous at the same time. "What's the big deal?" I kept telling myself. "You practically talk for a living anyway." But I was afraid that I might like him more after we spoke...

When he called, I was busy painting the inside of the coat closet. There was rarely ever a time that I would take a call from anybody without doing something else at the same time. I prided myself in all that I was able to accomplish, never wanting to appear as if I couldn't do it all. I was a wife, a mother of two, and caretaker to a dog, a saltwater fish tank and

Signs Surround You

a rabbit (actually, the agreement was that the kids would take care of the rabbit, but it occasionally fell to me). I also volunteered on the Park District Pool Committee Board and was an officer in the school PTA, as well as having a fulltime, demanding career selling pharmaceutical drugs. I was as busy as anyone.

Mark was a California guy, to be sure, and I wasn't used to his California ways. He wanted to know my sign and he talked about things I was only vaguely familiar with, like past lives and life contracts. I could tell from the emails that he was a deeper kind of guy, and even more so from our live conversations.

The phone conversation flowed for probably 30 minutes. I had finished painting the coat closet and was on to cleaning the saltwater fish tank when I reached a point in the cleaning where I needed to go. In truth, it was a good excuse to go. I hung up the phone intrigued by the conversation but thinking Mark was sort of "foreign" and different from anyone I knew. He also swore a lot, and I can blame him for bringing back my potty mouth. When we first started talking, I was shocked by his language. He threw F-bombs all over the place.

Not that I was stranger to swearing – I had gotten an early start at the ripe old age of ten. But when my kids started talking, I gave up the cursing. I had once heard someone say: "If you say 'fuck' when you burn the toast, what do you have left to say when the house burns down?" That started me on the path to cursing abstinence. And it wasn't like Jason didn't drop a few bombs here and there, but mostly I wasn't used to hearing that kind of language, so it was a little shocking to hear it from Mark. Still, it didn't keep me away and I made the decision to attend the concert.

I had planned on taking Ryan to see Mark play, but before Jason left he asked me not to let Ryan miss any football practices. The concert was during the middle of the week, and I wanted to keep my promise. Ryan was bummed; he really wanted to go with me. Rachel was happy to stay home, as her favorite babysitter would be coming over.

Earlier in the week, I had taken on a project of cleaning out the crawl space, which was about four feet in height and concreted. I hauled out a bunch of old stuff we had been storing down there and did a massive

Signs Surround You

throw-away. I used the shop vac to clear away cobwebs and vacuum the entire area, about 1,500 square feet. Then I put back and rearranged a few items we still wanted to store down there. We had been in the house for about eight years and I had never touched the crawl space. It was a huge undertaking, but one I was really proud to have accomplished.

Two days later – the day before the *Starship* concert – massive thunderstorms hit our area, resulting in severe flooding. For the first time ever, the sump pump in our crawl space failed and we got about a foot of water down there. It figured – something like this always happened when Jason left town. The last time he left, the dog got sprayed by a skunk!

I was able to buy a new pump and get all the water back out, but we had also lost power. My father-in-law got the generator going so we wouldn't lose everything in the refrigerator and freezer and so my saltwater fish would be okay. But on the day of the concert, I couldn't even take a shower or do my hair.

Good news for Ryan – the football fields were still under water and his practice was cancelled, which freed him up to go to the concert. He was elated. And I was relieved. I was becoming a little nervous about attending the concert by myself – what would Jason think? Ryan's concert attendance had always been a possibility, but I'm sure that on some level Mark was hoping I would show up alone...

Signs Surround You

Signs Surround You

Chapter 6

Guitar Man

~Song by Bread

https://open.spotify.com/track/0gZXockVcE7rEhSf4mcGLO?si=rWX-ktSKRFa198tT5qsO3A

The town where the concert was to be held was about a 45-minute drive from my house. I wanted to be sure we didn't get stuck in traffic, so we left a couple hours early just to ensure we wouldn't be late. As we found a place to park, I texted Mark to let him know Ryan would be attending with me. "*No way out,*" I jokingly added – a play on the song title from one of *Starship's* songs.

In reality, I was very happy to have Ryan there with me. It made my attending a concert much less dangerous in a couple of ways. For one, I didn't want to put myself in a situation where I would do something I wasn't ready to do. And two, I was happy to have Ryan there to mask any measure of inappropriateness.

Big, black, heavy clouds were threatening overhead and I was worried that the outdoor concert was about to be canceled altogether. But after all the rain the previous day, the Village of Homewood was smart enough to move the concert inside.

As we arrived, only a handful of people had already entered, ahead of us. Mark and the band were onstage doing a quick sound check, since the stage had just recently been moved inside. He nodded to us in acknowledgment. We found a front-row seat on the left side of the stage where Mark would be performing. Mark disappeared backstage as soon as the sound check was over. I texted him, asking him to come out to say "hi."

Signs Surround You

After a couple minutes, Mark arrived. To my dismay, he smelled like he had bathed in an ashtray! Ugh – reality check. I had forgotten about the smoking thing. It's not that I disliked the smell of cigarette smoke – it's that I hated it! Yes, HATE is the right word – I couldn't stress that strongly enough. I had spent my whole life as an anti-smoker, avoiding being around cigarette smoke in any amount because I just couldn't stand it.

Growing up I had three rules about boys: (1) they can't smoke, (2) they can't do drugs, and (3) they can't have hair longer than mine. Oh, my God, what was I doing? Three strikes, right off the bat! Well, okay – technically, two strikes. It was true that Mark was a smoker and an occasional pot smoker, so that was two strikes. But the third rule – no long hair – had mainly been because, well, I didn't really care for long hair on guys. And although his hair was *not* longer than mine, it was still what I would consider long hair. But it was actually a great look for Mark. I couldn't picture him any other way, nor have I ever seen any photos of him without longer hair. His hair was naturally curly, which probably would've been somewhat difficult to manage in a shorter style – and his longer style fit him just right anyway.

Mark visited with us for a few minutes and then had to run back to get ready for the-show. This show was somehow even better than the last one, although the lineup of songs was identical. At one point during the performance, Mark was facing Jeff, the bass guitarist, and while they were wailing away, the two of them were in kind of a back-and-forth exchange. Mark would look at me, look at Jeff and yell "beautiful!" And Jeff would nod his head and respond back. I could somehow feel that Mark was talking about me, and that made me feel very special.

Mark had a way of making me feel like the most beautiful woman in the world, and I'll admit it was something I had been craving. I knew Jason thought I was beautiful, but he rarely said it. Not even on our wedding day, and to a degree, that still bothered me. I had once confronted Jason about why he rarely told me I was beautiful and his reply was "Why should I tell you you're beautiful? Everybody else already does." Well, I don't care who you are or what you look like, it's always wonderful when someone tells you they think you're beautiful – it's one of those things you can't hear too many times.

Signs Surround You

After the encore ended to raving applause, the show was over and people started to clear out pretty quickly. Ryan and I just sat there waiting, once again not quite knowing what to do with ourselves. Eventually, Mark came out and led us backstage with him. We walked down into a kind of sub-basement room, where the entire band was sitting around, drinking and munching on snacks. There was quite an assortment of hot and cold food, drinks, and of course beer, which Mark already had in his hand. Now that I was near him again, he not only smelled like cigarette smoke but beer, and it was clear he had had a few already.

We all sat around talking for a while, and then the band decided it was time to load up and head to the hotel. Mark said he would ride back to the hotel with me in my car and Ryan could have his spot in the van with the band. Ryan almost couldn't get into the van fast enough – he was so excited at the chance to ride with the band. They were all very nice and also very normal, unlike what you might expect rock band members to be. Ryan had a good time on the 15-minute drive to the hotel; he was the center of attention.

Meanwhile, Mark settled into the passenger seat next to me and off we went, closely following the van. I didn't know the area very well and the hotel was fairly far from the venue – not to mention the fact that I had my ten-year-old son in the van ahead of us, and I had no intention of letting him out of my sight. So I needed to stay focused.

Unexpectedly, Mark grabbed my hand in his, looked at me and said, "What are we doing?" "I know..." was all I could respond. I felt the electricity of our connection as soon as he touched my hand.

We casually chatted, and at some point Mark grabbed my hair in one hand, pulled it into a ponytail and playfully jerked back on my head. My stomach dropped at the thought. His entire being exuded sexual energy. It was really something to feel, being this near to him.

The van pulled up to the front door of the hotel, and Mark and I found a place to park the car. When we reached Ryan, he was grinning from ear to ear, clearly having enjoyed every minute of his van experience. After a few exchanges of "nice to see you again" with the band,

Signs Surround You

Mark, Ryan and I headed up to his hotel room, "his home away from home" for the night.

Mark asked Ryan how he would feel about getting a guitar lesson, and Ryan excitedly agreed that would be a great idea. We sat there on the floor of the hotel room, Ryan holding Mark's guitar and Mark instructing Ryan. I kept staring at Mark – studying every feature of his face, committing it to memory, while he completely avoided any eye contact with me. Instead, he focused all his energy and attention on Ryan's lesson.

When they finished, we sat around talking for a few more minutes and then decided it was getting late – and since there was school the next day, Ryan should be getting home to bed. It actually didn't matter; I knew that as soon as we started driving he would sleep the whole way home.

Mark walked us down to the hotel lobby. I remembered I had something in my car I wanted to give him. The company I worked for had recently launched a smoking-cessation drug that I was now selling. Mark and I had discussed smoking on the phone a couple of times, and he agreed that it was really not in his best interest. He said that he had already been thinking about quitting and asserted, "I can quit at any time." Then to prove that theory, he paid a visit to the local drug store and bought some Nicorette Gum – a complete failure in helping him "quit at any time."

Mark wasn't sold on the idea of taking a drug to help him quit smoking, but he was at least interested enough to want to read the information I had brought for him. Ryan and I went out to the car, and I drove the car up and parked it near the hotel entrance. Ryan stayed with the running car while I quickly ran back into the hotel to give Mark the information.

I didn't see him at first. He had moved off to the side in a little area where the payphone was. I walked up to him and handed him the info and he promised to take a look at it. Then he grabbed me and kissed me, thrusting his tongue into my mouth. I had not been expecting that and it caught me off guard. It had been 20 years since I kissed any man other than my husband, but my feelings for Mark had been building and the kiss was not completely unwanted.

Signs Surround You

When I walked back out to the car, I couldn't see Ryan inside, which made me panic for a minute. I couldn't imagine that he had gotten out of the car – and I hoped if he had that he had not seen me and Mark! I quickly opened the door – there he was, on the floor, frantically searching for the dropped guitar pick Mark had given him from the show. I felt a huge flood of relief in knowing there was no possible way Ryan could have seen Mark kiss me.

Signs Surround You

Chapter 7

Help Me

"When I get that crazy feeling

I know I'm in trouble again…"

~song by Joni Mitchell

https://open.spotify.com/track/0tVzXGFyNPusa1VkHmYDLd?si=k-_6JT0yQJqDWk2tBv6Lpg

In the weeks following the concert, my mind never got far from the thought, "I'm having an emotional affair!" It was all I kept saying to myself over and over again – in complete and utter disbelief of the situation I found myself in. This isn't how I am – I've always been such an open book. For the first 37 years of my life, I could've run for any office. I didn't even have a parking ticket in my closet-devoid-of-skeletons. No transgressions whatsoever; I was squeaky clean. And loyal! But I was watching my loyalty fade away…and for what?

To be fair about it, I had been emotionally starved in my relationship with my husband, for a very long time. And my feelings were no secret. I had said to him many times, "When the kids are gone – I'm gone!" But this wasn't the way I had envisioned it playing out in my life.

Regardless of all that – there I was. Now what to do? It was getting to the point where Mark and I were talking and/or emailing every single day. We settled into an easy pattern of communication, spending 45 minutes or more each day talking on the phone, and more time at night emailing each other back and forth in streams of communication. He was on my mind constantly, constantly, constantly – and I was on his. One of our many deep communications began like this…

Signs Surround You

~~To: Laurie Majka

From: Mark Abrahamian

Sent: Monday September 17, 2007 11:57pm

Subject: thoughts

Hi Laurie,

No worries on consuming my time. I create my time! Still up playing guitar, hanging with the cats. Working on an amp...enjoying my time off!

I could feel you coming into yourself, actually, earlier today. Was quite kewl to be a part of! ...I do want to get inside you...

You are correct, u must figure out what you are going to create...it's your world.

I look forward to hearing what you wanted to share about thoughts you have had of me, always...u know the answer to hurting others or not...what's true for you is true for you.

Sorry if I missed you just now. I look forward to being with you tomorrow.

Always curious of your thoughts. Know u are always in mine.

Mark

p.s. I'll give it some thought as to what solo Ryan could learn. ~~

With Mark, it was easy to be an open book. I never withheld my thoughts or feelings from him – he always knew where he stood with me. Mark was deep and insightful, and a lot of times our conversations would actually revolve around my relationship with Jason. It was funny how Mark would sometimes defend Jason's actions. Even though he cared deeply for me, at his core he was trying to help me find ways to "live in my truth" and have real, open, honest conversations with Jason. He said that if I would just open up and speak my truth, I would be surprised what would happen. Things would get better, he told me, and then I might be able to have the relationship with Jason I had always wanted.

Signs Surround You

But the truth was hard for me with Jason. I didn't feel we were on the same page and talking to him was never easy, the way talking to Mark was. At that point in time, Jason and I spoke about ten minutes a day and usually about the kids. Hesitantly, I did begin to try opening up with Jason. My heart would pound as I began such conversations. I was afraid to rock the boat – or to reveal myself about Mark.

I remember one night sitting at the table talking to Jason about how I wanted to have these deeper conversations with him, how I felt that this was what was missing in our relationship. Jason's response was to say that what I really needed in my life was a lesbian relationship, because I was never going to find a man who could talk the way I was suggesting. Hah! If he only knew. The shock of his response made it impossible for me to hide my smirk – but he didn't seem to notice.

On some level, Jason did know something was different, because I didn't keep my conversations with Mark completely hidden and had been very open at the start about maintaining a relationship with him. I remember Mark sending me a guitar tab (written music) for Ryan to learn to play a guitar solo in a song. I printed it out on paper and presented it to Ryan. Jason remarked, "Oh, so *that's* how you're communicating with him – on your work email."

In the beginning, I wasn't trying to hide things, but now that things with Mark had escalated, I really didn't have any choice if I wanted to continue my connection to Mark. I knew the truth of what was happening with us had more potential to destroy than to help.

Music was my salvation. On my daily walks, I listened to a lot of songs! The lyrics of a song would hit me and I would listen to that song over and over and over again. The song *"Help Me"* by *Joni Mitchell* was one such song. I had been listening to it on my walk one day, and that night I emailed Mark and asked him what he was up to. He said he had been listening to a certain song. Yep, he was online looking at the lyrics and listening to *"Help Me."* The lyrics had somehow caught his attention – the way they had mine. We were so incredibly connected, it scared me.

Mark's feelings for me were increasing too and he was becoming bolder with his words, both on the phone and in emails. One time, before leaving on my daily walk, I checked my email to find this one:

Signs Surround You

~~To: Laurie Majka

From: Mark Abrahamian

Sent: Tuesday, September 18, 2008 3:11pm

Subject: RE: thoughts

Want to see you smile

Want to whisper in your ear

Want to feel your face in my hands

Want to hold you in my arms

Want to hold your hand

Want to kiss your lips

Want to kiss your neck

Want to see you when you laugh

Want to watch you when you walk

Want to watch a sunset with you

Want you around...

Want to make love to you

Want to laugh with you

Want to be with you

Want to make you feel good

I love you.

Mark~~

As I began reading it, I felt three drips of sweat pour out of my arm pit. My head started spinning and my breathing quickened. I wrote my reply, then headed off on my walk to think.

Signs Surround You

~~To: Mark Abrahamian

From: Laurie Majka

Sent: Tuesday, September 18, 2007 4:10PM

Subject: RE: thoughts

OH MY GOD, what are you doing

to me ?????????????????????????????????

I can't breathe.

I can't think.

I don't even know where my stomach is.

I am exhilarated.

I am terrified.

I am aroused.

I am numb.

I am awestruck.

You have a way of communicating with me that touches my Soul. ~~

~~To: Laurie Majka

From: Mark Abrahamian

Sent: Tuesday, September 18, 2007 6:25PM

Subject: RE: thoughts

breathe

think

feel

embrace

experience

enjoy

listen

look

Signs Surround You

...ah life. ~~

~~To: Mark Abrahamian

From: Laurie Majka

Sent: Tuesday, September 18, 2007 8:10PM

Subject: RE: thoughts

Ok, I took a walk. I am breathing again and thinking again. I keep reading and rereading your email.

I don't have words, only feelings. Call me tomorrow. I don't need to leave until about 10:00. I can't stop thinking about...everything. My head is spinning... Is that what you wanted? ~~

~~To: Laurie Majka

From: Mark Abrahamian

Sent: Tuesday, September 18, 2007 11:15PM

Subject: RE: thoughts

I know the situation but I still express to you that I want you. I want more. I would gladly have more. I would love to love you Laurie. ~~

~~To: Mark Abrahamian

From: Laurie Majka

Sent: Tuesday, September 17, 2007 11:25PM

Subject: RE: thoughts

How do you know me so well, know what to say to make me melt? It is as if you hear my thoughts and know exactly what I feel. ~~

~~To: Laurie Majka

From: Mark Abrahamian

Signs Surround You

Sent: Tuesday, September 17, 2007 11:31PM

Subject: RE: thoughts

You allow me to see you. You draw me in. I'm drawn to you. ~~

~~To: Mark Abrahamian

From: Laurie Majka

Sent: Tuesday, September 17, 2007 11:36PM

Subject: RE: thoughts

I am drawn to you, I want to stop... I can't stop. ~~

~~To: Laurie Majka

From: Mark Abrahamian

Sent: Tuesday, September 17, 2007 11:45PM

Subject: RE: thoughts

maybe it's time to stop. ~~

~~To: Mark Abrahamian

From: Laurie Majka

Sent: Wednesday, September 18, 2007 12:08AM

Subject: RE: thoughts

I want you. I want more. I don't know if we can have more. I am falling for you...good night Mark ~~

~~To: Laurie Majka

From: Mark Abrahamian

Sent: Wednesday, September 18, 2007 12:11AM

Subject: RE: thoughts

I have fallen for you Laurie. ~~

Signs Surround You

~~To: Mark Abrahamian

From: Laurie Majka

Sent: Thursday, September 18, 2007 12:21AM

Subject: RE: thoughts

I know. I lied...you already knew that; I have too...~~

It's strange looking at correspondence in hindsight. My gut reaction at the time was fear and the feeling that I needed to pull away. Mark scared me. He was a threat to everything I had built over the last twenty-plus years – but I wanted and needed our connection.

After several agonizing hours of mulling this over and hashing out the pros and cons with a few of my closest friends, I decided I needed to pull back. I needed to quit Mark cold turkey for one week – to have time to think, really think. I told him there would be no more phone calls, no more emails, no more contact for one week. Mark was not thrilled, but he understood that this was something I needed to do.

He made it to two days and eight hours before he broke my no-contact ban. He called, but I let it go straight to voicemail. He then sent me an email that included two pictures of him, almost identical – presumably so I wouldn't forget what he looked like – and a note that said:

~~To: Laurie Majka

From: Mark Abrahamian

Sent: Monday, September 22, 2007 3:13PM

Subject: Oops

~~ I know I know...I called... Thinking about u Laurie. My will power to stay away for a week from u is not so good... I miss talking to u, I must admit. In Memphis, on my way to Oklahoma.

Mark ~~

Signs Surround You

The thought made me smile, but it did not make me want to call him back. I did respond with...

~~To: Mark Abrahamian

From: Laurie Majka

Sent: Monday, September 22, 2007 3:21PM

RE: Oops

~~ *I know, I saw. Travel safely! Thank you for the pictures* ☺ *We'll talk on Thursday – Laurie* ~~

Mark was cooperative after that. And so the week went. It was pretty difficult because I had gotten very used to the daily conversations with him. I felt in my heart the absence of those conversations. But even though I still wanted to reach out to him, I didn't. The agreement had been that we would go for one full week with no contact, and then I would call him on the drive to attend my 20-year high school reunion in Kansas.

I made two phone calls to kick off the trip. The first was to Mark. I had to get it out of the way – I had been dreading it all day. My stomach hurt, my head hurt, and even though I knew it was for the best, I still wasn't sure I was making the decision my heart wanted me to make. After much contemplation, I decided I was in no position to move forward with *any* type of relationship with Mark. Our connection had become semi-dangerous in my eyes. I loved the way he made me feel about myself and the depth of our conversations – something I had been craving. I already loved *him*, but I was afraid of what this connection had the potential to evolve into, and I didn't want to destroy my marriage. I decided to sever ALL ties with Mark before it was too late.

When I told him the news, he said he already knew what was coming. He had been able to feel my decision for the last several hours. It was coming as no surprise to him. That was always one of the special things about our relationship; we could really feel each other. It was kind of crazy and I had never experienced *anything* like this with any other human being – ever! Not wanting to prolong the inevitable, we kept the

Signs Surround You

conversation very short, ending in "If you ever need anything..." And that was the end.

I started crying before I could even fully disconnect the call. I felt a small sense of relief, but a bigger sense of sadness. On a Heart and Soul level, I knew that we were *very* connected – drawn to each other very specifically for a meaningful purpose. It was so hard to explain, and that's what made the thought of ending it so hard.

My second call was to one of my close friends, who squealed in delight at the news. It wasn't that she didn't want me to be happy; it was that she understood what this connection had the potential to destroy. I spent the rest of the drive on my phone, calling a dozen or so friends – not to talk about Mark, just to catch up and keep my mind off of him. Those calls filled the void for the rest of the drive to the reunion.

My 20-year high school reunion was wonderful and at the same time served a greater purpose – keeping my mind off Mark. Twenty-four hours had passed with no contact, then 25, 26, 27, 28, 29, 30...and there he was, calling me on my cell phone. I let it go straight to voicemail, but I was so curious that I couldn't resist listening to his message the instant it arrived. I knew he was at a show that night, and that his show would be over and he would've had a couple of beers by then. His guard was down and he called me. This kind of thing never would have happened during the day, when he was completely sober – in that condition, like me, he possessed a will of steel.

The message was short and sweet: "Love you. Call me back!" Wow, what do you do or say to that? It was a good thing I was so busy. There were some parties to go to, which would keep my mind occupied. The next day there was a tour of my old high school, and then our formal reunion event. I spent so much time visiting and catching up with old friends that I actually didn't have Mark close in my thoughts.

On Sunday morning, before embarking on the long drive home, I had a nice breakfast with my parents. I then headed out – now left with only my thoughts. I made it all the way to the middle of Missouri before I finally talked myself into it being a good idea to return his call – how rude not to, I told myself. He answered on the first ring. "I knew you would call me back..." We talked for over two hours – as if the past 60 hours had never happened.

Signs Surround You

Chapter 8

Fool If You Think It's Over

~Song by Chris Rea

https://open.spotify.com/track/4Eq54SqWdCWCprJIRqwK8h?si=yVXNfK57T1y7ozFSWcKCIQ

The next few months were filled with lots of phone conversations, emails, texts, photos, flirtations, propositions, and several ups and downs. Mark and I would talk nearly every day during the week. Weekends were hard because neither of us was very available.

A month before I met Mark, Jason and I had bought a log house six hours north of us. The intention was for it to eventually be our summer retirement home. I saw it as the baby to save the marriage. A cabin was something we both wanted, something we could work on together and be excited about. It was still under construction and we had a big hand in finishing a lot of the interior work. There were many weekend trips up north after I met Mark.

The log house was pretty remote, so we didn't have a phone or internet or even a TV antenna. Additionally, no cell phones had internet back then and email was unavailable on the road. In the log house, our cell phone reception was horrible. With one bar of service, I would have to stand next to a window, moving the phone all around to keep the one-bar signal available to even send a text message.

The only way to communicate was by texting, but it was still rather new – and that old kind of texting would take forever to compose a 160-character limited text message, as phones didn't have full keyboards back then. The technology was very slow, but better than nothing.

I always felt so sneaky, texting. I was afraid of getting caught, and it heightened my awareness that what I was doing felt wrong. I wanted to

Signs Surround You

come clean with Jason but was talked out of it numerous times by those closest to me, who were afraid it might not be the right approach to salvage my marriage.

As my relationship with Mark progressed, I became keenly aware that it was not based in reality. Talking on the phone and emailing was not the same as spending time with someone in person. I began to pressure Mark into coming to see me. After all, he was single with no kids and free of commitments outside of his two cats. Also, he traveled for a living and possessed more frequent-flier miles than he could use in a lifetime. But all he did was make excuses. In early November, we had several email exchanges:

~~To: Mark Abrahamian

From: Laurie Majka

Sent: Saturday November 3, 2007 12:42AM

Subject: Re: camera

Why are you waiting? Are you afraid our meeting will lead to more or less??

~~To: Laurie Majka

From: Mark Abrahamian

Sent: Saturday November 3, 2007 12:48AM

Subject: Re: camera

anything is possible...I stated what I was concerned about as far as I go...as far as u go I'm concerned like I said that maybe this will bring u back to reality and you'll go "WHAT AM I DOING??" so both scenarios I'm concerned about.~~

~~To: Mark Abrahamian

From: Laurie Majka

Sent: Saturday November 3, 2007 12:51AM

Subject: Re: camera

Signs Surround You

If I am honest with you, which I always am, it is my hope that our meeting brings me back to reality.~~

~~To: Laurie Majka

From: Mark Abrahamian

Sent: Saturday November 3, 2007 12:52AM

Subject: Re: camera

Thanks for being honest with me~~

~~To: Mark Abrahamian

From: Laurie Majka

Sent: Saturday November 3, 2007 12:54AM

Subject: Re: camera

I hope that wasn't sarcastic – can't tell on email.

I said it is my hope – I am not sure how realistic that is though...

Does my 1st comment make you nervous? Less likely to make a visit happen?~~

~~To: Laurie Majka

From: Mark Abrahamian

Sent: Saturday November 3, 2007 1:01AM

Subject: Re: camera

That yer hoping that our visit brings u back to reality? Well yeah...the thanks for being honest with me had a tone like uhh ok. Like there is no feeling for me in all of this?? It's just something u have to do for you...?~~

~~ To: Mark Abrahamian

From: Laurie Majka

Signs Surround You

Sent: Saturday November 3, 2007 1:10AM

Subject: Re: camera

Mark that is not what I meant. I know where you would like this to go. If it does, I am in big trouble – then the next question will be, now what. If there were not feelings for you I would have no interest in seeing you! I am at a point in all of this where I NEED to know, need to see you. Yes, need a reality check because the phone and email is not reality! I care deeply for you and for your feelings – you KNOW that. It is crazy to imply that this would be only for me. You get to see too. Maybe when you see me, it will be a reality check for you that I am not what you thought or how you are thinking. That you don't want someone who is already in a relationship and you can't deal with the distance, and maybe I say yes while you say no. It is a risk that way too...~~

~~To: Laurie Majka

From: Mark Abrahamian

Sent: Saturday November 3, 2007 1:41AM

Subject: Re: camera

Ok, sleep time. I hear ya Laurie.~~

~~To: Mark Abrahamian

From: Laurie Majka

Sent: Saturday November 3, 2007 1:46AM

Subject: Re: camera

Do you want me to censor what I say?? Long time between replies – I know you don't feel good about this and I am sorry.

I can't predict the future and what my reaction to you will be. Hell, my friends are all over the place with would this relationship work? They are supposed to know me best. I am getting a range of between 10-70%!! All I know is that phone and email only cannot go on forever. We just need to find out, one way or the other – sooner rather than later. You

Signs Surround You

can call me tomorrow before noon if you want. Just answer this email and we will call it a night. ~~

~~To: Laurie Majka

From: Mark Abrahamian

Sent: Saturday November 3, 2007 1:55AM

Subject: Re: camera

Never want u to censor what u say. I'm ok. I hear ya. Have a good night Laurie :) ~~

~~To: Mark Abrahamian

From: Laurie Majka

Sent: Saturday November 3, 2007 1:59AM

Subject: Re: camera

I'm glad you are ok. I am worried about how you feel. Sweet dreams, Mark

The next day he called me while I was sitting in the Ace Hardware parking lot. The conversation led to more of me pressuring him to visit, which escalated into me yelling, "I'm married!" And him yelling back, "Well then, good luck to you!" and hanging up. As soon as the phones disconnected, I had knots in my stomach and that awful dissonance feeling that would not go away no matter how much I told myself I was better off without him. I was pissed and stubborn and had no intention of emailing or calling him back – ever! I made a playlist of songs to commemorate the occasion:

"When It's Over" by Loverboy

"Let Me Go" by 3 Doors Down

"Should've Known Better" by Richard Marx

"If You're Gone" by Matchbox Twenty

Signs Surround You

"You Won't Be Mine" by *Matchbox Twenty*

"If I'd been the One" by *.38 Special*

"If You Love Somebody" by *Sting*

"Turn Me Loose" by *Loverboy*

"Fool (If You Think It's Over)" by *Chris Rea*

I spent that Sunday playing them on my walk and in the car at top volume. That night I had to travel to a three-day meeting that was located only ten minutes from my house, but we were required to stay overnight at the hotel for the duration. When I parked my car, the song *"When It's Over"* was playing and I was singing it defiantly at the top of my lungs:

"'Cause deep, deep down inside

You're living in a life in total lies

What did he ever do for you

What's he trying to put you through

I don't understand

You showed him love and tenderness

Touched him with your sweet caress

Now he's leaving you..."

IT'S OVER, IT'S OVER, IT'S OOOOOVERRRRR..."

By the next morning, my defiance was replaced with defeat. In my heart of hearts, I didn't WANT it to be over. My body responded in kind with a sore throat, hoarse voice and that sick feeling like I was getting the flu. I couldn't concentrate in the meetings because Mark wouldn't leave my mind. I could feel *him* too. My heart and head were in a brutal battle of "call him / don't call him." And my body was losing. By lunch time, everyone was telling me how pale and sick I looked and that I should go

Signs Surround You

to my room. I'm sure they didn't want to catch what I had – but no one was in danger of that. This wasn't a virus; this was lovesick.

I went to my room, but instead of resting I called him. He didn't answer, of course, so I left an apologetic message requesting a call back. He called me within minutes, and after a short conversation, we had patched things up. The call also brought my body quickly back to equilibrium. Within an hour I felt immensely better and was able to rejoin the meetings.

He later said, "I knew when I heard your voice what was up. And from my side of this – I'm in love with a girl I haven't spent time in the flesh with." He was so insightful and understood what havoc emotions can wreak on the body. And he knew what to say to keep me coming back for more. But to this day, when the song *When It's Over* plays, it transports me right back to that day and those feelings. I usually hit the skip button!

Those last few days had been very telling. I realized both of us were in pretty deep. I would toggle back and forth between that "walking on clouds" feeling in love and a "walking the plank" feeling of doom. One thing was for certain, my feelings were gaining strength, and I really needed to see Mark in person, to see how I felt when I saw him.

In a way, I hoped that seeing him would "snap me out of this," because I had not lost hope in my marriage. I was still in a position where I wanted to see if Jason could rise to the situation and be that deeper emotional connection I needed. I wasn't sure it was possible. Mark and I – mostly Mark – came to the agreement that he would not make a trip to see me. The band would be performing nearby on January 12, 2008 – exactly five months to the day we first met. We would wait until then to see each other.

Mark and I continued to have deep philosophical conversations, which I loved the most about us. We explored concepts that were both familiar and new to me. One time, while talking about Soul Mates, Mark said, "I do believe we hang out with each other through lifetimes."

This is something I have come to hold in my mind as truth. Soul Mate relationships are not always romantic ones, the way Hollywood portrays them. They can be, and often are, *very* challenging – pushing

Signs Surround You

you toward Soul Growth or helping you find your way towards your life purpose. I don't believe in accidents – and when I look back at all the

things that had to align for me to even meet Mark and then form a relationship with him, that point becomes very clear to me.

I believe we all have a "life contract" that contains not only our bigger life purpose but lessons we want to accomplish while we're here on this Earth. We can't learn much without interacting with others, and we have Soul Mates who sign contracts to interact with each other. They are Souls we know very well. We don't have to seek them out; they show up when we are ready for the lesson. And it is always two-sided – we are both student and teacher. I also believe that God or Universal Consciousness or Creator – whatever name makes sense to you – is behind all of creation.

From an email, I learned Mark's take on God:

"I do believe in God. I believe God is behind everything. Words are and can be confused of their meaning. God is a concept, to begin communicating something that can't be comprehended in this game we call life. It's part of the game. It's a concept, God, we are it. We create worlds, we are a part of each other. Heaven and Hell is a state of mind created by the being. We answer to no one but ourselves. And I mean that in the broadest way one can possibly think what ourselves means. As a whole as well as individually. We are all part of each other. Individually we make up the whole concept of God. By ourselves and together as one. I could go on and on and on and on. Does it really matter? No. What's true for u is true for u so why ponder it?"

We continued our many conversations and our many ins and outs, ups and down, sharing – and eventually withholding – both of us fading in and out between fantasy and reality. A week later, he was out. Ending it all at 2:07 p.m. Sunday, November 18, 2007 with...

"I'm stopping this. Take care of what u have to get everything u want. Think about it. I wish u well. I'll never forget you Laurie"

...and we were back again by early December.

But the closer January got, the more Mark pulled away. He would say to me over and over that he didn't want to be "the cause" of my relationship ending. It wasn't as if I was working toward ending my

Signs Surround You

relationship – I felt like I was finding my voice with Jason for the first time, becoming less and less afraid to rock the boat.

We ended it again on a phone call New Year's Day. Mark did not want me to come to his concert on January 12. Nevertheless, a few days before the concert, I decided I was going, whether he wanted me there or not. In my heart and in my mind, I had to see him. I thought if I saw him, I would be able to resolve this once and for all. I called him two days before the show to share my intentions. He was less than thrilled and put up his objections, but in the end said I could do whatever I needed to do.

They were to play at a casino in Milwaukee, about an hour and a half away from my house. He again said not to come. I said I would anyway. It was over for *now*, but with our history that could change next week. I wasn't going to miss the opportunity to see him when he would be so close, and I wasn't taking no for an answer. Create my world!

Signs Surround You

Chapter 9

I've Been Searchin' So Long…

"There's a strange new light in my eyes

Things I've never known

Changing my life

Changing me…"

~song by Chicago

https://open.spotify.com/track/3z9pBucv2HHp1gYaTcQwil?si=POOiKnx7RPyYQO-b0ifvtQ

January had been a particularly cold month and that day was no exception. I couldn't believe Mark was going to be arriving in a matter of hours. I was extremely nervous about so many things. What if I didn't get the answers I needed…?

But I couldn't think about that now. I was busy picking up a supply of drugs in my storage unit to deliver to my doctors, and as usual was running low on Viagra samples and needed more of those too. I really had to get going because I wanted to finish up early so I could head an hour and a half north to Milwaukee for the concert.

My phone vibrated in my pocket. I almost didn't look at it, but at the last second I couldn't resist the temptation. It was Mark. He was at the airport, ready for his full day of travel from Austin to Atlanta to Milwaukee. The call was short. He said he didn't want me to go to his concert that evening – something about not having a lot of time to spend with me and us seeing each other not being a good idea. I told him I appreciated where he was coming from but that I had already made all

Signs Surround You

my plans and was going to be there. I shouldn't have been surprised by the call, but I still felt slighted – how could he not want to see me!

The concert would end around 9 p.m. I would have to leave Milwaukee by 11:00 in order to be home by 12:30. That was rather late to be arriving home in the middle of the week on a work night, but I had all the bases covered. Ignoring my conscience, I told Jason I had a work program about erectile dysfunction that evening in downtown Chicago– 40 minutes from my home – and that a few of my work friends were going to hang out after the doctors left. Based on that explanation, my ETA home would be between 11:00 and 11:30 p.m. I also needed to add the illusion of a late-night impromptu grocery-shopping trip to stretch my arrival home to 12:30 a.m. Late-night shopping was something I did quite frequently to avoid the crowds. As a long-standing night owl, it was nothing out of the ordinary for me.

I got my work day done early, as planned, then headed to my local grocery store. It was going to be several hours until I would be returning home to put the groceries away, but that didn't matter because the temperature in my trunk was well below zero. My only worry was that some groceries might actually freeze, being in there for that long. I had to take care in what I bought that day to make sure there were no food issues. Then I began the drive north.

I found a highway rest area about 20 minutes outside of downtown Milwaukee, where the concert would be held. I needed to make my transformation from savvy business woman to concert vixen. Changing out of my business pantsuit, I put on my favorite blue jeans and a cute top. I accessorized with some chunky jewelry and touched up my makeup, smudging and playing with the eye shadow until I had just the right look. Now the only thing that needed revamping was my hair. I got out the curling iron, hairspray and brush and started in.

There was more than one curious look elicited from other women passing through the rest-area bathroom. I didn't care. I needed to look my best – flawless, really. I wanted Mark to take one look at me and remember why he *really did* want me there tonight. When I was fully satisfied with my concert look, I carefully hung up my suit for the return trip home and got back in the car to finish the drive to the casino. I knew

Signs Surround You

exactly where it was; we had passed it on our way to the cabin a dozen times since last July.

Damn – I was early by almost 3 hours. Rarely early, I was more of an "on-time" girl. I liked to push the envelope, cramming in as many things as I could before I had to be somewhere, so as to avoid any downtime – or, as I saw it, "wasted time" in my day. I spotted a place to park my car where I could wait and make a phone call to pass some time.

Just as I pulled over, Mark called me. He sounded very somber and not quite himself. His plane had been heading from Houston to Atlanta when everyone started smelling smoke – knowing it couldn't be cigarette smoke, since smoking was prohibited aboard aircrafts. The smell was more than a little disconcerting; it had an electrical burning odor that stung the nostrils. Before long, the flight attendants transformed into emergency-landing mode and the passengers were hurried into emergency-landing positions. Mark said it had really scared him.

They landed safely in Charlotte, but Mark had to do some fast maneuvering to get himself on a plane that would get him to Milwaukee before the concert started. Attending sound check would be out of the question; he would be lucky just to arrive on time, before the concert started. He was now on a new plane, ready to push back from the gate. I told him I was already in Milwaukee and he seemed genuinely glad to hear that. Funny how your perspective changes when your life flashes before you...

As the time of the concert neared, I became progressively more nervous. Talking to friends on the phone took the edge off, much like alcohol would for a drinker, and the calls made time pass fairly quickly. After a while, I decided it was time to head into the venue.

When I arrived and was just about to get out of my car, I glanced at my hand and saw my wedding ring. I couldn't wear it. Having it on my finger was like wearing a huge exclamation point: "MARRIED – shouldn't be here!" The ring had to go.

I didn't want to put it in my purse; what if it got lost or stolen. No, the car was safer. I had self-parked, so there was no danger of a parking attendant needing to be in my car. But I still had to find a safe place to

Signs Surround You

stash it where no one would think of looking, in the event my car was broken into. Aha – my half empty Carmex lip-balm container. Perfect. The ring with its three marquis diamonds and soldered wedding band was a perfect fit. I had always taken pride in my things and would clean my ring with a toothbrush every morning. But today, I wasn't even worried about it getting all gunked up in the lip balm. At this point, it was becoming less and less important to me...

I walked and walked, all through the giant casino, finally locating the lounge where *Starship* was set up to play. It was a fairly large room with three levels surrounding the stage so that all the dining room tables had a great view. The concert was to begin in about an hour, and there were already several people lined up waiting to get in.

It wouldn't have made any sense for me to get there any earlier as Mark had not yet arrived, and I didn't have any band members' phone numbers to call and hang out with, wherever they were. So I just stood in line like everyone else. I recognized a group of five women from the last show, standing in front of me. Wow – groupies. I *so* did not want to be viewed that way. Mark finally texted me that he had landed, had his guitar and luggage in hand and was in a cab moving my way. Luckily, the airport wasn't far away and rush hour traffic would have died down by now.

I saw him walk in through a door at the opposite end of the room from where I was, then disappear and reappear without his stuff. The next thing I knew, he was coming at me so quickly, pushing me off balance and turning my entire body in a summersault through the air, I ended up landing – in heels – on my feet. Without a single item falling out of my purse! (I was even gladder that I hadn't stashed my ring in there.) We were on the top level of the room, with people seated at tables around me facing the stage, eating their dinner. Mark's little caper took me and everyone around by surprise, and a few people close by even applauded.

Mark then grabbed me and hugged me hard. He took my hand and pulled me out of the room, venturing into the smoke-filled casino area. He pushed me up against a wall and kissed me hard. I could feel all our combined tension falling away – the tension caused by my wondering if he would be happy to see me, and his tension from nearly coming down in a smoky crash landing. We stared into each other's eyes and the whole room disappeared. When he talked, it was strange connecting his face

Signs Surround You

with his voice – his voice was all I had known all these months, and I was unfamiliar with all the facial expressions that accompanied it. We talked and kissed for a few minutes and then he had to get on stage.

I took a seat on the lowest level, at a cocktail table that butted up against the stage. I would be directly in Mark's line of vision from his place on stage. He barely took his eyes off me all through the performance, and I felt like he played it all for me. I was so present during that show. I didn't let my mind wander any farther than the music and Mark. I needed to absorb it all – the way he looked, the way he played, the way his body moved, the way he looked at me.

When the show ended, Mark walked to the edge of the stage and held his hand out to me. The only way for me to get up there was to stand up on the table. In my scramble to join him, I dropped my phone. It hit the ground and fell apart, with the battery landing somewhere under the table. I hurriedly groped around to find the pieces. Assured that I had them all, I threw them into my purse. I then hopped up on the table, took his hand and he pulled me up onto the stage. I grinned at Stephanie as Mark and I passed by her and headed out the back door down an unknown "Employees Only" hallway. Neither of us had any idea where we were going. Mark just wanted to get as far away from the concert as possible, to avoid having to visit with any fans. We both knew we would have precious little time together.

As we entered the parking garage, the shock of the freezing cold air made Mark shout out, "This is why I could never live here!" It was a far cry from the Texas warmth he was used to. We found my car and navigated out of the casino's parking garage onto the city streets. Mark had gotten directions to the hotel, so he was doing the navigating. Somehow, his directions took us into the deserted, industrial part of town. We had to pull over to call the hotel for directions. Before we continued on, Mark grabbed my arm, turned me to fully face him and said, "So, what now? Do you have your answers and it's over between you and me?"

I thought I would gain some clarity seeing Mark in person. I thought I would get an overwhelming "it's wrong" feeling, but instead I had only a vague feeling of that. Part of me wanted this to be over – it would be so much easier and safer for my marriage. Up to this point, I

Signs Surround You

hadn't done anything horribly unforgivable – tons of talking, a little bit of sneaking, and a few kisses.

"Of course it's not over!" I replied, and got a giant grin and a very big kiss in return.

We finally arrived at the hotel and Mark checked in. His first order of business was to find Mickey and get paid. Money had to be his priority – he was working, he reminded me, as his kind of work never seemed like work to me. I was left behind in his room, to wait and watch the clock – which was ticking away all too quickly. I was feeling a bit like Cinderella waiting for her prince to return while at the same time trying to avoid turning into a pumpkin.

Mark returned and smothered me with more kisses. We only had about 30 minutes before I would need to head out, back on the road. We used our time wisely. He pushed me down on the bed and lay on top of me, fully clothed, and proceeded to kiss me. He gently kissed my face and lips and neck.

Want to see you smile – check.

Want to whisper in your ear – check.

Want to feel your face in my hands – check.

Want to hold you in my arms – check.

Want to hold your hand – check.

Want to kiss your lips – check.

Want to kiss your neck – check.

Want to see you when you laugh – check.

Want to watch you when you walk – check.

We had made it more than halfway through his "Want to..." poem in one short visit.

The whole world fell away when Mark kissed me. I was the proverbial putty in his hands. Our faces fit together so much differently

Signs Surround You

than my face did with Jason's. It's funny what you get used to, being with just one person for 20 years. But now my thoughts remained focused on Mark, knowing our time together was short. I would have plenty of time to think about Jason on the drive home. Mark and I kissed for as long as we could before I needed to go. It was almost that time when I remembered that I had left the suit I planned to change back into in my car. We interrupted our make-out session to make an unplanned run to the hotel parking garage. Hand in hand and laughing, we ran down the stairs to retrieve my suit. I changed in his room, not bothering to move to the privacy of the bathroom. He didn't move or take his eyes off me, except to let out a low whistle in response to what he saw.

It was time to go. Mark insisted on walking me back to the parking garage to retrieve my car. The walk was somber this time, both of us knowing there was a long stretch of time ahead of us before we might see each other again. I drove out of the parking lot and parked in front of the hotel lobby. We both got out of the car and hugged each other tight. He passionately kissed me one last time, and as he pulled away from me he looked in my eyes and said "I love you." I said it back and really meant it. He stood there in the cold with no coat and watched me drive away.

I would have to keep a heavy foot on the gas pedal if I was going to make it home by 12:30 a.m. I drove at a steady pace and the drive went surprisingly fast. My thoughts were constantly occupied with all that had transpired that evening – along with thoughts of the past and of the future and all the obstacles that loomed in front of me. I kept rolling the window down to let the cold air blow on me – not because I was falling asleep but because I knew that remnants of cigarette smoke still lingered in my clothes and hair. Smoking was not allowed indoors anymore – except in casinos – and the smoke clung to me like a tattletale, reminding me that I had not been a good girl.

I arrived home to a dark house. I carried all the groceries inside in two trips and put everything away, then checked on each of the sleeping kids before walking into the bedroom to sounds of heavy sleeping. Jason had most likely been asleep for hours. I set my alarm for the next morning and climbed into bed. It woke him and he softly asked how the program went. I said it was good and we both drifted off to sleep, side by side...

Signs Surround You

Two days later Jason was working in the garage with the radio playing in the background. I walked out there to ask him something just as the song *"(I've Been) Searchin' So Long,"* by *Chicago,* had begun playing. The lyrics stopped me in my tracks:

"As my life goes on I believe

Somehow something's changed

Something deep inside

Ooh a part of me

There's a strange new light in my eyes

Things I've never known

Changing my life

Changing me

I've been searchin'

So long

To find an answer

Now I know my life has meaning

Now I see myself as I am

Feeling very free

Life is everything

Ooh it's meant to be"

It was all true! And it resonated deep within my Soul. The thing that had really changed was ME. My feelings for Mark were changing my life – and changing me. For the first time, I was really seeing myself. But how free did I want to be? That was the biggest question of all...

Chapter 10

Seasons Change

~song by Expose

https://open.spotify.com/track/0f24hVOA4gLM8imuvoQ0Uh?si=QStrF4sGTKKcw_hKuBTeKA

Seeing Mark in person strengthened our connection a thousand percent. In a sense, it created the opposite of what I had thought it might. Our connection now had an easy, breezy feel to it – the back-and-forth, in-and-out tug of war had completely dissolved. For the first time since those early days, Mark was showing his true feelings for me – not holding anything back. It may have been because we didn't have any looming pressure around an upcoming visit, as it looked like his band wouldn't make it back to my area until the summer festivals began – and it was just January.

Mark was once again a part of my daily routine Monday through Friday. We explored so many fascinating topics and really got to know each other. It was clear to me, based on the spiritual growth I was undergoing, that Mark was a Soul Mate. By "Soul Mate," I am not referring to the Hollywood version – the love of your life, the be-all and end-all, one true love who completes you. No, I believe a Soul Mate is a close Soul connection you may have experienced many lifetimes with, in many different roles. We have many Soul Mates – male and female, young and old, friend and adversary – who "contract" with us to teach us something or to help us learn an Earthly lesson for Soul Growth. Everyone involved understands, on a Soul level, the purpose. I believe this is why you have that familiar feeling sometimes when you meet someone for the first time and feel like you already know them – it's a Soul recognition. A Soul Mate appears when the Souls are *ready* for the lessons. The one caveat, of course, is free will – which keeps things unpredictable.

Signs Surround You

When I look back on my relationship with Mark, I realize how many stars had to align for us to even meet each other, let alone begin a relationship. I had always had my guard up where men were concerned. I didn't have any male friendships, because I never let any man get close enough to be my friend. I hadn't grown up with brothers or had very many boys around me, so close male friendships were something I never sought out. Sure, I had some casual guy friends in high school and college, but nothing significant.

The friendship Mark and I had formed was something I was really enjoying. It was so different from my female friendships. Mark had a perspective that only comes from being a male – and a unique perspective, at that. Our conversations were deep, deep, deep. Deeper than anything I had ever experienced. It was as if there was no "bottom" to our deep well of discussion – and no ceiling, for that matter. Our conversations had no beginning, no end, and nothing was off limits. It was like an oasis in the desert of this lifetime and it had become my sanctuary for learning.

Time passed, and I felt the familiar longing to see Mark again in person. I would bring it up and he would shoot it down. One day, I was feeling an uneasiness the whole day – it was that familiar pulling-away feeling I had come to recognize through all the ins and outs of our relationship. I knew what was coming and every part of me dreaded it. It's hard to explain my connection to Mark with mere words, but when he was really happy about us, I could feel that energy – and when he was ready to exit, I could feel that too.

It was now April and spring was in the air. Mark called me to say, "I've been thinking about all this. You need to decide what you are doing in your relationship, without me in the picture. We need to take a season."

"What in the world does that mean – 'take a season'?" I responded.

He explained that he felt we would both get some perspective if we could take a break that lasted a season, as in the length of a season – as in three months. It was interesting to me that he picked that word – season – since just a week before, I had said to him, "I like this new season we are in. It feels like summer to me, and you know how much I enjoy summer." He responded with "I know what you mean. It's exactly as you

Signs Surround You

think it is – beautiful summertime, baby." I realized I might have brought on the season idea myself.

I really didn't want to discontinue the conversations and connection with Mark, but he wasn't leaving it up to me. Mark's band would be in my area on July 3, and he wanted us to have no contact until then. When I hung up the phone, the gravity of the situation hit me. I had already pulled over and parked my car so that Mark and I could finish our conversation without distraction. Now I sat there, in a parking lot three miles from my house, staring at the Dunkin' Donuts sign and crying as I realized what was ahead. No contact for three months!

I didn't want to think about ending things with Mark. He was on my mind constantly, and I knew how much more he would occupy a space in my head if we couldn't connect daily. And now I would also be plagued with thoughts of losing him.

I called my mom for consolation. She made me feel a little better by suggesting that it would give me a chance to work things through with Jason without distraction – as if I would ever be able to get away from my thoughts...but yes, this was going to be a good thing, I told myself – it would give me some much-needed perspective. I blew my nose, dried my eyes and headed home.

A few hours later Jason and I sat there on the couch with the TV playing some crappy show I had no interest in. I was too distracted to watch anyway – I was working on my courage. I had decided to ask THE question: was he happy...with our marriage...with us? I felt I already knew what his answer would be, and it wasn't really his answer I was seeking anyway. I was just hoping he would ask me the question in return, so we could have a conversation that exposed *my* true feelings. The question sat there stuck in my mind: "Are you happy?" – playing on repeat, waiting to be given a voice.

This was scary! I was reminded of times when I was a little girl in my bed with a noisy thunderstorm raging outside my window. I wanted to get out of bed and run to my parents' room for comfort. I would hide under the covers and say to myself, "Ok...ready... one...two...three... GO." But I would chicken out, remain in my bed and start counting all over again. Finally, I would build up enough courage to make my move and

Signs Surround You

run into their bedroom – only to have my mom say there was nothing to be frightened of and to go back to my bed in my own room.

So there I sat on the couch with Jason, silently repeating, "one...two...three..." without even a blanket to hide under. "Just do it," the brave self in my mind implored. "Ask him quick – like ripping a Band-Aid off."

Mark's pulling away had somehow given me courage – the courage to even be sitting on the couch with *this* question in my mind, ready to spill out. Finally, I abruptly threw it out there: "Are you happy?"

Jason's response left me speechless: "I'm happy enough."

My mind responded loudly, "Are you fucking kidding me?!! With all I do for you, you are only 'happy enough'? I've been doing all T-H-I-S for 'happy enough?'" It was like finding out you're getting a C in a class you had exerted a lot of effort in and the grade didn't match the effort – at all. I sat there in pissed silence.

After a minute, he questioned me, "Are *you* happy?"

I didn't respond right away, letting the question hang in the air until it got too heavy and came crashing down, forcing me to answer: "No."

I don't think he was expecting my answer, and the conversation ended as quickly as it started, with me storming out of the room in frustration. I had never done anything like that before – storming out in avoidance was not my style. That was Jason's style, to run away and never want to bring something up again. I had always been the confrontational one, wanting to finish what was started. This time, I knew instinctively that if I stayed, I would say too much – show my hand. So I just folded. I grabbed my purse and my keys, jumped in the car and started driving.

I didn't have a plan. I only knew that I was driving – didn't have a clue where I should even go. I headed to the parking lot of the forest preserve a few minutes from my house. It was dark and deserted, but it was private and I was alone.

My first instinct was to call Mark. But we were taking a season. I called Dawn instead. She listened and I talked – until I was interrupted by a forest preserve officer standing at my car window. Great. I rolled the

Signs Surround You

window down. He could see that I was crying and first asked if I was OK. I explained that I just needed a place to talk. He said to finish the call but then I had to leave. The forest preserve parking lot had closed an hour after sunset. I quickly finished my call and thanked Dawn for listening.

Having no place else I could think of to go to, I drove home. I had only been gone for 45 minutes but Jason was already in bed, although not asleep. He had written me a note saying that he felt I had something going on with someone else (thinking that was why I left and where I was) and that I didn't want to be a part of this family anymore. He felt that all I wanted to do was talk and argue, and that I was looking for a way out of our marriage.

He was right on one count – I wanted out of the marriage. I just didn't want to hurt anyone in the process. Would that be inevitable...? This was the dilemma that kept me immobilized. I went to bed without telling Jason good night.

Signs Surround You

Signs Surround You

Chapter 11

The Voice

"Make a promise, take a vow

And trust your feelings, it's easy now

Understand the voice within

And feel the change already beginning..."

~song by The Moody Blues

https://open.spotify.com/track/0iGNd4z2m800jE2JcWmBSs

L ike the song says; it is hard having your "...arms around the future, and your back up against the past." I was going to have to "face the music – and the song that was coming through." The trouble was that I had already fallen...

Mark and I started our season with a few text messages back and forth:

~~ 4-11-08

Mark: *I am thinking about you*

Laurie: *I will ALWAYS be thinking about you!*

Mark: *;-)*

~~4-12-08

Mark: *I wish it wasn't so complicated...I wish...*

Signs Surround You

Laurie: *I know...it's all I'm thinking about...the rainy weather outside matches my mood – sad...*

Mark: *I'm in Las Vegas...it's hot and sunny...I'm inside with the curtains drawn...I can't sleep...*

Laurie: *:((((I am sleeping more...it's an escape...did you notice today is the 12th??*

Mark: *It's all I want to do, thoughts of you keep me...I did notice...of course I did*

Laurie: *Of course you did :) I am grateful 4 every second of the last 8 months with you...thoughts of u still bring me to tears... there goes the mascara!*

Mark: *I wish them to be tears of joy...I am grateful to have had our paths cross...*

Laurie: *;)*

Mark: **-:*

Laurie: *No matter what happens, I love you in my heart for eternity!! That will never change for me...*

Mark: *Me too Laurie! ;-)*

~~4-13-08

Laurie: *Do you have any idea how hard it is, physically existing with someone you love but emotionally & mentally existing with someone u r in love with??*

Mark: *I don't understand what you are saying to me*

Laurie: *I am here physically with Jason. I do love him, but mentally & emotionally I am with you Mark. I am in love with you!*

Mark: *I know...but there is so much more there where u are than being in love w/ me*

Laurie: *I now have 15 pages of pro/con list...I am f**d. My head wants to explode*

Signs Surround You

Mark: I'm sorry...I never ever want u to feel that way...the pros and cons will tell you the answer

Laurie: *No clarity, no answers, only confusion. How r u doing? R u sleeping – I've been worried about u!*

Mark: *You need to wait and figure out what is important. I will sleep*

Laurie: *I know...I had a serious talk on Thurs nite. This is very hard on many levels <with tears in my eyes> I miss u terribly!!! I keep listening 2 Kenny Loggins' song "This Is It". It is one of those songs I can apply 2 u both*

Mark: *I miss u. Its late u should sleep*

Laurie: *Yes! Sleep well love or at least sleep ;-)*

~~4-14-08

Laurie: *Mark, this is sooo hard! I miss your presence in my life! I have added another 5 pages 2 pro/con list. To see your pros on paper shows me that...u r truly a beautifully amazing human being! It is quite a list, I know so much about who u are! Wow, wow, WOW!!!*

Mark: *and about the pros and cons of your life that u created before I came along is something to pay attention to*

Laurie: *;-) yes, yes I have not forgotten the importance of that as well. I have been working on the pros of my life & have several pages already. Thoughts of losing u worry me...*

Mark: *I understand Laurie-the whole thing is that u figure what is up with you and the life u have created before me and you*

Laurie: *I am emotionally trashed! I've got 2 get some sleep...*

Mark: *Sleep well Laurie*

Laurie: *nite*

Mark: *gnite*

Signs Surround You

78

~~4-15-08

Laurie: *it's not that there are differences we can't overcome. there was no fight or argument or disagreement, no anger or things we can't live with about each other...it's not you, it's not me, it's not us...it's circumstances...I wish it wasn't so complicated cuz u & me – that part is easy, effortless – right. with nothing else involved there would be no choice...only you and me*

Mark: --- [no response]

The next day I was on my walk at the ponds, thinking and crying, when I noticed a robin that tried to fly in front of me. Its foot was stuck in twine and fishing line, only allowing it to fly a foot off the ground. With no struggle from the robin, it took a few minutes to free its foot. I felt immense joy when I let it fly free – I had the biggest smile on my face and just started running! I had never had the chance to free a bird before. My first thought was that I wanted to share the experience with Mark. Then I started to think... *Are you the robin? Am I the twine that keeps you? Was that a sign?* I succumbed and sent Mark an email, explaining the story.

No response.

No response was just what I needed. Jason and I had begun to have some serious talks – about us *not talking*. The problem was that when I would try to explain to Jason what was missing, what I needed and why I needed it, the conversation would go off the rails and get turned around – usually ending in frustration for me. Why was it so easy for me to talk to everyone but Jason?

I had just begun reading a new book: *The 5 Love Languages* by Gary Chapman. The author explained how everyone has a "love language" that they respond to, and knowing the love language of your partner helps you fill in gaps that might exist without you knowing. The five languages were Quality Time, Words of Affirmation, Gifts, Acts of Service, and Physical Touch.

When I read the chapter on Words of Affirmation, it screamed "me!" No wonder I was feeling emotionally starved – my love language

Signs Surround You

was words and I was married to an introvert who preferred silence! No wonder Mark was filling gaps I didn't realize were unfilled by Jason. Further on in the book, I read about how someone with the love language of physical touch could only feel love from their partner through sex and other types of touch. Hmmm... Jason and I were in a catch-22 situation: I needed words of affirmation to feel love – and wasn't getting them – so I was withholding physical touch because I wasn't "feeling it." And he was doing the same, but in reverse. Finally – something in writing that I could share with Jason to explain what I had been unable to articulate on my own. I sat there in wonder at the timing of the universe...

Jason and Ryan would be leaving the next day to go turkey hunting in Iowa for four days. I wrote a note indicating my desire that Jason read both chapters of the book on his trip. I highlighted and underlined passages and wrote a note in the margin relating to how someone lacking in their love language might want out of the relationship. I wrote: "I already feel like I have one foot out the door." It made me feel both scared and relieved to put that in writing. I sealed the envelope and sent Jason on his trip with the discovery information. I hoped I had found it in time...

Ten days later I finally got a text back from Mark

~~4-26-08

Mark: *Hi Laurie just to let you know I received your email. On my way home from the airport, a long 2 weeks, I am beat. Anyways, hope u r well*

Laurie: *All is well. We are BOTH the robin! True love's purpose is to set the other free. That kind of Love is giving, not consuming. I spent the first week & half in a panic – feeling like I was losing you, afraid you found/would find someone else...I am past that. You stepping back was what I needed to really explore my feelings/needs. I have had several conversations with Jason. He knows where I stand, what I want, what I need and where I'm going if I can't get it. Now I just need time to see what the possibilities are. I have made arrangements to see you July 3rd if you would like that...I know by then I will have many answers. I miss u every day and I only wish the best for you Mark*

Jason read every word of *The 5 Love Languages* chapters and notes I had sent with him on his trip. We had some very long discussions about them when he returned home. He had come back with a big attitude adjustment. Before he left for the trip, we had gotten into a huge fight over what I was trying to explain to him that I needed. He didn't get it and passed it all off as selfishness on my part. Now the thought of losing me coaxed him out of his defensive posture into a whole new stance. Suddenly, he was fully engaging, wanting to sit and have talks, go on walks, and most of all to plan dates.

In the meantime, the month of May arrived. Mark and I had been making contact through texting about every other day until my birthday on the 13th. Our texts then assumed a more playful tone, with Mark and I flirting and once again crossing lines. It was clear that "taking a season" was only marginally effective. Mark's mid-May text began with "I want to touch you again, Laurie" and was followed with some very suggestive pictures. I took full advantage of the new playful Mark and was fully back in the game too.

On May 16, I took a trip to Florida with my "twin" Kelly and two of my other close girlfriends. The amount of contact I had been getting from Mark was surprising, and once I landed in Florida he actually called me. It was the first time we had spoken live in over a month. The band was performing on the opposite side of the country and Mark was getting ready to head out for the show, but he promised to call me later that night.

The four of us girls were staying in Kelly's beautiful, 19th-floor condo, and Kelly and I were sharing a bed. She noticed that I had gone to bed with my phone held tightly in my hand. I had never taken things so far, or been so desperate to receive a phone call – from anyone. Mark texted me at 2:13 a.m. to say goodnight, figuring that I had probably gone to bed by that time. I crept out of bed and went out onto the condo balcony to talk to him. The humid Florida night air was a sharp contrast to the conditioned air inside. It felt so good to have real contact with Mark again, and we easily fell back into our natural rhythm. I stared at the ocean, now fully awake.

The next day the girls planned an intervention for me. Kelly had been shocked and mad that Mark had that much control over me that I

Signs Surround You

would sleep with my phone so as not to miss a call from him. They also noticed I had lost a few pounds and that I was rationing my snacks – instead of taking a handful of M&M's, I counted them. One of them remarked how bony my back felt when she had applied sun screen. I explained that I had always been a conscientious eater, but I felt like my life had spiraled out of control and food was now the only thing I *could* control. They wanted me to know that they loved me and understood the situation, but that they would be keeping their eyes on me.

Mark consistently texted me for the rest of the trip, which made it easy for me to keep my promise to my friends not to sleep with my phone again. Mark had become very playful, sending more suggestive photos, and I responded:

~~5-19-08

Laurie: *I like the pictures ;)*

Laurie: *I like u ☺*

Laurie: *a lot, a Lot, A LOT ;)*

Mark: *reality, reality, reality*

Laurie: *What does that mean? Don't make my stomach drop in a bad way....staayyy*

Mark: *LOL What else? Married, situation, life*

Mark: *All of a sudden it's as if something has changed. It's still something u need to figure out as far as your life – your family – your situation – reality*

Laurie: *I'm still working on it. I know what u mean. I want you to stay in, not out...*

Mark: *I don't think u look at how much your life would change, and if you're going to change it I don't want to affect that decision. U have to figure out what u r doing*

Laurie: *It is all I think about. I think u underestimate my analyzing. I am telling you I don't want u to pull away from me*

Signs Surround You

Mark: --- *[nothing for three days]*

That was how it would go: pull away, come back, serious, frisky, move towards me, I move towards him, he pulls back. The one thing I heard over and over again was how much he didn't want to be "the cause" of the dissolution of my marriage. It was much too late for that. He was certainly the catalyst, but in reality I wouldn't have made a decision about my marriage based on moving on *to* someone else or *for* someone else. The problems in my marriage were there, and had been, long before Mark entered my life. He just helped shine a floodlight on them when I thought they were safely buried in the backyard – out of sight, out of mind. But once exposed, they could not be covered back up.

Signs Surround You

Chapter 12

Right Back Where We Started From

~song by Maxine Nightingale

https://open.spotify.com/track/00s8dO3RWrFkBqC9Jly6ag?si=W4IB2vM5QbudAgZ4CVjUKQ

The "season" Mark and I were taking was winding down, and each day brought me closer to seeing him again. I was to be on my own when he arrived in town. The kids and Jason were heading to the cabin early for the July 4th holiday, and my parents would arrive in town late on the night of the concert.

I was hoping to see Mark as soon as he arrived, but the friendly skies had other plans and the plane delays had him arriving at his hotel after 10 p.m. He said he would call me when he got in. I waited. No call. I waited some more, still no call. I texted him – no answer. Feelings of dread began to set in. He was not going to be calling me as promised. I slept with my phone again, just in case. It was a good thing Kelly wasn't with me.

Vibrations originating from my phone at 2 a.m. roused me from a light slumber. He had made it in after 10 pm. He was sorry he hadn't called me. He had eaten, then collapsed in exhaustion and just now awoke to see my text. I texted him back, hinting that I was available to cuddle with him if he wanted – which he didn't. I called him. He didn't pick up, but he texted me saying he thought it best that we didn't see each other on this trip due to my situation and his harried travel schedule not letting him feel his best self. Then he relented and called me. Aggggh – it was the usual pattern. Hard to believe this was the same guy who a few weeks earlier had been sending me suggestive photographs.

It was always his fear getting in the way. Fear that I would see him and then want to end things. Fear that I would see him and want to

Signs Surround You

change my life for him – making him feel that he was the cause. Always a million fears that crept in from the shadows as an impending visit approached.

We didn't talk long. He did a good job of making me feel his decision really had nothing to do with me personally. But it didn't change my motivation to make a visit happen. I went back to sleep; I would need my beauty sleep if I was going to see him the next day.

The venue was in Hoffman Estates, a suburb of Chicago just 20 minutes from my house. Dawn and I were meeting for lunch five minutes from where the show would take place. I had been on the fence about seeing Mark, debating whether I should comply with his request. But driving by the location now, I felt even more resolve not to let an opportunity pass. After lunch, I drove back to the area where the band was to perform and parked my car. A carnival was being set up when I arrived, and with so many people milling around, it was easy to walk to the stage area without anyone noticing.

As luck had it, I arrived about ten minutes before the band did, having had only a vague guess as to when the sound check would be scheduled. Mark saw me immediately and raced towards me saying "I knew you would be here!" with a big smile on his face as he rotated me off my feet with his trademark air summersault. Again I wasn't expecting it and again I marveled at his ease in effortlessly lifting my body off the ground.

I watched Mark do his thing with the band during sound check. Sitting in the grass talking to Stephanie while he was up on stage, I really felt a part of his world. When they were finished I gave him a ride back to the hotel. We talked and kissed in his room for about 30 minutes before he kicked me out so he could focus on show preparations – which included a nap, a shower and a shave. I promised to return an hour before the show started with a hamburger single from Wendy's, his favorite, and we would ride with the band from the hotel to the show.

When my phone rang a couple hours later, showing his name on the caller ID, I figured it wouldn't be good news. He cancelled his Wendy's order and told me the band's van was too full to take us both because Mickey had extra people attending the show with him. He asked me to meet him there, reminding me that he would be working.

Signs Surround You

At the show, he was even more standoffish and didn't want me backstage, even though I had been invited back by someone else. He was clearly in work mode today and I was a distraction. My excitement for the show diminished steadily. The sole consolation was that Dawn, my partner in crime, sat next to me through the whole thing. I thought to myself; the only way to get through this life is with good friends. But Dawn was more like a sister to me and had supported me through this entire ordeal with Mark.

When the show ended I offered to drive Mark back to his hotel, half expecting him to decline. Surprisingly, he accepted and as I had no intention of going to his room – having been made to feel like a distraction – we stood outside in the parking lot to say our goodbyes. Things hadn't turned out like I thought they might, and I was left with my feelings towards Mark dampened – his cool attitude was contagious. I drove away wondering why I had been so excited to see him in the first place. The good thing was that the results of the night were just what I needed to help me on my journey of "figuring things out." I decided I really needed to forget about Mark and focus my attention on Jason this coming weekend.

The next morning, I headed up to our cabin with my parents for the Fourth of July weekend. Jason and the kids had gone up two days earlier. The day after I arrived, early in the morning, Jason and I snuck away by ourselves to go on one of my favorite hikes along Pictured Rocks Lakeshore on Lake Superior. At the end of our hike, we stood on the beach, bathed in the morning sun, and kissed for a long time. My feelings for Jason were different now, but not gone. I remembered a friend who had been in a similar situation, telling me that once you felt nothing when you kissed him, you would know things were truly over. They weren't over, but I was torn between what my heart wanted and wanting to keep my family together – two things that could not coexist. Jason's increased affection towards me didn't change the fact that we still didn't spend much time talking, and I was keenly aware that the lack of a deeper emotional connection was still missing in my relationship with him.

Signs Surround You

Signs Surround You

Chapter 13

Lessons in Love

~song by Level 42

https://open.spotify.com/track/3EGl5qmVmGlfgy9BmNb1R8?si=RV9y93PQSQGEdoHYeE5Onw

On July 12, 2008 a company picnic at Great America amusement park placed me next to the suburb where *Starship* would be playing that night. It had been nine days since I saw Mark play with the band in Hoffman Estates, and by the time I dropped him off at his hotel parking lot after the show, the visit had left me with the resolve to really try with Jason – to see what he and I had left to salvage in our relationship. But now, in spite of my attempts to force myself to make a concerted effort with Jason, I couldn't deny the feeling of excitement at the thought of seeing Mark again.

Mark knew about the company picnic, and he was under the impression that I would *not* be attending his concert – so he was freely texting me all day. What he didn't know was that I had driven separately from my family and had made arrangements to meet Dawn at the concert venue after the picnic. She was getting there early to save us seats close to the stage directly in front of Mark.

I texted him: "How do you feel about wind-blown hair?" hinting that I would be there. He didn't answer and I got a little nervous about showing up unannounced but thought he would be thrilled to see me regardless. "Thrilled" was not exactly his reaction…

I knew just enough about how these concerts worked to find someone to take me to the band's holding area. None of *Starship's* concert venues was actually a normal concert setting, so the band was never in a predictable area like they would have been in a regular concert

Signs Surround You

arena. Today they were in the Village Hall building of the town of Waukegan, and they had free rein in the place. Catered food and drinks were in the main room, which was where the majority of the band was hanging out when I walked through the door. Only Mark and Jeff were missing. The others were happy to see me, and I chatted with everyone for a couple minutes.

I was anxious to see Mark. I had taken time to fix my hair, reapply makeup and change into jeans and the shirt I had worn when I met him at that first concert. After a day of riding roller coasters, my hair still had the messy, windblown look despite my best efforts to tame it. But I was sure he would still like the look.

The band guys pointed me towards a back door with a one-word explanation of "smoking," and off I went. I opened a door that led to a small courtyard and saw Mark standing there with a cigarette in his hand and a genuine look of surprise on his face. Despite my texting hint earlier, it was clear he had not been expecting me. I hugged him hello and said hi to Jeff.

Mark blurted out, "I thought you weren't coming." He seemed annoyed more than anything. Jeff, sensing Mark's agitation, made a quick exit.

Mark was surprised that I had found them and didn't try to hide his annoyance at my presence. He explained that he didn't feel he was "at his best," feeling very road weary, and that he hated surprises – and that he had made a point of telling me he hated surprises. I didn't remember him saying that and I figuratively threw the texts at him in my defense – letting him know I thought he would have deduced from the cryptic messages that I was coming. The hints had missed their mark.

Mark's words felt like a dagger in my heart, and I could feel tears stinging my eyes. I got defensive and let him know how surprised I was that he wasn't happy – no, that he wasn't *thrilled* to see me. I raised my voice: "Do you have any idea what I had to go through to even be here with you today!" making more of a statement than a question.

I stormed out of the courtyard and back into the building as the tears started to fall. Rushing by Stephanie, I caught her eyes – she had not missed that I was upset. As I walked out the front door, I could hear

Signs Surround You

her yelling at Mark, who must have followed behind me: "What did you do to her?"

I called Dawn and found her outside. Several emotions overwhelmed me at once: embarrassment, anger, sadness, resentment. I was ready to leave and *not* stay to see the concert, *not* stay to see him play – everything felt ruined. I was upset, Stephanie was upset, Dawn was upset, Mark was upset – and I knew it would affect his show.

Dawn talked me into staying. But when the show started, I kept back away from the stage so that Mark couldn't see me, wouldn't know if I had gone home or stayed. I could see him scanning the crowd every so often. I was still mad, but towards the end of the show my emotions had calmed down and I was enjoying the energy and the music. I moved closer to the stage. Mark found me instantly and smiled.

After the show, I waited with a few of the band members, not sure what would happen next. Within a few minutes, Mark was there beside me, apologizing for what had happened earlier. He said he had felt my energy all along and knew I hadn't left. He then explained that since he thought I was not going to be attending the show this time, he had made arrangements to meet a friend from music school who lived in the area. His friend planned to attend the concert, and afterwards they were going to grab a beer together and catch up. My arrival had complicated things; Mark wanted to see his friend and he wanted to be with me too.

He introduced me to his friend and we all walked over to see the friend's new car. I felt bad about intruding on their visit, so I stepped away to give them some time together and to call Dawn and tell her things were fine. After a much shorter visit than Mark had planned, his friend said his goodbyes and left.

Mark and I walked hand in hand to my car and then drove to his hotel. When we parked, he turned to me and said "I don't like how the band treats me when you are around." I was puzzled and asked him what he meant. He explained, "I feel like they treat me differently – they treat me better. It's like they like me more because of you." I was thinking that should be a *good* thing, but Mark didn't like the fact that he felt validated in their eyes because of me. He felt it somehow diminished him.

Signs Surround You

After Mark checked into the hotel, we got on the elevator and he pushed the button. Then he looked at me very seriously and said, "I don't know why you are with me. You could have anyone." I responded with a passionate kiss and whispered, "I don't want anyone else."

We spent the next several hours talking and making out. I loved the way I felt being in his arms. All the events leading up to this moment faded away. I stayed longer than I should have, not wanting to end our time together.

Mark texted me on my drive home: "You move me in a way no one ever has. I love you." That message alone made every negative emotion I had felt that day melt away.

I arrived home well after midnight to an unexpected sight – a dozen red roses in a vase on the kitchen table with a Happy Anniversary card attached. Kissing someone other than my husband in the early morning hours of my wedding anniversary was, to say the very least, a first. And flowers were an unusual gift from Jason – clearly he wasn't going to let me go that easily. He was just beginning to step up his game.

Signs Surround You

Chapter 14

If You Leave Me Now

"You'll take away the biggest part of me…

You'll take away the very heart of me…

Baby please don't go

Ooohh girl, I just want you to stay…"

~song by Chicago

https://open.spotify.com/track/0KMGxYKeUzK9wc5DZCt3HT?si=QTmmmQkLQUi9vSKK4S60FA

On the way to the restaurant, Jason excitedly declared, "I feel like we're dating again." As usual, he and I were on different pages of the same book. He was looking for ways to save us; I was looking for ways to tell him I wanted out, because that's where I felt things were headed.

Jason was engaging – which was good, and what I had wanted all along. But it was too little, too late and it just made me feel bad. I saw the potential of what we could have been if he had showed up in our relationship like this all along – and that made me feel sad. Sad, because Mark had been right – Jason, if given the truth, might have responded in ways that would have surprised me. But now, when his hopes were high, I was in the position of having to knock him back down again by being honest with him – the exact reason I had always avoided saying what I really felt. Hurting someone I cared about was not something I wanted to do. At dinner, I stood in my truth and explained to Jason that I appreciated his effort but, to be honest, I was afraid it was too late for me. The conversation deflated his enthusiasm and we drove home in complete silence. Our new mood matched the stormy weather outside.

Signs Surround You

My resolve to work on the relationship with Jason was diminishing with each passing day as I was realizing it didn't hold enough of what I felt I needed. My thoughts focused more on leaving than staying, and Mark's impending visit to my area on August 3rd wasn't helping.

The next day I was out for a few hours and came home to an empty house. I heard music as soon as I walked through the door. It wasn't Jason's style to leave a radio on when he left – and besides, this music was coming from upstairs where there was no radio. I walked up the stairs to see that i-Tunes was open on the computer, playing the song *"If You Leave Me Now"* by the band *Chicago*. *"...Oooohh no baby, please don't go..."* was pleading from the speakers.

This was big. Jason was semi-computer-illiterate. I was only aware of his ability to turn it on and get online. Jason knew nothing of i-Tunes, and this song had not already been downloaded into my i-Tunes library – which meant he had to have figured out how to download a song, too. He had then set it to "repeat" and left the house, letting it play – apparently hoping to appeal to my emotions and my love of music and the band *Chicago*.

I was completely blown away by the romantic gesture, another thing Jason was not – romantic. I was so impressed by his grand gesture that I let the song keep playing on repeat over and over again. After a few hours, it reached top-10 status of most-played songs on my i-Tunes play list, and it would be a few years before it was knocked off that list. I had to admit, it was a genius move by Jason.

Signs Surround You

93

Chapter 15

Shattered Dreams

~song by Johnny Hates Jazz

https://open.spotify.com/track/5KXKhCfPNS4342ly8tTf6w?si=OqgwnDIVRliiKrbKSIWpwA

The anticipation of seeing Mark again was overwhelming and I thought of little else. This trip would be different from all the earlier trips, because of the fact that Mark was playing near my area on two consecutive days – which meant he would be staying overnight and I would have an entire 24-hour period of time to spend with him in person. I no longer felt like I was looking for reasons to push him away – although I still wasn't IN one hundred percent. But I was IN love.

I had been playing it cool for a few weeks, knowing an anticipated visit was what made Mark the most nervous and had the most potential to push him away. We had had a few phone conversations lately, but nothing more, and I was looking for a good excuse to get in touch with him. A couple days before the show, my sister called to let me know that *Starship* had sent out a blast email announcing the birth of the bass guitarist's little girl – Jeff and his wife had their first baby. This was a perfect segue, I thought – a reason to reach out to Mark, since he and Jeff were really close. I fired an email off, asking Mark to congratulate Jeff for me – and at the same time confirmed I would be there to see him at his concert on Saturday.

Things then began to unravel. Mark's reply was not what I had been expecting. He became very jealous, accusing me of being interested in Jeff and using him just to get nearer to Jeff. I remembered Mark mentioning, early on, something about all the girls liking Jeff and wanting to get close to him. But that was not me! Nothing against Jeff; I

Signs Surround You

was sure he was a great guy, but all my interest was always in Mark. Come on – he *had* to know that. How could he even imagine anything else!

Mark then brought up that I had mentioned Jeff in our last phone conversation too. Now he thought he clearly had the smoking gun, proving him right. I then went into a more detailed explanation, trying to dispel the conclusions he had jumped to, but Mark was having none of it. He ended the conversation with "Don't even think about coming to the show." Great!

I was fuming mad – how could he even think these things about me! But I wasn't mad enough to reconsider attending his show – I was going! There were tears, there was frustration – but *"Nothin's Gonna Stop Us Now!"* became my mantra. I knew if we could just see each other in person that everything would be ok.

My friend Gina and I had arrived so early at the venue in Elgin, another suburb of Chicago, that we were both able to find parking on a hill almost directly behind the stage. Never had I procured such a nearby parking spot at a show. We staked our claim on the lawn close to the stage and in front of where Mark would play. Dawn and her entourage would be coming a little later, so we saved their place as well. The band had not yet arrived and I had decided not to let Mark know I was there.

When the van arrived and *Starship* took to the stage, I was situated back where Mark wouldn't see me. From my vantage point, I could see him occasionally scanning the crowd. I was doing a good job of not letting him see I was there, but I knew he probably felt my presence anyway.

The band fed off the large crowd's energy and put on a fantastic show. I held out until the fourth song and then wound my way back in through the crowd to where my friends were sitting just as the band was playing the song "Sara". *"Sara, Sara, storms are brewing in your eyes..."* It perfectly captured how I felt. Later, Mark said that one minute I wasn't there, and the next minute he looked up and there I was. He said he wasn't surprised in the least – which was a good thing since he was very clear about not liking surprises.

When the concert ended, Mark didn't run off back stage like he usually did, but instead visited with fans within my field of vision. He

Signs Surround You

didn't make eye contact with me or acknowledge me as I stood there talking with my friends. I was becoming impatient with being ignored by him and was torn between wanting to stay and wanting to leave. Dawn, sensing my agitation, urged me to join her group at the casino. All I *really* wanted was to join Mark. But I was NOT about to make the first move – he had made it clear that he didn't want me there, so if he wanted to talk to me, HE would have to initiate it.

After about 20 minutes, the crowd had mostly moved out of the stage area, and my friends were packing up getting ready to move on as well. I made the difficult decision to walk back to my car and leave. It was the only move I could make that would allow me to live with myself – I had acted so uncharacteristically with Mark over the last few months.

Gina and I slowly walked back to our cars together and talked for a few minutes next to her car. I had planned to stay with Mark that night and did not have a "plan B." Gina offered for me to come home with her. I declined but told her that once I got into my car to leave, no matter what Mark did or said I would not return to meet up with him. I had decided to meet Dawn at the casino – not the decision I wanted to make, but the decision I *had* to make.

As I left Gina at her car and began to cross the street to my vehicle, my phone rang. I expected it to be Dawn asking me where I was – but it was Mark. "Where are you!" he animatedly asked as if it was the most natural question in the world and he had not spent the last 20 minutes ignoring me.

I explained that I had just dropped Gina off and was about to get in my car to leave. He asked me to stay, to come back and meet him behind the stage. I said again that I had decided to leave; he again asked me to stay. My heart wanted to stay more than anything – and it overruled my brain.

I walked back down the steep hill, against the flow of the still-exiting crowd. A police officer was positioned at the intersection, helping people cross safely. As I waited to cross, I spotted Mark, who had already spotted me and was moving in my direction. He had his guitar slung over one shoulder with his left hand clamped around the shoulder strap, and a beer in his right. He was only able to move a few feet at a time before

Signs Surround You

someone would stop him to shake his hand or pat his back and congratulate him on an awesome show. We kept moving in the direction of each other, and since I was better able to navigate the crowd, the gap between us was closing. When I reached him he lifted me off my feet in an enormous bear hug, and I could feel the beer bottle press into my back. He then kissed me hard and I could taste his smoky warmth.

People around us hooted at our public display of affection, and some were still shouting out to Mark in appreciation as they moved past us. Mark asked where my car was and suggested we "get out of here." The cop wouldn't let Mark cross out of the concert area with his beer, so he chugged it and threw the empty bottle in the overflowing trash can. Then he grabbed my hand in his now free hand and pulled me across the street, stopping on the other side to kiss me again – we had several starts and stops up the hill. I then spotted Gina, who had waited in her car to make sure I would be okay. Mark and I walked over to her window and I introduced them. Seeing that I was fine, Gina bid us goodnight and drove away.

Mark and I got into my car and drove to the Holiday Inn Express, where the band would be staying that night. Mark said Mickey was having a get-together at the Bennigan's restaurant located inside the hotel and asked what my thoughts were on joining them – while making a remark about being starved. I wholeheartedly agreed that we should join them, as I realized my missing appetite had suddenly returned.

I ordered a Killian's red beer, and with no food in my stomach I could feel a buzz after only a few sips. The restaurant had cordoned off a portion for the band, who were all still buzzing with the energy from the show. We walked around, talking to everyone, and then settled into a booth – seating ourselves on one side of it, practically in each other's laps.

We looked at the menu, placed our order and settled into a benign conversation. We were barely able to keep our hands off each other, and by the time the food came out, all I really wanted to do was go back to his room where we could be alone – I had already waited such a long time for some alone time with him. But I reasoned that a few more minutes wouldn't make much difference.

Signs Surround You

As we finished our meal, Mark looked at me, suddenly more serious, and said, "If you didn't have kids I would ask you to move to Texas to live with me." My stomach dropped. This was the most Mark had expressed his feelings towards me in person. His feelings hadn't changed, even with all our time apart and all our ins and outs. He and I both knew there was no possibility of me moving to Texas, but I was touched that he had even considered it. The gesture of saying it out loud was one of the most special he had made, and I understood how significant it was for him.

We went back to his room and broke all records for talking and kissing. The "Want to" poem had one final check mark missing: *Want to make love to you.* I had dreamt of this night for over a year and it was finally becoming my reality. I had always imagined it with the ecstasy and intensity of the lyrics from the song *"Miracles"*. *"So we're makin' love, and you feel the power, and I feel the power...you ripple like a river when I touch you, when I pluck your body like a string..."* He was a skilled guitar player after all. But his expressed desire many months earlier of wanting to...kiss...every...inch of my body fell short. All of the ups and downs of the relationship over the past year had taken its toll, somewhat diminishing the passion that had had a life of its own in the days when "figuring yourself out" was not our reality. Exhausted by the day's events, we fell asleep side by side.

In the morning, I awoke first. Mark had never seen me first thing in the morning and, like most people, it wasn't exactly my best look. I went to the bathroom to freshen up, then got back into bed but couldn't fall asleep. When Mark woke up, he practically jumped out of the bed. Shirtless, wearing only his underwear, he perched on the back of a chair near his side of the bed. I could feel a distance that hadn't been there the night before. He had not been wasted, but he was completely sober now and his whole attitude was different – somber, as if the morning light brought back with it the reality of my situation.

We talked and dressed. I felt badly, knowing that if I hadn't been there, he would have had the chance to sleep in. I knew he had precious few days off during the summer concert frenzy, and it was a rare opportunity for him to not have to be up early, rushing off to the airport

Signs Surround You

to catch an early morning flight. The band would be performing in the next state, but it was less than a two-hour drive away. Mark's lack of sleep made him slightly grumpy, and I knew he wasn't happy about not beingable to sleep in longer. But I had not made the decision to stay overnight by myself.

In the lobby, we talked for a while with Stephanie, who had ventured out with friends and used my GPS the night before. By the time we got to my car, it was closer to lunch than breakfast. I treated Mark to his favorite meal at Wendy's – a single hamburger, no cheese. We then set out on the long drive to Wisconsin. I called a few of my friends, who had been waiting with bated breath to see how the evening turned out, and put each of them on speaker to say hello to Mark.

The drive was full of small talk. It was just a normal day, something we had never experienced together, and neither of us was in the mood for a deeper conversation. We ran out of small talk about an hour into the ride. I had purposely steered us away from more serious topics, not wanting to remind Mark that my situation was not much different than the last time I had seen him.

When we were about 20 minutes away from our destination, the energy in the car changed for the worse and I got that sick-to-my-stomach feeling. I knew it well – it was the feeling I would get when Mark was ready to pull away from me. I told him what I was feeling and asked him if I was right. He didn't admit to it, but said nothing to refute it either. I knew my gut was right. I knew he had begun pulling away, and I got the very distinct feeling that this visit would be the last time I would see him for a very long time. I even remarked that I felt like this was the last time I would *ever* see him. He actually said, "Time will tell." It had the unmistakable feel of Mark letting me go...

Signs Surround You

Chapter 16

Should've Known Better

"I gave you all of my body and Soul

Never believing we might lose control

I took my hands off the wheel..."

~song by Richard Marx

https://open.spotify.com/track/5j1zOOvkxxe4uZZ2Jgl8r4?si=4Q9leXaNSV-LMPkfpSa5xA

After my visit with Mark, I decided to be low key with our communication. I had so many mixed feelings, and I still had so much to deal with in my life, before Mark. We had little contact and exchanged only a few text messages here and there.

As Labor Day approached, he called me that Friday afternoon. It wasn't a long conversation. He wanted me to know that after much thought he felt it best we move on, away from each other. He had come to the conclusion that what he needed in his life was to have a relationship with someone who lived in Texas. He wanted to have a girlfriend he could come home to, and although there was no one at the moment, he wanted to start looking. Not that he needed my permission, but out of respect for me, he didn't want to leave things hanging.

It wasn't relief, but there was a calm feeling that came over me. I had needed someone else to make the decision – the draw I had for Mark was so strong I had been unable to cut the cord. His call was finally enough for me to begin putting up a wall around my heart.

The next day Jason, Dawn, Dale and I went to the Schaumburg Festival to see *Richard Marx* in concert. The more Jason moved toward

Signs Surround You

me, the more I seemed to pull away from him. *Richard Marx* sang the song *"Should've Known Better"* and it reminded me of Mark – who was still never far from my thoughts.

The song catapulted me back to the time Mark and I had been in a communication dry spell – our "season." One day, I texted him the lines *"I gave you all of my body and Soul, never believing we might lose control. I took my hands off the wheel."* Mark responded with "LOL," and that text temporarily reopened our communications. We exchanged texts back and forth for the next few hours. Later on, every time I heard that song, it brought back the same forlorn feelings.

My intentions with Mark had never been to enter into an affair. I was such a controlled individual in all areas of my life – until I met Mark and he worked his way into my heart. I never saw it coming until it was too late and I was in too deep. Had it always been inevitable? Had we planned it in advance before we entered into this lifetime, and was he my destiny? Or was he just here to be my teacher, meant to show me something, help me with a lesson – a lesson that had gone further than planned, in a direction it was never meant to go. These questions rattled around in my head, but they were unknowable.

For the first time since I'd met Mark, I really felt things were over. It was clear that he was unwilling to rearrange his life for me and I was unable to rearrange my life for him, because of my kids. Unwilling vs. unable – to me, there was a big difference. It was time now to close this chapter and focus on what I had already built in my life and the decision I needed to make – to stay or move on.

After I created my pros and cons list, I realized that I needed to bounce things off a neutral third party. At the urging of my "twin," I began seeing a therapist a few weeks later, who was helping me sort things out. My initial decision had been to file for divorce, but I didn't want to take such drastic action without being completely sure I had done all I could to save the marriage. After the last series of talks with Jason, which were not moving us forward on any path, I decided we needed marriage counseling. My therapist continued to see me separately on a weekly basis and agreed to see the two of us jointly to help us sort through our marriage issues. Jason was open to anything that would keep us together,

Signs Surround You

but I was still unsure that "together" was where I wanted us to be. With those viewpoints, we began the sessions.

After a few weeks, it seemed clear to me that this union was not going to work. The sessions turned into a way for me to explain to Jason *why* I wanted out, instead of being a way to figure out how we could stay together. A neutral third party had a way of explaining how and why the damage that had been done made it seem impossible for me to stay.

I had not been able to give Mark what he wanted by making a decision quickly. It wasn't that he had given me an ultimatum – in fact, he had made it very clear that he wanted no part of being my "cause." But I knew on some level that if I had made the decision to leave sooner, Mark and I might have actually had a chance. I had moved at the speed of molasses. My situation was far too complex and Mark understood the complexities – but not really, not in the sense that they could be understood by someone who lived them.

How do you undo quickly what had been done over a period of 20 years? How do you break vows when you promised forever? And how could I have promised forever to begin with? The person who made those promises all those years ago meant them, but that person wasn't me anymore. I had been young – too young. People tried, at the time, to warn me against trusting youthful disposition, but the impetuous mind of my youth thought I knew better than they – they who didn't really know me. I did the best I could at that point in time, and what was done was done.

If I had had a magic wand, I honestly wouldn't have undone the past – not even to change things so that I could have been with Mark. My past made me who I was, and I came to like that person. I never would have attracted Mark in the first place without all the experiences that made me, ME. Happiness comes from within and I wasn't *un*happy – just dissatisfied, and not willing to settle. I was now ready, willing, and able to announce to the world that I was up for more. Whatever that would mean...

Signs Surround You

Signs Surround You

Chapter 17

Harden My Heart

~song by Quarterflash

https://open.spotify.com/track/3CSLUIrl2KPMulHR5bh170

One day in mid-October, on my daily walk around the ponds, I noticed that one of the few houses visible from the forest preserve path was boarded up and had a big red sticker on the front door. I was curious and went to check it out. I realized the house had been foreclosed on and was now for sale by the bank. The wheels in my brain started turning...

On this very walk, several weeks earlier, Jason and I had had a conversation where I asked him if he would rather keep our house or keep the log house. He thought for a moment and said "our house." It surprised me, but his answer was good – it made more sense for me to find a new place to live that I could make beautiful and make feel like home for our kids. I *wanted* Jason to keep the house we had together, because it would always feel like home to them. I felt that if Jason had to move someplace new, he would never be able to make that place feel homey.

I drove back to the foreclosure house later that same day and wrote down all the details so I could call the realtor. Walking around the property, I noted how much disrepair the house had fallen into. There were several buildings: the house had a detached two-car garage, an old, rusted metal shed, a small wooden storage shed and an above-ground pool with a nice deck built around it. The pool was green and full of leaves, and upon closer inspection I saw that the deck was warped and splintered. A lot of work to do, to be sure. On the other hand, the lot was huge, with beautiful mature trees, and was surrounded on two sides by forest preserve. The property was located at the end of a quiet, dead-end street, and was only a ten-minute walk from our house.

Signs Surround You

The next day I called the realtor to get more information and to make arrangements to see the inside of the house. I discovered after a few calculations that this house was not only within my price range but would allow me to comfortably keep the log house too. Perfect. Now the only obstacle was telling Jason about my new plan. We had a counseling session coming up, so I told Jason I wanted to take him on a "field trip." I didn't know how else to put it – a poor choice of words, in hindsight, because it set him up for a letdown

I pulled into the driveway of the foreclosure house on the way to our session and told Jason I wanted to buy it. He threw me a "you've-got-to-be-kidding-me" look of shock and disapproval. This house was clearly in very rough shape, and we hadn't even talked about divorce yet; having honest talks was still our core issue. After showing him the house from inside the car while sitting in the driveway, we drove the 30 minutes to our therapy session in silence.

Upon arriving Jason directed his displeasure in the only direction he felt he could – he threw the paperwork our therapist had asked him to fill out for this upcoming session into her lap in utter frustration. He had thought we were moving toward resolution, and now he was realizing that I was moving toward dissolution. It was the beginning of Jason letting me go – kind of. At least he had decided not to try to stand in my way, which would have been futile anyway. He agreed to let me have my part of the equity in our house, and he refinanced it to take me off the mortgage. He even went so far as to accompany me during the purchase and closing of my new house.

I had never experienced so much red tape in my life as I did buying that foreclosure house. These houses are sold "as is" by the bank. Mine had a hole in the roof, covered by a tarp to keep the weather out, and a family of raccoons was living in the attic. My plan was to gut the house to its studs, lob off the roof and replace the trusses with new ones, changing the roof pitch to add a large attic for storage. I would then build a one-foot knee wall around the perimeter to extend the inside to nine-foot ceilings, giving the house a more open, bigger feel. I would leave the furnace, air conditioning and sub floor, but everything else had to go

During the sale process, I got a call from the bank three days before I was set to close, informing me they couldn't close on the

Signs Surround You

mortgage. Apparently, an appraiser had noticed the blue tarp on the roof in a photo of the house's addition, and he assumed roof damage. The bank was refusing to finance the house until the roof was replaced. Now I was in a bind: A new roof would cost about $4,000 – yet I was going to be ripping off the roof and trusses as soon as construction started. Replacing and tearing the roof off again was out of the question for me. However, the bank wasn't open to any reasonable negotiations

A friend of mine who was a mortgage broker made a suggestion that just might work. I quickly sprang into action. I went to the house that day in 12-degree winter weather, armed with a small step ladder, a shovel, a serrated knife and a pair of scissors. I hadn't even bothered to change my clothes and was still dressed in a business suit, boots and a long winter coat. I threw snow up onto the roof with the shovel to cover the exposed blue tarp and cut off all the excess tarp that still hung over the roofline. Then I retook pictures of the house and sent them to my broker – who quickly applied for a new mortgage with not one but two other banks, hoping to increase my odds of getting an approval. Bingo! A few days later, I was accepted and approved by a new bank. This was one of those times where creativity and initiative were my strong suits.

The house had taken so long to close that I exceeded the guaranteed close date that would have locked my interest rate in, and I had to pay an extra $100 a day to keep from losing the low, locked-in rate. At one point, I got a call when I was out of town that the house had been broken into. Someone had thrown a rock through a window and broken a door getting in. There was some broken glass inside and a little graffiti, but nothing else. Regardless, the bank wouldn't close until that damage was repaired – repairs that were going to be ripped out when reconstruction started. Finally – 75 days after I had put in my original bid to buy the house – it was mine! All smelly, moldy, raccoon-occupied, 1250 square feet of it.

Dawn came over to see my new purchase. She didn't have to say a word – the shocked look on her face of "This is yours? Are you crazy?" said it all. I would find out later that she cried all the way home, thinking that I had made a *huge* mistake. I was the only one who saw a vision of what that house could be – and I was determined to make it beautiful.

The picture of what my life would look like without Jason was complete. All I had to do now was gather the courage to file for divorce...

Signs Surround You

Signs Surround You

Chapter 18

Feelin' Stronger Every Day

~song by Chicago

https://open.spotify.com/track/3hfqqSWS52Vucr4S0mLqUN

Divorce had been on the horizon for a long time; pulling the trigger had long been the issue. Like the bullet from a gunshot, divorce leaves a hole in your heart. The only good thing is that it's not fatal – the heart will eventually heal...

I filed in February 2009. I didn't have the "heart" to have Jason served; that always felt like such an uncivil thing to do. I delivered the papers to him myself – he didn't bother looking at them. I hoped that we would avoid using separate attorneys. I had been more than fair and left more than my fair share on the table. I wanted things to be as easy and pain-free as possible, and I would rather Jason have our hard-earned money than give it to a second attorney.

I also wanted to be fair about custody of the kids. One of my friends and her ex had an unconventional arrangement: they split their time with the kids completely in half. He would have them for a week and a weekend; then she would have them for a week and a weekend. Holidays were also alternated equally. Jason and I agreed that this option was the fairest way to do it. As a father, Jason was getting a good deal. Usually, dads got every other weekend and every Wednesday, amounting to eight days out of a 30-day month – not such a good deal if you want to spend time with your kids. Jason was a great dad and I didn't want to take that away from him, or from them. It was a controversial arrangement, but it would work for us.

It was going to be especially challenging for me. When the kids were young, I had quit my job to stay home with them and spent every day with them for five years, until I went back to work when our youngest

Signs Surround You

entered first grade. Being without them for half the time was going to be *very* difficult for me, but I really believed I was doing the right thing – the best thing, considering the circumstances.

All winter, I spent time keeping the driveway of my new place snow free. It kept me connected to the future while I waited for the new house plans to be completed. I was still living in the old house with Jason and the kids – *his* house, now that we had refinanced and taken my name off the mortgage. My new house was unlivable in its current condition and would have been condemned if anyone with any authority to do so had visited it.

One day, Dawn suggested I go on a blind date with a friend of Dale's they thought I had a lot in common with. Dawn thought it would take my mind off the divorce and off of Mark. The friend's name was also Mark and that was part of the draw. I agreed to go. We double-dated with Dawn and Dale; the four of us having dinner at a nice restaurant. I assumed it would be a simple outing to appease my friends and would also serve as a much needed, one-time distraction. Surprisingly, Mark T. and I hit it off, and we began talking and occasionally dating – adding complexity to my life yet again.

I decided to begin on my newly purchased foreclosure house with some demolition work, and the bathroom seemed like a good place to start. Armed with a sledgehammer, a crowbar, a ventilator mask and some muscle, I got to work. A double layer of drywall, covered with chicken wire in the corners and plaster over the top, made it double the work and double the mess. When I took down the bathroom vanity-light fixture, I was amazed that the whole house hadn't caught on fire from the half-assed electrical work. What other surprises would I find, I wondered. I spent the day demolishing the bathroom, making the best use of time I could by doing demolition myself while waiting for my moonlighting architect. He was doing this job for me on the side, and on the cheap, in order to get my remodeling plans finished so I could submit them to the Village and get my permits – and get going on getting my life back.

I planned on adding a second bathroom to the house but the existing plumbing was pretty shoddy, not to mention that the house had been "winterized" by a company hired by the bank to take care of such

Signs Surround You

things. They butchered the job by cutting the conduit and flexible pipes to drain them, rendering the entire plumbing system useless. My plan was to completely rip out and replace the old plumbing.

The plumbing system was in the crawlspace – a muddy, gravelly, snake-infested hellhole. I decided to first concrete the crawlspace, which ran the entire length of the house. It wasn't going to be cheap, but it would accomplish two things: make the house easier for my subcontractors to work on, and take care of the musty, wet-basement smell in the house. The crawlspace had been a dumping ground for the former occupants: garbage and long-forgotten bags of clothing, along with corroded old pipes, rusted plumbing, and a tangle of yellow and white electrical wires plus miles of abandoned old cable wiring. It was a disaster. Armed with my "love" of cleaning crawlspaces, I got to work.

After working on the project for some hours, I decided to take a break. The previous week, I had been reading the book *Three Magic Words* by U.S. Andersen. There was a chapter where the author talked about connections and how we are all connected by energy since we ourselves are made of pure energy – which made sense to me. He suggested an experiment to prove the strength of our connections. You were to think of your target person for ten minutes straight – while willing them to contact or call you. It was advantageous to look at a picture of them or to hold an object (such as jewelry) they once possessed, while you focused your energy and thoughts on them.

It had been Labor Day weekend when Mark and I last texted and talked to one another, and that was six months earlier. I missed him every day but had resisted contacting him. However, I believed in the experiment U.S. Anderson suggested. After all, who hasn't had the experience of thinking about someone, only to have the phone ring *while* you were having those thoughts – and that person would be on the other end of the line. I decided to try it. I had at my disposal an empty, silent house where there were no interruptions. So why not? Nothing to lose. I also had a guitar pick that Mark had used while playing the "*Rosanna*" guitar solo. I kept it in my purse wallet and always carried it with me.

Sitting there on the faded, wooden floor in the living room, I thought about Mark and willed him to call me, while my fingers toyed with his guitar pick. Ten minutes doesn't sound like a long time until you

Signs Surround You

sit down to focus your attention on something for that long. I had to keep reeling in my wandering mind, but I did do it for the full ten minutes. When I finished, I didn't feel any different – I couldn't *feel* him and I wasn't sure if it had worked. I went back to finishing the crawlspace project, only occasionally letting my mind wander back to thoughts of Mark.

Three hours later, I was taking another break from the smelly, dirty crawlspace, when my cell phone vibrated in my pocket. *Holy shit!* It was Mark calling me "out of the blue" – after an almost six-month absence – to see what I was up to.

He was surprised to learn that I was cleaning out the crawlspace and asked, "How dirty could it have gotten since you last cleaned it?" Then, wondering aloud about my crawlspace obsession, he added, "What is it with you and the crawl space? I've never even *heard* of anybody cleaning one."

He was even more surprised – shocked, really – to learn that this was a NEW crawlspace in my NEW place. He said he wasn't surprised that I had *bought* a place, but I didn't believe him. My other news – that I had filed for divorce – was met with stunned silence. I could almost feel him thinking that he had been the cause. He wasn't – but I couldn't deny his contributing role. The news of forward progress rekindled our connection, and Mark and I began communicating again...

Sometime in late May, Jason discovered – by looking through my cell phone – that I was dating Mark T. I had not really been hiding it; all my friends and family knew about him. But neither did I feel like throwing it in Jason's face. Jason was NOT happy with the discovery. But it was my life now – my life to do what I wanted, when I wanted and with whom I wanted.

Jason didn't see it that way. He wanted to control my life and threatened to kick me out of the house – which was now refinanced in just his name, making it technically his house even though we were still married. He told me I couldn't see or talk to Mark T. until I moved out. I told Jason he was crazy if he thought he had the right to control who I saw or spoke to. But out of respect for our living arrangement, I made the decision not to see Mark T. even though I didn't agree that Jason should

Signs Surround You

have any say on the matter. The divorce delay was all his doing, as he had refused to sign any papers until the state of Illinois was going to make him – which was two years from the filing date. (Thank you, Illinois!)

I also had delays in getting my Village permit to begin construction, and it wouldn't be resolved until the week after July 4th! I was *soooo* anxious to get the construction going so I could move out and get my life back.

Signs Surround You

Signs Surround You

Chapter 19

Obsession

~song by Animotion

https://open.spotify.com/track/3N7GqZMpZJW69Te1bfUTc3?si=Fh-SVPWLSGqGb8JWp_dQdA

Early summer was the kickoff to many Village festivals, which once again would bring Mark and the band to town. He was to be in my area in July for back-to-back shows. On the day of the first show, Mark called me at 11 a.m. from the airplane before it even arrived at its gate, to make sure I was still planning on attending the show that night. The attention felt good.

It had been a very long time since I had seen Mark in person, nearly ten months, and I was really looking forward to seeing him again. I thought it ironic that I had restrictions on my freedom to see Mark T. but none on the only man who had ever been a threat to my marriage. Jason was evidently more focused on the local threat.

The show was to take place about ten minutes from my house. It would be the first time Mark and I would see each other with me untangled from my marriage. But now I was involved with Mark T. and wasn't exactly available – although that had also been the case with Jason. However, my relationship with Mark was now on the level of friendship only, though there would always be undercurrents of attraction that would never vanish.

I offered to meet Mark early, at his sound check, so we would have more time together. He said he would wait to see how things were set up when he got to the venue. I was reminded by that of how things had been before: move toward me, then push me away. In the end, Mark declined my offer to attend the sound check, and for once I didn't push things.

Signs Surround You

I arrived at the concert about an hour before the show started, with Dawn and Dale in tow. They were always up for a *Starship* show. Right as we sat down, I saw Jeff walk by on the other side of the ropes, in the backstage area. I jumped up and called to him. He came over to say hi and hugged me across the ropes. I asked him to let Mark know I was here, as I knew Mark might not have his phone with him. Jeff promised to pass along my message.

I stood waiting by the ropes for a few minutes, thinking Mark may have been near enough to come and say hello. After a few more awkward minutes of waiting there, I decided to sit back down with Dawn and Dale and let Mark find me. I texted him, to cover all the bases, but got no response. By the time the show was ready to start Mark still had not made his way out to see me. I was confused by the mixed signals he was sending. Why bother calling me so early this a.m. to make sure I would be here – and then not want to see me at the sound check, and not come out to see me before the show. What was so pressing that he wasn't making the time? I didn't get it. And my ego was feeling slightly bruised.

By the time the show started and Mark walked out on stage, I wasn't even happy to see him. But after a couple songs, I decided to let it go and just get into the energy of the show. He *had* made the effort to call me, after all, and had indicated he wanted me to be there.

After the last encore song was over, the band left the stage. Dawn and Dale offered to stay there with me but I declined, telling them to go and assuring them I would call later. I went back to the roped-off area that was now a deep row of fans hoping to see the band. A few band members were there talking to people in the crowd and posing for pictures. But no Mark. I decided I would wait exactly five minutes, then leave – not wanting to repeat old habits.

One minute later Mark appeared and got my attention just as a guy in the crowd asked me if he could have his picture taken with me. It was a strange request, but I obliged and we snapped a quick pic. I then hopped over the rope to walk to where Mark was waiting for me. He was standing back a ways from the crowd, not really wanting to be accessible to them. He grabbed me in his arms in a huge hug, lifting me slightly off the ground. He explained that he didn't have his phone with him but that he had gotten the message from Jeff, and then apologized for not coming out to see me before the show.

Signs Surround You

When I called him out on the mixed signals he was sending, he sighed and turned serious. Without making eye contact, he said, "I have traveled all over the world performing with *Starship*, and I am never nervous before a show..." Then, fixing his eyes on mine, he added, "...unless you are there." After a moment's pause, he continued: "I don't know how to explain it, but you being here to watch the show made me nervous – I just couldn't see you before."

I was stunned – and flattered, really. And also puzzled, never having heard him say anything like that before. It sure explained a lot! I wished I had known sooner how he felt – it would have quelled many of my apprehensions.

How could I be mad after that explanation! But it was hard to understand how I – lil' ol' me – could make HIM nervous. He was a professional musician and superb at his craft – what could there possibly be for him to worry about? Besides, I was his biggest fan. He could have totally messed up some part of a song and, unlike–him, I probably wouldn't even have noticed. That's how biased I was. Or is it just that love is blind?

Mark picked up his guitar from where it had been lying in its case on the ground next to him. I took the cue and grabbed his hand, and we walked to my car. When we got to the hotel, but before heading to his room, Mark made me wait with him while he had a cigarette outside. Once in his room, we fell right back into that comfortable space that existed effortlessly when we were together – as if we had seen one another the day before instead of ten months before. Mark confided that when we were together – just the two of us, alone – he felt more comfortable in his own skin than he had ever felt with anyone else. I said it was because he was my closest Soul Mate on Earth and that it made perfect sense to me! It was truly astonishing how I still felt about him, in spite of all the ups and downs we had experienced with each other. We were still drawn to one another like magnets.

I had always felt Mark's purpose with me was to help me with my Soul growth, and for me to help him with his. He had functioned as my teacher and I absorbed every lesson like a sponge. In the time I had known him, I had grown more than I had in all my previous years on this planet combined. That night, we had deep conversations about life, and I left feeling happier than I had felt in a long time.

Signs Surround You

I was hoping to spend some extra time with Mark the next day, since the band would be performing only about 45 minutes away from where I lived. But the next day Mark decided to sleep in and relax before sound check. I thought our contact the night before would have made him want to spend more time with me, and I had cleared my schedule in anticipation of that. But instead, he asked me to meet him at the show.

The show was on a Saturday night and I took the kids with me. Kelly agreed to meet us there, as she had never seen *Starship* perform live and she wanted to finally meet Mark. It was a beautiful summer evening and the show rocked. Often after shows, Mark would post on Facebook: *"We rocked their faces off!"* Tonight, in response to those Facebook comments, about 20 people in the crowd carried images of blank faces glued onto popsicle sticks – held up in front of their own faces. It was a clever gesture and the band loved it.

I was so pleased to have both Kelly and Dawn, plus the kids, at a show with me. Mark knew they would all be attending the concert tonight and that they would want to say hi to him. When the show ended, we walked over to the backstage access area. I could see Mark about ten feet away, visiting with people I didn't recognize. He stayed there talking with them for quite a while, knowing we were standing there waiting for him. He didn't acknowledge us or gesture that he would be right there. Kelly thought it was incredibly rude of him. She already felt rushed and the need to head home, as she had plans to spend some time with her daughter.

It made me feel bad, knowing we were waiting and Mark was taking his time getting to us. But I also understood how these shows worked – and that Mark had never been at my beck and call, regardless of how important he sometimes made me feel. He was working, and visiting with the backstage fans was part of the job. He finally made his way to us – him on one side of the gated area, us on the other. He hopped the barrier and visited for several minutes, giving special attention to Ryan and asking him how the guitar playing was going.

Kelly had agreed to drop my kids off at home after our visit with Mark, so that I could stay and spend some extra time with him. By the time Mark gathered his guitar and was ready to leave, the venue had completely cleared out and darkness was setting in. We walked across the

Signs Surround You

lawn that had previously been packed with people but now had only a smattering of workers left, picking up trash. I drove him to his hotel, in the opposite direction from my house. When we got there, we saw Phil having a smoke. Mark joined him and we visited for a while. Then I waited in Mark's room while he went to find Mickey so he could get his paycheck.

Meanwhile, Jason was having a fit about Kelly dropping off the kids instead of me bringing them home. I was surprised when I looked at my phone and saw all the missed calls and text messages from him. He called and texted me over and over until I answered my phone. The bigger surprise was that he had taken issue with Kelly bringing our kids home – she was my "twin," after all. But I was not surprised that Jason was mad about me staying to visit with Mark after the show.

About the time I called Jason back and was having a heated discussion with him, Mark got back to the room. By then, Jason was threatening to throw my things on the lawn and lock me out of the house if I didn't come home immediately – and I believed him. I was trying to calm him down, but at the same time I didn't want Mark to see what was going on. He would not have been able to relate to the situation: Jason didn't "own" me anymore, but he was doing a pretty good job of controlling me.

I decided to make a quick exit – no visit was worth the repercussions Jason was threatening. His attitude had shifted from trying to win me back to being confrontational and mad at me most of the time. At least he was starting to move through the stages of loss; he had arrived at anger. I didn't like dissonance and the feeling of someone being mad at me, but it was a good change for Jason.

On the hour drive home I thought about construction on my foreclosure house having barely begun. I was still several weeks away from moving out of Jason's house. Sure, I had options – both Dawn and Kelly had offered to let me stay with them. But it would have made spending time with my kids difficult. I only had a few weeks left to play these silly games until I had my life back again, and I felt sorrier for Jason than mad at him – he was grasping at straws as his world kept shattering around him.

I arrived home to a quiet, dark house, with nothing of mine thrown on the lawn. The front door was unlocked and the front-porch

Signs Surround You

light was on, beckoning me inside. I felt relieved that I could just go to bed.

The incident with Jason on the phone took its toll on my relationship with Mark. He somewhat distanced himself again. It was fine – I had plenty of other distractions in my life at the moment. I turned my full attention to remodeling my new house and my new life.

Signs Surround You

119

Chapter 20

It's My Life

~song by Talk Talk

https://open.spotify.com/track/4jhsuQCUCJKA5fObXb6XdJ?si=Yfa76Ew_TCe7RJLqj7aVSg

For as hard, and as long, as I tried to grow into deeper feelings of love for Mark T., they never developed as deeply as I needed them to. We decided to call it quits but mutually agreed to remain friends. I dated a couple of times after that, but my heart was never really in it.

One of my dates was with a guy who had contacted me on a dating website. He had been trying for a while to make arrangements for us to meet, but it was just not jiving with our schedules. One Friday afternoon, he asked me to accompany him to a street festival in the city (Chicago), but I had already made plans of my own to be at home. It was mulberry season and I wanted to pick some berries in my yard and make a mulberry crisp. I planned to watch a movie and eat my crisp at home alone, as the kids were with Jason that weekend.

As soon as I arrived home from work, I changed from work clothes into berry-picking clothes and hurriedly started picking berries. Storms had been forecast and were fast approaching – the sky already looked threatening. I was about ten minutes into the picking when heavy gusts of wind began to blow through, ahead of the storm. Berries were being knocked off their branches, splattering their juices all over my shirt – good thing I had changed first. I kept picking until large drops of rain began to fall, barely making it into the house before a heavy downpour hit. The sky grew darker and 40-mph gusts of wind began to break off tree limbs across the road. I prayed that none of my trees would fall onto my newly remodeled house.

Signs Surround You

I was just starting to make the mulberry crisp when the power went out and stayed out. I wouldn't be able to use the oven, so I threw the unbaked crisp into the fridge. No internet or TV worked in the house, but I could still watch a movie on my partially charged laptop. I watched it until the power died on that too. It was still early and the open invitation from the website guy still sat on my cell phone, waiting to be answered. I decided to return his call and accept his offer to meet him at the street festival in the city. It would be better than sitting alone in the dark.

My date suggested parking my car near the festival, then meeting. When I arrived at where he told me to park, he was walking his dog there. He introduced himself and hopped into my car, suggesting I park at his nearby house so he could drive us to the festival. He seemed nice enough. He showed me around his newly remodeled "summer" home and explained that he lived the rest of the year in California. He had retired at the age of 42, after managing a prominent family's portfolio and dabbling in the stock market on the side.

From what this guy had shared with me, he seemed like a good catch – financially stable, well-educated, with a master's degree under his belt, and several cool hobbies. He said he was a triathlete and participated in extreme sports – which was believable, as he looked to be in great shape.

After the tour, he mentioned that he was supposed to have his 14-year-old son that weekend and wondered if I would mind if his son tagged along to the festival. I thought it odd that he had made plans with me while already having plans with his son. I was fine with his son coming along, although I didn't particularly like the idea of being introduced to someone's kid this early in what wasn't even a relationship yet. I had waited for nine months before introducing my kids to Mark T.

After 30 minutes on the phone with his son, back and forth, they decided to delay getting together until the next day because the son wanted to hang out with friends. I then learned that if his son would have come, we would have had to drive 40 minutes to pick him up and 40 minutes to bring him back. That would have been weird.

He then shared with me – a perfect stranger – a big "super-secret" project he was working on. He and a few others were to present this grand idea to OWN (the Oprah Winfrey Network) in less than a month's time.

Signs Surround You

He name-dropped some of the people involved with this endeavor and had to explain several names I didn't recognize, who might have had some notoriety in the world of technology, but did not register in my world. He showed me a printed, 15-page synopsis of the idea – which just happened to be in his car. The idea sounded good – great, in fact. It would have been cutting-edge technology, but that was five years ago and the technology he was talking about still doesn't exist.

While driving us to the festival, his conversation covered the history of his teenage son and ex-baby-mama, including openly expressed hatred for her – which made me extremely uncomfortable.

We parked the car and began walking around, with the mouth-watering smells of food wafting through the air and the sound of live music playing in the background. As we walked, he started asking me questions about how things had been going so far, dating people I'd met online. I said that besides him I had only been on two dates with two men I met at the same dating site he and I met on, and that I had a date with a new guy planned for later that week. I told him that this guy and I had had a few conversations, but since he was a TV camera man, at the beck and call of his job, we hadn't been able to coordinate our schedules to go out on a date yet.

With that barely out of my mouth, my date stopped us in our tracks and stood up on the curb in what felt like an attempt to intimidate me. He became very angry that I had another date planned – even if it had been planned before he asked me out. He accused me of serial dating and told me how lucky it was for me that he had chosen to reach out to me, since so many women on the site had shown interest in dating him and he turned them all down. He asserted that he had only reached out and been interested in me.

All that seemed pretty bizarre: I thought it was called "dating" because you could decide *after* meeting someone if you liked them and had enough in common to go out again. Maybe I was mistaken – maybe I had applied to a mail-order bride site, where he picked and I just had to go along with it...?

Needless to say, I was not digging the various sides of anger this man was comfortable in showing me so soon after meeting. Most people showed their best self, only revealing their worst after they knew you

Signs Surround You

better. I couldn't help but be reminded of the typical patterns and signs that an abusive person shows. Warning bells were going off in my head. I decided that if he was the abusive type, I would need to play along so that I could make my escape without incident.

We eventually returned to his house, and I assured him that I would cancel my date with the other guy. He made plans to call me the next day so we could get together again. I left with a "See you tomorrow," with no intention whatsoever of following through. I felt relieved to make it out of there safely, and when the song "Miracles" came on the radio during the ride home, I felt sure my Spirit Guides were letting me know I had done well.

The next morning Kelly chastised me for even going to his house. My defense was that I had been tricked into that, as he had originally suggested meeting me but was there waiting where he had instructed me to park my car. Then, without asking, he got into my car with his dog and insisted I drive to his house to park so he could drive us to the festival. He was a con artist – I felt sure of that.

Later that day Jason came over to borrow some tools. When I saw him, I hugged him really hard – thinking about how much the date the night before made me feel vulnerable and scared. Jason made me feel safe; he hugged me back and whispered "I've missed you." We talked for a while and then he and the kids decided to stay for the rest of the day to swim in the pool. We picked up pizza and ice cream and ordered a movie to watch at my place. It was a lovely family day, and Jason and I talked a lot that day. We had evolved our relationship into a nice friendship.

The next day was Father's Day. I went to the store to buy Jason a gift from the kids. On my way, I called a guy I had had a date with and we had become friends. He was interested in dating me, but I had clearly placed him in the friend zone. The night before, an upcoming date was to have taken place and he had been very excited about it. I called him, curious to see how it went. Unfortunately, she stood him up. He spent the next 20 minutes trying to sell me on why he would be a great catch for me and why I should date him. Something he said during the conversation made me think about Jason and everything we already had together... It might be something to consider.

Signs Surround You

I called my dad to wish him a Happy Father's Day and told him and my mom all about my scary date and about my nice day yesterday with Jason and the kids. Dad asked, "Have you been thinking about getting back together with Jason?"

"Not until today," I answered.

Then he said, "Your Mom had a premonition two weeks ago that you and Jason would get back together."

That was strange because the idea had never even crossed my mind until that day. The only reason Jason and I were still not divorced, after my filing 16 months earlier, was because Jason *still* refused to sign the divorce papers. Dad then asked if I was worried that they (my parents) wouldn't approve of me getting back together with Jason. I laughed – how could I have a thought like that when I had never even considered it as a possibility before that very day? Dad went on to say that he and Mom had discussed it at length and, knowing the positive changes Jason had made, they would be thrilled if we got back together. He said how wonderful us getting back together would be for our kids. I got off the phone with my mind turning like a hamster on a wheel...

When I took Jason his Father's Day gift, he asked me if he could go with the kids and me to the cabin for the Fourth of July holiday. I said, "Sure, why not." Then I had to go, even though it was a Sunday, I had a full day of study ahead of me. I was learning about the disease state of Alzheimer's so I could take a test on a new drug that I would be selling for work. I tried really hard to concentrate on my new task, but my mind kept wandering to Jason, and the discussion with my friends. And to my terrible, scary date that made me *never* want to *ever* date again. And to my parents comments...

I remembered a dream I had had two years before. The thought lit up my mind, and I recalled that I had actually written the dream down. I spent the next hour tearing my attic apart looking for the notebook where I had recorded the dream. I was afraid that it had been thrown out or lost in the move, but I finally found it. It was actually in the nightstand next to my bed, where I kept a dream journal that I had not written in for a long time. The dream was even more telling than I had remembered...

Signs Surround You

Jason and I are leaning against a car that is parked on a sandy beach. I can hear the waves of the water crashing onto the shore behind me. Jason is softly kissing me and I have the odd feeling that I have a lot of time to kill. After a while, there is an Asian guy standing next to us, and I recognize him as the actor from the TV show "Lost." He is making Jason and I sing a song to each other that goes like this:

"I didn't know it could happen, happen – I didn't know it could be this, be this – I didn't dream it could be this..."

Then Jason puts his arms around me and is holding me from behind. We are both still singing: "...I didn't know we could have this..." The Asian guy is laughing at us because we can't always figure out the rhyme and how the song is supposed to go. He keeps saying things to us like "Come on, guys, you're going to be here a long time.

When I woke up from the dream, I felt calm and secure and, in spite of the kissing, was not in any way sexually aroused. I immediately wrote down the dream in the notebook. As I was writing, I suddenly realized that the Asian guy from the TV show "Lost" was part of the <u>rescue team</u> on the show! When I remembered that, I understood that his being on the rescue team was the important thing in my dream.

This dream took place in April 2008 when Mark and I were in our "season," and Jason and I had begun having more serious talks about our relationship. Jason still didn't "get" where I was coming from with regard to our conversations, and at the time of my dream I didn't have much hope for our marriage. I remember feeling perplexed by the content of the dream but didn't really think about it again after I wrote it down.

The sudden urge to find this recorded dream was surprising to me, as it had been so long since I'd even thought about it. I only had a vague sense of the dream's content, yet I felt compelled to find the notebook and read it. I dropped everything to do so, even though what I should have been doing was studying for the test I had to complete by the end of the day

The dream read more like a premonition than a dream, and I had a sudden epiphany – I clearly saw in my mind my life as it *could be* now with Jason. I envisioned us gutting his house and redoing it so it looked new, like my new house. I saw us all working on the project as one big

Signs Surround You

happy family, then moving into that house and selling this one. It was incredible how I saw so much in one split second – kind of like how people describe their lives flashing before them when they have a near-death experience. Perhaps I had tapped into that. I decided to keep the dream to myself for now. I would wait to see how the trip to the cabin went in three weeks...

Jason pulled out all the stops that holiday weekend and was at his best. We had an ease in being together that comes from having shared life with someone for over 20 years, counting the four years we dated. The kids clearly enjoyed us being together too. On that trip, Jason invited me to go on a date with him to see The *Moody Blues* in concert the following weekend, and I accepted. I love The *Moody Blues*!

Jason took care of all the arrangements for our date. We had lawn seats and took our own picnic-style dinner. We talked and laughed about old times and thoroughly enjoyed the music and the atmosphere. When the concert ended, to avoid the hordes of people all leaving at once, Jason and I just sat there in our lawn chairs talking.

Our discussions then took a more serious turn and we began talking about us. I asked Jason how things would be different if we got back together. He had a very detailed response ready – which surprised me because Jason's standard response was "I don't know." I was impressed with his answer – he had clearly given this much thought and had learned a lot in our time apart. We talked so long that the cleaning crew had to kick us out.

Over the next week, Jason and the kids and I spent every day together. The following week Jason came to my house to stay with the kids while I attended a two-day overnight work meeting. He never left.

We decided to get back together on our 19-year wedding anniversary. It had been nine months since I moved into my remodeled foreclosure house and over 16 months since I filed for divorce. However, Illinois recognized the time you entered into counseling as the starting point of the two-year waiting period to get divorced when both parties didn't agree. Fitting that into the calculation, in another three months I would have been free of Jason, whether he liked it or not – and now I was

Signs Surround You

going to reset the clock to zero. It was a little scary, but I decided I was "all in."

Jason had been gung-ho about getting back together, but now that I fully agreed, he seemed gun shy. He marveled that I had made the decision so quickly and was worried that I might change my mind. He didn't want to get hurt; his heart had barely recovered from the first time. I really felt, after all that had happened and also because of the dream epiphany, that the stars had aligned to show me what we could now have. At my core, more than anything, I wanted my family back together, and so did Jason.

I wanted our new relationship to have a fresh start, with no skeletons in the closet, so I sat Jason down to have a candid talk about Mark and what he had meant to me. Jason already knew most of what Mark's and my relationship had been, but I wanted him to also know the changes that had been brought about in me. I told him I never wanted to be in a situation like that again and that we would need to be so much more open and in communication.

Jason agreed, with two conditions: I had to sever all ties with Mark Abrahamian as well as with Mark T. I was taken aback and told him I needed to think about it, because it felt to me like he was trying to control me again. I wanted "us" back together without losing "me." Would that even be possible?

I talked to a few friends about Jason's conditions and garnered mixed reviews. In the end, my dad made the most compelling argument to comply with Jason's wish. He presented the case in a way I could accept where Jason was coming from. He got me to understand that it wasn't just a matter of Jason controlling me – understandably, Jason felt he had reason to be concerned.

I cherished my friendship with Mark T. Things hadn't worked out with us romantically but I loved talking to him, and he filled part of the void that Mark had left. There was never a chance of us getting back together, and as far as I was concerned he posed no threat. I called him to break the good news about Jason and me. He was surprised, knowing all I had gone through with Jason, but he was happy for me and happier for the kids. He really loved my kids and remarked that there was nothing

Signs Surround You

better for a kid than having their parents get back together. I still hadn't made up my mind about Jason's conditions, so I held off saying anything to Mark T. about it.

The next day I reluctantly told Jason I agreed to his conditions but that I didn't like him putting conditions on me – it had almost been a deal breaker for me until my dad intervened. Jason then informed me that he had erased both "Marks" from my phone and expected that I have no further contact with either of them. I had no choice but to comply – it was a small concession in the scheme of things...

Signs Surround You

Signs Surround You

Chapter 21

I Wanna Go Back

~song by Eddie Money

https://open.spotify.com/track/0gqy8H7byrHRhBVtKkMVKy?si=x7P1rGuDS-6RiiqhBYBbbQ

Labor Day weekend 2012 was here. Over the years, Labor Day weekends with Mark held so much significance. He had said things were over between us on Labor Day of 2008. One year later, Labor Day 2009, he played that awesome guitar solo for me at the Schaumburg concert. It was now three years later, and the holiday made me nostalgic for him and our time together.

I had plans to attend the *Hall and Oats* concert with Kelly on Saturday night. She and I hadn't had much time to connect since our discussion on August 12, just a few weeks before – the discussion about the anniversary email that I had ultimately never sent to Mark. It was still on my mind, and we talked about it on the drive to the concert. Kelly was sure I had made the right decision in not sending the email and in not contacting Mark.

Nevertheless, after I had ruled out the phone call option that Kelly had suggested, I toyed with the idea of talking to Mark in person. Mostly, I wanted to set the record straight with him. As time passed and I had hindsight vision of our time together, I realized the damage that most certainly had been done when I didn't introduce him to my parents, especially my dad. More than anything, I wanted to explain to him what really happened that night, so that he would know the truth of the situation – the truth that not introducing him to my parents had nothing to do with him or my feelings for him.

I looked at the band's upcoming schedule for the first time in years and saw that *Starship* would be playing in Kansas on September 9. Hmmm...that could work. My parents lived in Kansas City, and I

Signs Surround You

seriously thought about going. I looked at flight schedules, talked to my parents about it, and devised a plan. The only thing left to do was put it all in motion. But after much deliberation I decided against it – too risky on too many levels. I think I was mostly afraid that Mark would be open to seeing me in a way that was more than friendship. We had not ended on bad terms; we had just faded away from one another. I knew, too, that he was in a relationship, and I didn't want to put him in an awkward situation with his band members. No, it wasn't a good idea to see him, too much to lose and not enough to gain.

After the *Hall and Oat's* concert was over, Kelly and I made plans to get together at my house with a couple of our other friends two days later, on Monday, Labor Day evening. Kelly was running in a half marathon on Monday morning and I wanted to celebrate her awesomeness.

Sunday, September 2, 2012 was a normal weekend day, except for the fact that it was exactly three years to the day – Sunday of Labor Day weekend – since Mark had played that spectacular guitar solo for me and I had last kissed him, our last physical contact. Rachel and I were the only ones at home; we hung out all day and watched movies that night, outside in our screened-in gazebo. The movie ended at about 10 p.m., and I suddenly got an idea for a new project.

Projects are kind of my thing. I have to have something in the works at all times, but this idea was unusual, even for me – I decided to document my life in music. When it popped into my head, it wasn't like I had been sitting there thinking about music or past concerts, or even about Mark's concert. It was just that music had been such a strong influence in my life that it now seemed fitting to document it.

I grabbed my high school scrapbook and the computer. I needed to first create a timeline of all the concerts I had ever attended, in chronological order. I found the perfect website, *Setlist FM*. You could type in any artist, then look up their entire concert history by date. Once found, you could see a "setlist," a list of every song the band played during that particular show. How cool (or "kewl," as Mark used to say). Through this site, I was able to recreate every concert I had ever attended since I was 17 years old! I stayed outside in the gazebo working on my newly created project until after 2 a.m. I was so excited working on it, I had to force myself to go to bed even though I wasn't tired.

Signs Surround You

I woke up that Labor Day Monday, anxious to work on the project. I had no other plans for the day. I got dressed and headed to the drug store to find a cool notebook to use. It was past back-to-school shopping time, and I figured there would be slim pickins for any school-type supplies. Surprisingly, I found a couple of rock bands on the covers of spiral note books – how perfect. I picked *AC/DC* and headed home to work on the project.

I kicked off "my life in music" by talking about the music experiences from my early years. To get an accurate snapshot, I called my dad and enlisted his help. I laid out in the sun working for hours – researching past concerts, printing set lists, and gluing dog-eared concert tickets into the notebook. It was all coming together very nicely.

I had invited three friends to come over to my place to enjoy homemade sangrias and celebrate Kelly's amazing finish in her half marathon, but in the end, only Kelly was able to make it. It was a beautiful summer evening and we sat outside. I listened to her recount the details of her race, while slowly sipping my deliciously fruity sangria. Afterwards, I excitedly showed her my new "life in music" project.

Our discussions eventually turned to the topic of Mark. I shared with Kelly a feeling I had been having all day. I told her I "felt" a trip to Austin, Texas was coming – the city where Mark lived. I had no intentions of booking a trip for myself and I had never had any business trips there before, nor had anyone even mentioned Austin as an upcoming destination. But somehow I "knew" this trip was going to happen.

Kelly didn't doubt my premonition, but she immediately asked, "Would you go see Mark if you went to Austin?"

I immediately answered, "Yes."

Before the word had finished coming out of my mouth, Kelly said in a quiet voice, "I don't think that would be a good idea..." I didn't reply, but in my head I said, "I don't care if it's a good idea or not – if I wind up in Austin, I will most definitely try to see Mark!" He might not agree to see me, but I would not let a potential opportunity to see him slip through my fingers because of not letting him know I was in town. I had spent five years fantasizing about making a trip to Austin.

A few years before, I had told Mark I wanted to visit him. At the time, I had already filed for divorce and was remodeling the foreclosure

Signs Surround You

house. However, Mark T. was the new obstacle to me going: I thought about where things might go if I visited Mark, and I wasn't about to start those shenanigans again while dating someone else. So I never made the trip...

Signs Surround You

Chapter 22

Always

"When I die you'll be on my mind

And I'll love you, always..."

~song by Bon Jovi

https://open.spotify.com/track/2RCheOr2cMoyOvuKobZy44?si=LGkgTzkPTqi3pdOAQ53Fuw

Sunday evening of Labor Day weekend, September 2, 2012, Mark rocked their faces off in Norfolk, Nebraska. It was a roasting ninety-degree-plus day, and much hotter on stage as he wailed on his guitar. Soaked in sweat, he went backstage after the show ended. Not feeling well, he laid down on the couch while making a phone call home. The call reached further than he may have intended as the massive heart attack took him unawares. He dropped the phone and dropped to the ground. He was gone before he would have fully processed what was happening.

The call had reached all the way to Heaven and he was done – this life contract was now complete. It was a remarkable life that impacted more people than most lives. In the days after his death, thousands of people reached out to his band from all over the world, and the news reached CNBC, TMZ, *Rolling Stone* and the Associated Press.

Signs Surround You

Signs Surround You

Chapter 23

You're Still Here

~song by Faith Hill

https://open.spotify.com/track/6ykV7Y99blpyNtQJXW6cOG?si=XsCOuG8VS1Sq5feEYfEr5Q

It was a cool, breezy morning, the Tuesday after Labor Day weekend. I was out early with my dog Storm to get a four-mile walk in before my meeting. I had just begun my second loop and was approaching the wooden bridge on the first of three ponds when a crazy thought found its way into my mind – an overwhelming feeling that Mark had died and that Phil from his band would be contacting me. It was such a significant thought that I can remember exactly where I was when I had it. In all the time I had known Mark, I had never experienced anything like this. I remember rationalizing it as preposterous and thinking "Wow, that's crazy!" I literally pushed it out of my mind.

I finished the rest of my walk, with nothing out of the ordinary occurring, and headed into the house to shower. Enjoying the warm water cascading over my body, I started lathering my hair with a coconut-scented shampoo – when another strange thought found its way in. This time I got the very distinct feeling that Mark had been in a horrible, fatal plane crash. Wow – the thoughts were getting worse!

I had never really worried about Mark with all his flying, because my dad and grandpa were both pilots, and in my youth our family spent a fair amount of time in the air in small Cessna airplanes. We would occasionally drive to the county airport before dusk and take a leisurely flight over Lake Michigan, just to watch the sun set and see the beautiful Chicago skyline lighting up. So I had a greater ease about flying and felt it was safer than most people might, based on my familiarity with it.

Signs Surround You

The kind of thoughts I was having about Mark had never entered my mind before – not even after the close call that occurred with his plane a few years earlier, when it caught on fire and they had to make an emergency landing. If *my* mind had imagined a death scene, Mark probably would have died from lung cancer.

When that second thought occurred, I held it in my mind a little longer, not quite ready to push it away. I wanted to examine it – wondering why I had had these two strange, related thoughts that didn't seem to originate in my own mind. This time, Phil didn't contact me but other members of Mark's band did. Of course. That would make sense – I would have to find out "outside of myself," from someone else, since I no longer had any contact with Mark. If something happened to him now, how would I know unless someone contacted me.

Wondering if I might actually be going crazy, I forced these ideas out of my mind so I could focus on getting ready to leave for work. I didn't want to be late for my meeting. I washed the shampoo out of my hair, quickly conditioned and rinsed it, and got out of the shower. I toweled off and began brushing my long, wet, tangled hair, getting it ready to be dried. I picked up my orange, super-fast blow dryer, which could dry my hair in six minutes, and began drying it.

A new thought now entered my mind – this time it was a very strong urge to go find my great-grandmother's ring and wear it today. Okay – now, that was really random. Great-grandma Gladys had died about ten years before. I owned two things that had belonged to her – a beautiful porcelain statue from the 1940s and a silver double-pearl ring with two tiny diamonds. I may have worn the ring once or twice, shortly after Grandma died, but it had been a long time since then and I wasn't even sure where it was.

I continued drying my hair, but the urge had become so strong I literally felt compelled to turn off the hairdryer, put it down, and run to my jewelry chest to find the ring. It only took a minute to locate it sitting in its white box cushioned with blue velvet. I slipped the ring on my finger and went back to drying my hair. In my mind, I said "There Grandma, are you happy now?" She didn't answer, although I half expected her to. It

Signs Surround You

was so bizarre – I felt my great-grandmother had actually *forced* me to find the ring and wear it today.

I was running a bit behind, between the earlier thoughts about Mark and looking for my great-grandmother's ring. I had to quickly throw on some make-up and clothes and head out the door.

Signs Surround You

Signs Surround You

Chapter 24

Fire and Rain

~song by James Taylor

https://open.spotify.com/track/3LcYYV9ozePfgYYmXvOP3r?si=utxxDY9FQUaMyyqREr1fWQ

I'll never know why some things happen and other things don't... I had about a 20-minute drive to my client's office that morning. As usual, I had the music blasting in the car. I never heard my cell phone ring – or maybe the music drowned it out and it never rang through my stereo speaker in the car, like it usually would when connected to Bluetooth. I also didn't see the text message my dad sent me around the same time. I suppose if I had heard the news while I was driving, I could have gotten into a collision or driven my car off the road...

I arrived at my client's office a few minutes early for our 9:30 a.m. appointment and met my colleague in the lobby. We asked security to call the woman we were meeting to come and get us. As we sat there waiting, I could not shake the feeling of impending doom that I had been having all morning.

Before my client arrived, I took one last look at my cell phone and still didn't notice the text message my dad had sent. But I saw a missed call from my mom and a voicemail. On a normal day, if Mom had called – and especially if she called while I had only moments before a client was to arrive – I would not have listened to the message. But as soon as I saw her voicemail in my inbox, I had a bad feeling. I actually thought the purpose of her call was going to revolve around my dad's health, so I pressed the voicemail play button.

As I listened to the 15-second message that was about to change my life, the impact of the words was like a tsunami, while everything

Signs Surround You

140

around me seemed to move in slow motion. I held up my finger in a "just a minute" signal to my colleague and ran out the front door of the building. Mom's message said: *"Hey Laur, Dad just sent me a text about Mark. Oh, Laurie, I'm SO sorry. I think you ought to take the day off to feel your feelings...I love you!"* Then *click.*

I don't even remember how I called her back. My mind had turned to mush as soon as I heard the words "...about Mark." I had absolutely no idea what she was talking about, and yet somehow I instinctively knew.

She answered my return call on the first ring, her voice full of empathy, leading with "I'm soooo sorry." I impatiently explained that I had no idea what she was talking about. She said she had received the same text message Dad sent me – saying that Mark had died of a heart attack...and she had called to comfort me.

So...that was the "...about Mark" part...a heart attack. I was in complete and utter shock. I noticed my colleague on the other side of the door, motioning to me to come back inside. I had to go. I quickly ended the call and walked back inside, still reeling from the shock.

Normally, emotional intelligence would have guided me to not say anything about my phone conversation. But this wasn't just *any* bad news – I had just discovered that my closest Soul Mate had made his exit. I apologized to my client and colleague for the delay and explained that I had just learned of a friend's death. The client asked me if I needed to leave, but I assured her that I was fine to stay, that I needed to be here for our product demonstration. I was in such shock that no tears had yet escaped my eyes.

We were the last to arrive in the small, packed conference room filled with our other colleagues and clients all ready to see our software demonstration. Luckily, I was there to observe that day, not to present. I took the only seat not surrounding the square table that accommodated ten people. All of the clients had their backs to me; only my colleagues faced my direction – a small blessing.

I tried to listen as the presentation began, but I couldn't concentrate. The news was slowly sinking into my brain, and suddenly I could not hold back the tears. They came slowly at first, with me quickly wiping them away, hoping no one would notice. I then remembered the missed text message my dad had sent and pulled my phone out.

Signs Surround You

141

~September 4, 2012 8:29am

~~I don't know how to tell you this but Mark Abrahamian died of a heart attack after a concert in Norfolk, Nebraska Sunday night. I'm very sorry~~

Tears began to flow in earnest now. How fortunate that I noticed a Kleenex box within arm's reach of where I was sitting. I grabbed one and dabbed at the tears. I saw my colleague, the one I had arrived with, give me a sympathetic look of "Are you okay?" All I could do was muster a faint smile and nod.

I answered Dad back:

~ September 4, 2012 9:42am: *I am sitting in a meeting completely bewildered – I am so sad... I didn't know.*

Dad: *I took the risk that this message might reach you at a bad time, but thought the need to know overruled that. Again I'm very sorry. I know how much he meant to you~~*

Me: *I know. How did you find out? I'm in a meeting and I can't stop crying~~*

Dad: *I monitor MSN.com all day and I saw it on there first thing this morning~~*

Since Mark had died on the Sunday of Labor Day weekend, the news feeds didn't pick it up until Tuesday, the day after the holiday. It was incredible to me that the news had reached me. I would not have found out on my own for who knows how long, as I never looked at the *Starship* concert schedule anymore, except for viewing it a few weeks earlier when I was thinking about seeing him. Dawn probably would have found out before me, because she never missed seeing *Starship* in concert when they came to town.

But Mark wanted me to know! I believed he had tried to prepare me with the thoughts that came to me shortly before the news itself. Then he found a gentle way for me to get the news –it was to be discovered by my dad and delivered by my own mom. Way to go, Mark!

I stayed in that meeting for 40 long minutes, with tears rolling down my cheeks the whole time. I texted four of my close friends, who all knew "the Mark story" well. Their messages kept me occupied until finally

Signs Surround You

Kelly sent me a text that said *"Leave that meeting!"* Kelly and I worked for the same company, and she was the one who had brought me in. Her words and direction were all I needed to hear. When the demonstration paused for a break, I didn't need to say much. The client who had heard the news when she came down to get me took one look at my red eyes and tear-stained cheeks and said, "Are you sure you want to stay?"

"No. I need to go." And with that, I made a quick exit.

I handed my badge in to the security guard on my way to the building's exit and practically ran to my car. Heavy sobs and a flood of tears poured out of me as soon as I got inside. I lay my head face down on the steering wheel and just cried for about ten minutes. All I wanted now was to go home. Kelly called me and I called Dawn on the drive. Both insisted on meeting me at my house. They both travel so much, it was a miracle they were in town on that saddest of days.

Kelly got there first, as she was working from home, a mere five minutes from my house. I fell into her arms and sobbed. She later told me that she had never witnessed anyone in such profound grief. When Dawn arrived we searched for news stories. With the initial shock now eased, I was hungry for the details. I got out my box of saved correspondence and pictures, and we talked about Mark for an hour. I couldn't have made it through that day without the contact and love of these two extraordinary friends – two of my closest Soul Mates on this Earth. I knew it was no accident that they were both available to be there for me in my literal moment of need.

Later that afternoon, I called my parents. They advised me not to attend Mark's memorial service. They said Jason would not take well to the news of me wanting to go, and that he would not understand how upset I was. I realized I would have to hide my emotions from Jason. He would never understand the Soul connection Mark and I had...

Signs Surround You

Chapter 25

Woman in Love

~song by Barbara Streisand

https://open.spotify.com/track/1pTGc8pwyo6xtgXBKCBcFn?si=pIMKEOLFSGGrGFsCTHlyQg

The first three months after Mark's death were the most difficult I have ever experienced. I had never felt such devastation, despair and utter abandonment at any time in my life. The three-year span of time since I had last seen him, on the amazing guitar-solo day, had not made the reality of losing him any less painful. In reality, it probably made the impact of his death even worse, because I had never grieved the end of our relationship – there was a complete lack of closure. I had always believed we would be together at some future point in time – sometimes even envisioning myself taking care of him later in life, when the toll of time on the road and smoking cigarettes might have taken his health. But those visions died along with Mark. I spent the entire day I learned of his death shrouded in grief.

But I had received the message loud and clear from my great-grandmother that I was not alone on this day – the Other Side was with me. In my heart, I already knew Mark was with me in spirit, probably even more so now that he was no longer on this physical, Earth plane. But my brain was having a hard time wrapping itself around that concept. It kept crying out, "He's gone forever!"

My brain was winning in the battle over what my Heart believed. Yet, in another sense, I was in complete *disbelief* – disbelief that he was gone and disbelief that he would choose to be with me now when he could be anywhere with anyone – disbelief that he even loved me still. But the signs had been clear! He had undeniably let me know that he was around me!

Signs Surround You

The tears came and went in waves that brought me to utter despair and heartbroken sobs. At one point, I caught my reflection in the mirror and almost didn't recognize the woman staring back at me with her red nose, puffy eyes practically swollen shut, and cheeks smeared with black mascara. She was almost unrecognizable to me. It was revealing to me that my immediate reaction wasn't to concern myself with the woman whose grim reflection was staring back at me, but to freak out that when Jason got home he was going to immediately see that I had been crying all day. He would start asking questions I wouldn't want to answer.

Sad to say, when Jason arrived home, he didn't seem to notice anything was amiss – *sad*, because he should have. But I knew it was going to be impossible to hide my grief for long – and why should I have to hide it? Someone I loved deeply had died – isn't that the "best" reason of all to be sad?

Later, while sitting outside on the back porch, Jason asked how my day was. "It was okay," I said – not my normal answer, as I rarely had a day that was "okay." My days were almost always "great," "fantastic," "wonderful," "interesting," "amazing," or "awesome". "Okay" was an out-of-the-norm response from me.

Jason may not have noticed my appearance, but the "okay" caught his attention and was quickly followed up with "What happened? I took a deep breath and told him. "Mark Abrahamian died." The first thing out of his mouth was "Drug overdose?" What an asshole! "Of course it wasn't a drug overdose!" To my knowledge, no one had ever overdosed on marijuana, and I defensively added, "Mark didn't do drugs." The response to that was a switch to "I hope you don't expect me to be upset about this."

Seeing that this was leading down a rat hole I didn't want to follow, I got up and went inside. I was standing by the refrigerator in the kitchen when Ryan walked into the house. As soon as he saw me, he immediately asked, "What's wrong?" I explained the situation and Ryan was very consoling. He remembered meeting Mark a couple of times, and especially remembered the guitar lesson Mark had given him about five years earlier.

Signs Surround You

Rachel arrived home next and was even more sympathetic upon hearing the news. I think she really understood how deep my feelings for Mark went. Her first question was "Are you going to go to his funeral?" That was the million-dollar question. Of course I wanted to attend the memorial. I had spent all day trying to figure out when it would be, where it would be, even looking at potential flights – and debating whether I should go or not. In an hour-long conversation with my parents, both strongly urged me not to go, for the benefit of my marriage.

At that point in time, I had not met Mark's family yet. I knew of them, of course, and if I went to the memorial I would know the band members. But my presence had the potential of being awkward for the woman who had become his fiancée. I pictured a ridiculous scene: "Hi, I'm Laurie. I was Mark's second closest Soul Mate on Earth, second only to his mom. Nice to meet you."

I had no idea when or where the memorial would be held. I assumed within a couple of days, and that it would be in Austin – wrong and wrong. I had sent a private Facebook message to Phil, Mark's band mate and close friend, and was awaiting his reply. When I had the details, I would examine the pros and cons and make my decision.

Then a realization hit me: Oh, my God – how would I have felt if I had actually booked myself to go to that show in Kansas! It was the first concert scheduled *after* the one that would turn out to be his last. I can't imagine how much further anguish that planned trip would have caused, not being able to see Mark one last time – missing him by one show. Fortunately, my cooler head had prevailed and I had not put that plan into action.

Mark's death hit me harder than anything I had ever experienced. How do you process something like that? The loss of a Soul Mate, young and seemingly healthy, was shocking enough. But I was realizing more and more that part of the devastation was due to never having grieved the ending of our relationship. In my mind, it had never really ended – I had placed it on hold. I had pressed the pause button and said to myself, "To be continued..."

So in addition to his death, I now had to sort through the ending of a dream that was never to be – although it never really felt like a "dream." Dreams may or may not come true, and I always felt certain that

Signs Surround You

Mark and I were "meant to be." I felt that sometime in the future when I was truly free, I would reach out to Mark and we would somehow pick up where we left off. That might sound unrealistic, but that was our relationship. Our connection was so deep that we might have not seen each other for years – and upon seeing each other again, it would feel like we had spoken just the other day.

I needed to find closure and there was only one way to achieve that without being able to see Mark in the flesh again: I was going to have to find him in the spirit world – behind the veil – on the Other Side. I knew just what to do and as "luck" would have it, I had two medium appointments scheduled, one for October and one for November. It was as if the Other Side, knowing what was coming, had already conspired to help me. But that was still more than a month away. I needed help now!

It was time to pay a visit to my own spiritual "library". I would find him again – through my books, my music, and my experiences. I was certain of it! The signs in the early morning of the day I learned of his death were a promise of what was yet to come. My longing to connect to Mark was as strong as his longing to connect to me...

Love never dies.

Part Two

Signs Surround You

Signs Surround You

Introduction

I've lost grandparents and other people I love who have sent me small signs over the years to let me know they were around. I hoped to hear from Mark after he died, but never having lost someone I felt *this* connected to and not knowing what to expect, I actually made no demands on him for reaching out to me from Beyond. But don't confuse that with not having hope – although it was more like *faith* that I would connect to him: I am very spiritual, and I deeply believe in God and Angels and life after death.

Mark and I had never discussed the possibility of our death, and we made no plans to reach out to one another between this world and the Great Beyond. Two days after I discovered he had left this Earth, I was keenly aware that my great-grandmother had reached out to me. I was her great-granddaughter; I knew she loved me and was connected to me; and I wasn't surprised to hear from her. But with Mark, I wasn't sure what to expect, since we had not spoken for the last three years. Did he still feel connected to me in the way I still felt connected to him? Or had time and other relationships eroded what we once shared, completely shoving me out of his thoughts? Time would tell...

Reality or Illusion?

Aren't they the same thing? Einstein teaches that time is an illusion and that time is relative. Scientists say time passes many times faster in some places in outer space than on Earth and that a person would age that many times faster. I think our World is like outer space compared to the Other Side. We spend 30, 40, 50, 60, 70, 80... years here on this Earth, but to the Other Side it is a small fraction of that time. So if time itself is an illusion, what else do we perceive with distorted vision? My guess is – everything! Most significantly, I think we misread how truly interconnected we are to everyone and everything – and I do mean **every single person and thing**.

Signs Surround You

Signs: What Are They to You?

Do signs exist? I am not here to attempt to prove that to anyone – no one can prove it, really. I simply want to share what feels and seems real to me, hoping it can help you recognize when you are receiving a sign, or help validate a sign you have already received. Evidential information will be presented, which you can choose to believe or discount. What's true for you is true for you, as Mark used to tell me.

I believe that when our loved ones pass away, they are anxious to connect with us to assure us they are ok and to let us know they have never really left us. They do this by sending us *signs* to validate their presence in our lives. This is the way they are able to "physically" show us love again.

Signs can take many forms. There are really no limits other than the limitations of the skills of those on the Other Side. From what I understand through the spiritual teachings I'm familiar with, our loved ones merely change into a different form of energy when they leave their body behind. They use their energy to manipulate things in the environment in order to send us signs. This has to do with their vibration level and finding a way to communicate with us that enables us to recognize and know it is them. And as we get better at receiving their signs, the way they communicate with us evolves. These are the reasons why signs can vary from person to person. We are all unique beings!

There have been several types of signs from Mark that have come up for me that I think are common signs people get from their loved ones on the Other Side. In the chapters that follow I'll describe some of the signs I have received, which include most of the common ones. For your reference, those types of signs and other common signs are described in the appendix in the back of the book.

Chapter 1

My Musical Signs

Music has the ability to bring out emotions we might not otherwise tap into. So much of what we enjoy about music is how it makes us feel – whether it's a soft, smoky beat that calms your nerves and puts you in a Zen moment, or an upbeat techno rhythm that makes your blood pump. Whatever it is, music seems to speak directly to our Soul.

To our human mind, it seems impossible to think that something outside our physical reality could determine *what, when,* and *where* music shows up in our lives. But we have to remember that Spirit is not limited by the laws of the physical world. And since music is created purely from vibration, it is something the Other Side can easily use to communicate with us. People commonly report hearing songs that remind them of their loved one. Songs can show up and catch your attention at home or when you are out somewhere, when you are thinking of the person or not thinking of that person, either way. You may even hear lyrics that feels like you have been given a special message or an answer to something you were thinking about.

Music is a wonderful gift from the Other Side. Every medium who has brought Mark through since his death has told me that Mark communicates with me through music, and the evidence for this is irrefutable. Music is definitely his primary method of communicating to me – which makes sense, as he was a professional musician, and music also connected us *before* he died.

I have omitted scores of examples of musical signs that I've received from Mark, since many of them would be repetitive. I will share some of the small, seemingly insignificant signs as well as the more

Signs Surround You

meaningful ones. You shouldn't dismiss the small signs you receive; think of them as a hug from the Other Side.

Hello, It's Me

When the wound from my loss of Mark was still fresh and I felt heartbroken, sadness was my primary emotion. But despite our being apart the last three years of Mark's life, I should have known he would still have feelings for me. The first week after his death was filled with signs, especially song-related ones.

The evening of the day I learned he had died, I had to pick my son up from hockey practice. When I got into the car, the first song that played was *"Heat of the Moment"* by *Asia*. Mark and I had not communicated during his last three years, and the lyrics really hit me:

"I never meant to be so bad to you

One thing I said that I would never do

A look from you and I would fall from grace

And that would wipe this smile right from my face."

That song was followed by *"Heaven is a Place on Earth,"* sung by *Belinda Carlisle*. Two days before, on the morning of the day Mark died (before I even was aware of his death), I had purchased concert tickets to see *Belinda Carlisle* and the *Go-Go's* perform. I felt that Mark was "showing" me through music that he knew I had just bought tickets to her concert. He was acknowledging events currently happening in my life – not to mention the significance of the theme of Heaven in the song.

The third song that played made me cry so hard I practically drove off the road. *"Hello, It's Me"* by *Todd Rundgren* began with the lyrics *"Hello, it's me. I've thought about us for a long, long time..."* It had been my hope that I was not alone in my thoughts of "us," that Mark had thought of me too and that the impact of our relationship on his life had been real. I wondered, *could it be that he was reaching out to me to say hello from the Other Side...?* My heart felt it was true!

Signs Surround You

Lastly, *"Help Me"* by *Joni Mitchell* started playing. This was such a special song during the period of time when Mark and I were together. One day back then, I listened to this song over and over for my entire walk. Later that night, when I emailed Mark, he shared with me that he was on YouTube at that moment, listening to *"Help Me."* Somehow, we were both drawn to the same song on the same day – and it wasn't even a current song! It had been recorded 34 years before, yet it spoke to both of us. The song represented where we were at that point in time in our relationship...falling in love and afraid of what that meant. It connected us to the lyrics:

"Help me

I think I'm falling

In love again

When I get that crazy feeling

I know I'm in trouble again...

And you love your lovin'

But not like you love your freedom

Help me

I think I'm falling

In love too fast

It's got me hoping for the future

And worrying about the past

'Cause I've seen some hot hot blazes

Come down to smoke and ash

We love our lovin'

But not like we love our freedom"

The words brought me to sobbing tears at the thought of having lost him – lost a love that was never to be again in this lifetime. I cried so hard I

Signs Surround You

could barely drive. I had to pull over to regain my composure before picking my son up from his practice. The music had given me some relief, but I decided it was best to turn it off at that moment...

The First of Many Miracles

It was now a few weeks after Mark's death, and I was still very raw. I needed some time to be alone with my thoughts, and I was thinking about going on an eight-mile walk in the forest preserve. The trailhead was only twenty minutes from my house, but I had never been to it before and was still undecided about whether or not to go. Suddenly, I felt compelled to leave at *that moment.* I hurried out the door and started driving.

Within five minutes, the song "*Miracles*" came on the radio station for the first time since Mark's death. Completely overwhelmed, I cried through the entire song. Its importance and significance resonated in every part of me. The station played the longer version of the song, lasting nearly seven minutes. When it ended, I remembered the compulsion I had had only minutes before, to leave my house immediately. I then realized that if I had been in the car ten minutes earlier or ten minutes later, I would have missed the song playing. I could not deny the timing or that this was indeed a sign from Mark.

Rock Their Faces Off

On our way to the cabin, with Jason driving, I silently asked Mark to send me a song. Moments later, Jason reached over and changed the radio station to hard rock music. I thought to myself, *"Great. Now I'll never get a song."* After about ten minutes, the radio announcer came on and said, "We're gonna rock your faces off!" In my entire life, I had only heard one other person use that phrase – Mark. He would post on Facebook after a concert: "We rocked their faces off!"

This sign was even better than getting a song. Sometimes Spirit exceeds your expectations in fulfilling a request and you don't always get signs in the way you were expecting.

Signs Surround You

Find Your Way Back

I was on Facebook a month after Mark's death and noticed a new picture a band member had posted. It was a picture of Mark and a girl he went to high school with. I clicked on the picture to enlarge it just as the *Jefferson Starship* song "*Find Your Way Back*" began playing on the radio. The day before, I had told my mom that I was feeling alone, like Mark wasn't with me. That song, in its serendipitous timing, felt like a big hug from the Other Side.

Just Remember I Love You

There was a time after Mark and I were no longer together, but before he died, when I spent a lot of time playing the song "*Just Remember I Love You*" and connecting it to him. Seven weeks after his death, Jason and I were driving in the car with the radio playing. I was singing along with a song and Jason commented that he didn't know how I could understand the words. I explained that I am drawn to the words of songs because I connect to them. Sometimes, the words will catch my attention and I will be laser focused on them, but as soon as I try to listen to them again, my mind wanders because of the connections – with the exception of the song "*Miracles*." That song gets and keeps my attention every time.

Ten minutes after our conversation, I dropped Jason off at the house. I had to run inside for something, so I left the car running. Three minutes later I returned, just as the last line of the song played: "*Just remember I love you and it'll be alright*." That was followed by the song "*Miracles*," which ended exactly as I reached my destination.

Once again, I had to marvel at the timing, considering I had talked about "*Miracles*" just 15 minutes before it played. And I thought it very special that I got an "I love you" to go along with it.

You Are Everything

As with the song "*Just Remember I Love You*", there was a time after Mark and I were no longer in contact, when I listened over and over to The *Stylistics'* song "*You Are Everything*," connecting it to Mark. After

Signs Surround You

he died, I found myself going back to that song often. When I woke up on the morning of October 26, 2012, that song was playing in my head as soon as I open my eyes. It was still on my mind as I left the house, and I played it twice on my drive into work that morning.

Later, on the way home, I stopped at the grocery store to pick up a few things. My last stop was the deli department. I took a number and stepped back to wait my turn. As I did, I unknowingly placed myself directly under a speaker just as the song *"You Are Everything"* began playing. Funny that I had not noticed *any* music playing in the store until that moment. As I had awakened that morning with the song already playing in my head, I realized that the idea for it to be played had not originated with me. It had to have been put there by "someone else."

When you think about the statistical probability of me hearing a particular song, in a location where I just happened to be, with the exact timing for it to be delivered? It is mind-boggling to see all the strings Spirit had to pull to get a message to me.

Good Heart

I was having dinner with a friend I used to work with when Mark was in my life. We had not seen each other since Mark had died, three months before. I told her about his passing and all the signs I had been getting over the past three months. When I dropped her off at her house, we sat there talking for a few more minutes before I pulled away to drive the 30 minutes home. I turned on the radio just as *"We Built This City"* by *Starship* had begun playing. I listened to the song, then made two phone calls. After the calls, I wanted to listen to the song *"Sara"* by *Fleetwood Mac*; I selected it and pressed play. The song played but throughout the entire time, the screen said *"Good Heart"* by *Starship*. When the song ended, the screen became normal and updated to the current song.

Only Time Will Tell

Four months after Mark died, I had the opportunity to see the band *Asia* in concert. Through a little bit of luck, I was invited backstage to meet the band before the show. They played their song *"Only Time Will Tell"* and

Signs Surround You

I wondered if Mark was there with me, enjoying the show. "Time will tell" was a phrase he had used over and over. The following day, when I went on my walk, the first song that played – on shuffle mode of my 1,100 song collection – was *Only Time Will Tell.* I couldn't help but feel Mark had answered my question.

You've Just Had Some Kind of Mushroom

Mark's mom Marilyn sent me a picture of her and Mark that was taken on a day Mark had set up a surprise visit to her. (Funny, he didn't have a problem surprising other people.) Marilyn was living in Florida at the time and was at work when Mark showed up unexpectedly. A co-worker of hers snapped a picture of them to capture the moment. It is my favorite of Marilyn because of how happy she looks, and my favorite picture of Mark too. He has a giant smile on his face and looks so vibrant and handsome and really happy.

While I was driving one day, the thought of that photograph entered my mind. I pulled it up on my phone at the next red light, and as I did the song "*White Rabbit*" by *Jefferson Starship* began playing on the radio. It was a song *Starship* played at every concert. I laughed at the song "choice": It has lyrics that says: "*One pill makes you larger, one pill makes you small...and you've just had some kind of mushroom and your mind is moving low.*" The day before, Marilyn had been telling me about a supplement pill she was taking that contained a derivative of medicinal *mushrooms.* I had to call her and share the sign Mark had sent to both of us, letting us know he had been listening to our conversation.

Five Minutes Earlier or Five Minutes Later

I was busy working on the *Soul Heart Art* website that I was creating and a mere two days from launching. I had asked Jason to take care of things so I could focus on it. When I saw that we were almost out of dog food, I asked him to go to the store to get some; the next day was Easter, and I was afraid the store might be closed. Jason said he would go, but later that evening, he said to me "Hey, let's go to Target." I was so annoyed because all I wanted to do was work on my project, but I said "Fine, let's

Signs Surround You

go." As Jason wasn't quite ready yet, I waited ten minutes for him before we left.

We were in the car for three minutes of the five-minute drive to Target when the song *"Miracles"* came on the radio. Five minutes earlier or five minutes later and I would have missed it. I made Jason wait in the car with me to finish listening to it before we went inside. There are no accidents.

When I Die, You'll Be on My Mind

It is never easy losing someone you love, and harder still losing someone you love and not having closure. If you never had the chance to say goodbye, or you hadn't been in recent contact for whatever reason, it might leave you wondering how they felt about you.

Love never dies, especially from a Soul perspective – we really are pure love. I knew that, but it had been seven months since Mark died and I still found myself seeking the answer to that one question: *Did he love me after all that time had passed?* I was mostly seeking the answer through medium connections: I just wanted to hear those three little words from Mark – *I love you.* I had heard it through four mediums, but it wasn't enough for me.

While on my walk one day, I found myself talking directly to Mark while listening to my music. I do that sometimes; I imagine he is walking beside me, and I have a conversation with him out loud (hoping no one notices). I have heard that our passed-away loved ones like us to talk to them that way because, although we can't see them, they really ARE there.

In the heartfelt talk I was having with Mark, I explained to him that what I missed the most was our deep conversations and him telling me he loved me; and even though I felt like he had answered me several times, through mediums, I still wanted to hear it again. When I finished my talk with him and was walking along, deep in thought for a few moments and not paying attention to the music, the lyrics suddenly caught my attention:

Signs Surround You

"I'll be there, till the stars don't shine

"Til the heavens burst and the words don't rhyme

*I know **when I die you'll be on my mind***

And I'll love you, always..."

"There's no price I won't pay

To say these words to you...

I, will love you, baby

Always and I'll be there

Forever and a day, always"

That song, *"Always"* by *Bon Jovi,* had come up a few times since Mark's death. In the talk I had just had with him, I had not asked him to send me an answer; I had not asked him to send me a song or lyrics or anything else. I had no expectations whatsoever; I was merely expressing myself to him. The instantaneous answer to my unspoken question amazed me: He didn't just say *I love you* – he said *"When I die you'll be on my mind and I'll love you, always."* Mark answered my question more specifically than I could have even imagined.

Anniversaries

On the one-year anniversary of Mark's death, I woke up at the cabin and, as usual, turned on the radio. The first song that played was "*Guitar Man*" by *Bread* – the song I had also heard on his birthday. I immediately texted Dawn to share my sign. She replied that she got goosebumps when she read the text. Mark likes to use this song on anniversaries, and I would be hearing it on subsequent anniversaries too.

Later that day, Dawn called to share an uncannily similar experience she had just had. She and Dale were in Arizona, driving and listening to Pandora on her phone. They hit a dead zone and had no cell service, so they switched to listening to music on the radio. Her phone was sitting on her lap and suddenly made a "weird" noise. She looked down and the screen was still off, but when she touched the screen it said *"Guitar Man"* by *Bread* – which then began playing. She was sure there

Signs Surround You

was still no internet availability where they were, but she couldn't explain how that song was able to play on her phone.

Birthday Miracles

On my birthday, I asked Mark to send me one of his home-studio recordings of him singing, as they rarely play on the music on my phone. After making my request, I played my music but never did get a song from him. Later that day, my sister Stephanie called to wish me a happy birthday and to tell me she had been watching the news and heard the song "*Miracles.*" It was played in the background of a story that featured twins who were born holding hands. Stephanie said she never hears that song, but when it played she thought of me. She found a link to the news video and sent it to me so I could see it too. I thought it was a beautiful way to receive the song "*Miracles*" from Mark, through my sister.

Later, while my music was playing and I was looking at some photos on my phone, one of the songs Mark home recorded – "*Ain't No Sunshine*" – finally played. Happy Birthday to me!

He Never Tires of Filling My Requests

It was a couple of days before the seven-year anniversary of meeting Mark and I was feeling nostalgic. I took out my binder of saved email and looked for the "Want to" poem. I read several pages of emails, reminding me of what would never be. Waves of sadness hit me. I talked to Mark out loud for a while and told him I wanted to feel his love for me. I sat there crying for several minutes.

Later, when I left for my walk, I picked up my phone to turn on my music. I didn't exactly ask him to send me a song, but I did say in my mind, "*Don't fuck around*" – as in "*I want a song; I want it now; and make it good, because you made me cry today. You had better send me a song to make up for what we will never have!*"

Before I pressed shuffle, I said in my mind, "*Miracles,*" then pressed the play button. *Even I* was shocked to hear the beginning instrumental of "*Miracles*"! And immediately after it started, I found a white feather

Signs Surround You

(feathers are another common sign). *"Miracles"* was followed by a *Van Halen* song, Mark's favorite group; and to me, it served as the cherry on top of a hot fudge sundae.

That night, I was recording the signs from earlier in the day in my notebook. I walked downstairs to my phone to see what *Van Halen* song had played, as I couldn't remember. When I returned, Mark's original song *"I Need Your Love"* was playing from iTunes on the computer – giving me that message, followed by the message in the last line of the song: *"I Love You."* The *Van Halen* song *"Can't Stop Loving You"* then began playing – which "coincidentally" was the same *Van Halen* song that had played earlier in the day.

Soul Mates

Driving home one night after a concert, I noticed the license plate on the car ahead of us read "SOLMATE." I immediately thought of Mark and took a picture of it. As Mark had been a professional musician, I didn't think he would have missed an opportunity to accompany me to a concert, and I took the license plate to be the sign that confirmed it.

The car with the license plate pulled ahead, away from our car. Had I been driving I might have been tempted to stay up with it. But I wasn't driving, so I watched it until it was out of sight. I sat there thinking about the concert and the amazing sign. I asked Mark in my mind if he had really sent me that sign. Moments later, the *Starship* song *"With Your Love"* began to play on the radio – I looked up and saw that the car with the "SOLMATE" plate was directly in front of me again! Will I ever stop doubting and questioning and second-guessing my signs?!

Toto Concert

My good friend Kim and I had lawn seats to see *Toto* in concert four days before the second anniversary of Mark's death. The weather forecast was calling for an 80% chance of thunderstorms on the day of the concert, which would not have been fun in the uncovered lawn area. By the day before the concert, it had long been sold out. I called the venue anyway to inquire about any available seats in the covered pavilion area. The

Signs Surround You

woman on the phone said there were a few tickets in the last rows that had been returned, but I didn't have the info I needed to exchange our lawn seats. I was going out for a while and told her I would call back.

When I got home later that day, I was busy and wasn't thinking about the concert. But in the middle of vacuuming, I got the overpowering inspiration to call the venue right that moment. I did so and was told that two tickets had just been returned for 9th row center – which I was able to buy. The night of the concert proved to be rainy, and I was so happy I had made the decision to upgrade our tickets – and that I had been inspired to call when I did.

At the concert, *Toto* had played their first four songs when the lead guitarist stepped forward and said, "This song goes out to a special girl in Chicago – I don't know if she is even here. Laurie Ann, this song is for you..." Kim started cheering and pointing at me: Laurie Ann is my first and middle name. Of course, I didn't know the lead guitarist of *Toto*, but I still took it as a sign from Mark when the song *"I'll Be Over You"* played:

"There are no guarantees

There are no alibis

That's how our love must be

Don't ask why

It takes some time

God knows how long

I know that I can forget you

As soon as my heart stops breaking

Anticipating

As soon as forever is through

I'll be over you

Remembering times gone by

Promises we once made

Signs Surround You

What are the reasons why

Nothing stays the same

There were the nights holding you close

Someday I'll try to forget them

Someday I'll be over you."

What a great song. I got goosebumps several times as it played.

When the concert was over, we walked back to my car, and as I started it up the song *"Miracles"* began playing on the radio. Thank you, Mark – it was a beautiful shout-out.

Van Halen Concert of 1988

Two days after the *Toto* concert, I went on my walk in the middle of the day, even though the humidity was 79%. I was still thinking about all that had happened at the concert and was talking out loud to Mark as I passed a man and his daughter. They were riding bikes but resting on a bench at the moment. Shortly after I passed them, they got back on their bikes and started riding to the parking lot that was about an eighth of a mile away. As they passed me, I noticed the t-shirt the man was wearing – a "vintage" 1988 *Van Halen* concert t-shirt. I ran to catch up to him and snapped a picture of the back of his shirt as he was pulling away from me on his bike. When I did, the song *"Miracles"* began playing on my phone – as if Mark were saying, "Yep, I'm here with you on your walk too."

Later that night, I got into my car to drive ten minutes to pick up some dinner. As soon as I started the car, the song *"Miracles,"* from the first note, started playing on the satellite radio station.

That day brought me a beautiful compilation of signs. I was also amazed at how many times over the past week I had heard the song *"Miracles."* Mark knew how hard the anniversary of his death was for me, and I was sure he had been working overtime sending me signs.

Signs Surround You

Marilyn's Birthday

The day before the second anniversary of Mark's death, I had it planned to go on a ten-mile walk so I could reflect on the past two years. It was now about an hour later than I had intended to set out, but I told myself, *"I am right where I'm supposed to be."*

The satellite radio station was playing when I got in my car to drive to the forest preserve. I felt an urge to turn on the FM radio station. When I pushed the button to change the station, the song *"We Built This City"* was playing. The lyrics of this song mention "the city by the bay," referring to *Starship*'s hometown of San Francisco. This was also the song that had played when I left Mark's mom Marilyn after seeing her for the first time in a suburb of San Francisco. I found it significant that it was Marilyn's birthday that day, as well as one day before the second anniversary of Mark's death. It felt like Mark was sending a message for both of us.

Location, Location, Location

As you have seen, Mark clearly speaks to me through music. The various examples I have given are just a fraction of what I have received from him. I'd like to end this chapter with the music sign that was the most significant and had the most meaning for me.

It had been more than two years since Mark passed. We were on our way to a hockey tournament for my son Ryan that was to take place 45 minutes from our house. Jason was driving, Ryan was sitting up front, and I was in the back seat diligently working on a Soul Whispers post.

We exited the highway and, for whatever reason, I looked up from my work – in time to see the Holiday Inn Express through my window. It was the hotel Mark stayed at back in August of 2008 after his concert in Elgin. Mickey bought dinner for the band at the Bennigan's Restaurant located inside the hotel. This was the only meal Mark and I ever shared, and the image of me sitting with him at that booth came to mind. I remembered that as we finished our meal, Mark looked at me, suddenly serious, and said, "If you didn't have kids I would ask you to move to Texas to live with me." Thinking of that night evoked strong feelings and

Signs Surround You

does so even today. It was the night of the end of everything between Mark and me.

The night before the hockey tournament, I had been listening to a top-40 countdown that I enjoy on "80's on 8" satellite XM radio. I don't listen to that station very much, but the radio was still tuned to it. Five seconds after we passed Bennigan's restaurant, it started playing "*We Built This City*" by *Starship*! When I heard it begin to play, I actually started shaking and got a full adrenalin rush. I had to text Dawn and Gina, who had both gone with me to that concert.

That sign was one of the biggest confirmations I had ever gotten from Mark, because of the significance of that night to me and because the feeling I got was that Mark was letting me know he felt the same. I had no control over the situation that allowed for the timing. It might seem like such a simple thing, but the complexity of the timing was what made this sign so special, and specifically my lack of control in the timing. A sign where "all the stars align" can give you so much confirmation and joy.

Later, after the hockey tournament, Jason was again driving and this time changed the radio station to one which, it so happened, wouldn't be playing any songs I would associate with Mark – further corroborating the fact that the satellite XM radio station had been "queued up" for me to receive the sign.

Signs Surround You

Chapter 2

Manipulating Electronics

We are surrounded by electronics, and loved ones in Spirit seem to like to play with electricity and electronics. After all, our loved ones are pure energy now. They are capable of turning the lights on and off, making the phone ring, leaving us voice messages, sending us texts and even changing our computer screen or freezing it with a special message. Electronics can also be used to send us a double sign, such as changing the radio station to a different one while playing a particular song just for you.

Signs that seem to be favored by many in Spirit include lights flashing in the room, the power going on and off or just staying off.

Freezing My Electronics

My vehicle has a touchscreen that shows radio information which includes the name of the radio station I am tuned to and the name of the artist and song currently playing. Four days after Mark died, when I started my car in the morning, the radio had last been tuned into an XM satellite station called "The Bridge." The screen said, *"With Your Love"* by *Jefferson Starship,* but there was no sound, only silence. Puzzled, I pressed a button to change to another satellite station. The radio then burst to life, broadcasting the song being played on that station – but the screen still said *"With Your Love"* by *Jefferson Starship.* I pressed the button again, to change to an FM station, and the same thing happened – the screen showed *"With Your Love,"* by *Jefferson Starship* yet played the song the station was broadcasting. I was both puzzled and amazed – nothing like that had ever happened before.

Signs Surround You

I continued pressing buttons and whatever was playing on the station whose button I pushed came through on my stereo speaker like normal – but the car screen *still* said *"With Your Love"* by *Jefferson Starship*. I kept pressing buttons and changing stations back and forth between FM, AM and satellite – with the same result every time. My heart was screaming "It's him! It's him!" But my brain still wanted me to find a "rational explanation."

I decided to call the Sirius XM Radio company, who broadcasts the station "The Bridge," to check on my satellite subscription. Perhaps it had expired and was turned off, which might explain why my screen was frozen. The customer service representative had never heard of such a thing happening. He checked on my subscription and verified that it was still good for another year. He then offered to reset my radio remotely from their end, which he assured me would clear and reset my frozen screen. Part of me wanted to leave it alone, so I could savor the message Mark was sending me for a while longer. But since I had waited on hold so long to talk to someone, I agreed to let him try. I waited on the line for five minutes while he reset the programming and confirmed it was complete. To my amazement, my screen was still frozen – it still read *"With Your Love"* by *Jefferson Starship*.

My car screen stayed frozen like that even after I turned the car off and back on again to run a quick errand. When I arrived at my friend Dawn's house for lunch, the screen was still frozen with the title *"With Your Love"* by *Jefferson Starship*. I brought her out to the car to show it to her. As soon as she saw it, she said, "Hi, Mark." Later, when I returned to my car after lunch, the message had vanished and my touchscreen was finally back to normal.

I don't know why I was so resistant to believing that Mark was trying to contact me, but Mark's death was still so new, and it had been three years since we had last spoken; I was afraid he might not have wanted to connect with me. I guess I needed to be sure there wasn't a logical explanation before I let myself believe something magical was really happening. In the end, I felt this was the first *really* big sign I had received from Mark letting me know without a doubt that he was around.

Signs Surround You

I Know You're Out There Somewhere

While driving home on the six-hour ride from the cabin, I was thinking about the day before when I had heard on the radio the song *"I Know You're Out There Somewhere"* by The *Moody Blues*. I felt strongly that Mark had sent the song to me, but at the time, receiving songs from Mark was still something new. I had never lost anyone this close to me who I felt would send me songs I could connect to. I wanted to hear The *Moody Blues* song again, so I could listen closely to the words. I queued it up on my iPhone music and it wirelessly connected to the car radio.

As the song was playing, the car's touchscreen changed, and instead of saying *"I Know You're Out There Somewhere"* by *The Moody Blues*, the screen now said *"White Rabbit"* by *Jefferson Starship*. My car radio screen had only acted like that the one other time – showing the name of a song that was not the one playing.

I switched to the satellite radio station and the screen now showed a different song name, matching what was playing. When I switched back to connect to my iPhone song again, The *Moody Blues* song was still playing, but the screen now said: *??? Jefferson Starship*. I had never seen question marks before either, and it still showed a different band than the one that was playing. What was happening was against all probabilities.

When the *Moody Blues* song ended, the screen switched to the name of the song that had just begun playing, in the normal mode. My heart knew that Mark was answering my question and confirming that he had indeed sent the song to me the day before, when I was at my cabin. I truly felt in awe at what I had just experienced.

We Will Be Connected for a Long Time

I "recycled" my old flip phone by using it as an alarm clock. Safely locked inside were ten significant saved text messages from when Mark and I were still together. One night, it was after midnight before I was finally heading for bed. I set my alarms for 5:45, 6:00, and 6:05 a.m., to insure I wouldn't oversleep the next morning. Before placing the phone on my nightstand next to the bed, I reopened two text messages from 2009 that read: *"Sweet dreams"* and *"We will be connected for a long time."* I

Signs Surround You

smiled to myself and silently told Mark goodnight, then placed the phone on the nightstand and hopped into bed.

No sooner had I laid my head on the pillow than the alarm began sounding. Not wanting to wake Jason, who had to get up super early, I scrambled to turn it off quickly – I'm not even sure how I got the alarm turned off that fast. Then, curious to see what I had done to set the alarm off, I looked at all the alarms to see if I had misset one of them, but they were all three correctly set up. I'm "guessing" Mark just wanted to say goodnight back to me.

April Fools

I was driving in my car when I was dialed into a conference call for work. The call suddenly disconnected, even though I had full cell signal. When the disconnection occurred, the satellite radio launched back into play mode and the song *"It's Not Over"* by *Starship* was playing through my speakers.

Now, what are the chances for that to happen? I thought it funny that Mark disrupted my call to play an April Fools' Day prank on me!

Sedona

Shortly after moving to Arizona, Rachel and I took a day trip to Sedona, Arizona. As we were driving, I was playing one of her favorite songs *"Down Under"* by *Men at Work* through my YouTube app – as it was not downloaded in my personal music. She asked me what kind of sandwich they were referring to in the song. I handed her my phone so she could read the lyrics on its screen.

Suddenly the song changed to "*Miracles*" by *Jefferson Starship* and the screen *in the car* now also mirrored my phone with the title "*Miracles*" just as the lyrics "...*If only you believe in miracles, baby we'd get by*" played. Then the screen changed again to *"Unknown Artist."* At that moment I felt Mark all over – like his Soul passed thru my body – and I felt goosebumps from head to toe! Then my phone music reset itself and went to the default beginning of my song collection. This was the first sign I had received from Mark since our move.

Signs Surround You

171

Chapter 3

Signs Designed to Reach You
With a Message

There are times when our loved ones in Spirit want to get a specific message to us. It might come through a dream or through a communication from a person here on Earth. Sometimes, it is an actual physical sign that you see, with an idea in writing that has been trying to "hit you over the head" to get across to you.

Signs can come to you in any way, in any form, at any time. When you are given the gift of information, don't ignore it; there are no accidents. By following the suggestion of a sign from the Other Side, you may even avoid a problem or a hassle.

What Dreams May Come

Since Mark's death three weeks earlier, I had been on a reading frenzy and was also spending a lot of time taking longer walks. I decided to download a few books on tape so I would have something to listen to besides my iPhone music; at the time, music was often too emotional for me to handle. The first book I downloaded was by Deepak Chopra, *The Seven Spiritual Laws of Success*. That book did a great job of feeding my mind while keeping my thoughts away from Mark, if only temporarily.

I was also searching for ways to connect to Mark, and I reread several of the books in my collection written by mediums. Along with that, I was on a quest to find books I hadn't read that were written by mediums I was unfamiliar with. I started with the audiobook *The Spirit Whisperer*, by John Holland. At one hour, 30 minutes in length, it was

Signs Surround You

perfect for one of my longer walks. In this book, the movie *What Dreams May Come*, starring Robin Williams, was referenced. The author stated that this movie depicted how he thinks the Other Side works, and that it had a good visual representation of what his Spirit Guides had told him regarding how the Other Side looks.

Next, I read a book by a medium from England, titled *The Survival of the Soul*, by Lisa Williams. She too referenced *What Dreams May Come*. With two random references to the same movie in the same week, I felt I had to see it. I didn't have it in my movie collection, so I ordered it from Netflix, to be delivered to my house in two days. It was disappointing that it would not arrive in time for me to take it to the cabin.

This movie was still on my mind when I came to the frozen foods section of a grocery store near our cabin, where the movies for sale were situated. Looking through the rack, I was dumbfounded to find sitting on the shelf a copy of *What Dreams May Come*! This was not a recent movie; it had been released 14 years earlier. It hadn't been a particularly popular movie, either. It had good reviews but had not won any awards or critical acclaim. And Robin Williams was still alive at the time, so the movie was not being carried in memory of his death. The store only carried a tiny movie selection of less than 50 movies – chosen from potentially tens of thousands of possible movie titles they could have selected. It was a tiny grocery store in a town of less than 2,000 people, and I was shocked to see this particular movie available for sale there. I bought it, of course, and watched it that very night.

As I was watching the movie, I remembered seeing it years before. But on that night I watched it through different eyes. One of the core messages that is always expressed in books written by mediums is that our loved ones on the Other Side never leave us. This movie did a great job of demonstrating how they know what is happening in our life even after they are gone. They still care about us, love us, and want us to know they are with us always.

Signs are designed to pique our curiosity and get our attention. The Other Side does not have the limitations we do in this physical world, and they can use many types of signs to get our attention and touch our heart. We only have to be open to receive them...

Chapter 4

Facilitated by the Other Side

The creation of new relationships can also be facilitated by the Other Side. Sometimes we need assistance in meeting a Soul Mate, or creating the circumstances perfect for "bumping into" one. We can't forget that we were all connected before we came to this Earth, and when the timing is right the Soul from the Other Side will move Heaven and Earth to make a needed connection.

New Friendship

I went to the store to buy a sympathy card for a friend of mine who had to put her dog to sleep. While I was looking for something "dog-appropriate," I picked up a card in the loss section. Instantly, I "knew" I was supposed to mail it to Mark's mom. I had not previously thought about sending a card to her, because of my own grief. There was also the fact that the relationship between Mark and me had been unusual. But it had been almost a month since Mark's death, and I decided that sending a card now would be fine.

I had not met Mark's mom before he died, but I was able to find her address, and I wrote her a two-page letter. Then I printed some pictures of Mark and me from when we were together and mailed them to her along with the card and letter.

The next day it occurred to me that the address might not be current, and I remembered that I had put my return address on the envelope. I began to worry that the card might be returned to me, and I didn't want Jason to see it in the mail – I thought he might open the letter and read it. That would have been uncharacteristic of him, but seeing

Signs Surround You

174

Mark's last name might raise too much curiosity. I didn't feel I had anything to hide, but I knew if he read what I had written he might be upset; Jason didn't understand the bigger Soul picture and connection Mark and I shared. I also felt he would think it took the Soul connection I had with *him* away, and it would hurt his Earthly ego. Added to that was the worry that if he intercepted the card in the mail, read it and never told me that he had done so, it would seem as though Mark's mom hadn't responded to my gesture, which would have been unfortunate for both of us.

Mark talked about his mom quite a bit; he was very close to her. He said she had been a very big spiritual influence on him, more so than anyone else in his life. When he was alive I had often thought that I would like to meet her someday. She was one of the biggest reasons I had wanted to attend Mark's memorial service. I wanted to tell her how much Mark had talked about her and how much he had valued their connection. Not that she wouldn't have been aware of that, but it's the kind of thing that's always nice to hear. One time when Mark and I were in a conversation about Soul connections, he shared with me that he thought his mom was his closest Soul Mate on Earth. What a beautiful compliment for his mom!

Later that same day, while driving Ryan to get his hair cut, I told him about the card I had sent to Mark's mom and my concern that it might be returned to me and intercepted by his dad. As we pulled into the parking lot, I was explaining to him that I was afraid his dad would be hurt if he read what I had written. Just as I was communicating those thoughts, the song "*Fooled Around and Fell in Love*" by the *Elvin Bishop Band* began playing on the radio. I considered this a *Starship* song because Mickey Thomas had been the singer for the *Elvin Bishop Band* when the song was recorded, and it was also played at every *Starship* concert I ever attended. I knew as soon as I heard it on the radio that Mark was letting me know his mom would get the card and everything would be ok. That particular day was also the one-month anniversary of Mark's death. I shared those thoughts with Ryan and he too was amazed.

The next day, I woke up to an email from Mark's mom! A feeling of relief washed over me as I realized my card had been received by her and that she had actually responded to me, and I no longer had to worry about Jason and the effect it might have on him.

Signs Surround You

Later that night, when the house was quiet, I sat down to respond to Marilyn's email. I had so many questions for her. First, I wanted to know if Mark had been buried or cremated. As I wrote the word "cremated" the song

"Miracles" began playing, and I could now feel Mark's presence around me. I immediately got goosebumps all over my body. As the song played, I noticed that there were hesitations before each of three notes – which had never happened before with this song or with any of my music. I couldn't help but feel that Mark was sending me another sign. Incidentally, as I would later discover, Mark's body had indeed been cremated.

Austin, Finally!

It was the day after I learned of Mark's death. My friend and colleague Melissa and a client of ours had met for lunch. I was still filled with grief and almost hadn't gone. After we discussed some business, the client mentioned a trip to our company's Innovation Center in Austin, Texas. He declared that this year he was finally going to go, after being invited and not attending for the last six years. My premonition from three days before about making a trip to Austin was beginning to look like a real possibility – *if* I was able to get permission to attend that meeting with my client.

After the lunch, I emailed my boss to confirm that I would be able to accompany our client to Austin. My boss wholeheartedly supported my going with him, and she approved the trip. It was scheduled to take place in less than a month. I would finally be traveling to Austin, Texas – the former residence of Mark and the town I had dreamed of visiting since 2007.

In Part 1 of this book, I wrote about telling my friend Kelly that I didn't know how or why but I "felt" a trip to Austin was coming. (That was the day after Mark died, but I didn't yet know about his death.) I had never before had the opportunity to travel to Austin, and when I now called Kelly to tell her the news that the trip was going to happen, she too was blown away.

Signs Surround You

176

Another sign occurred a few days later. I was driving along when the song "*Never Be the Same*" by *Christopher Cross* started playing on the radio. It had been many years since I had heard it, and I can't think of a song that better articulated how I felt about Mark and our relationship. The lyrics penetrated my heart and brought me to sobbing tears. I went home and downloaded the song into my music collection and played it many times over the weeks that followed, before my trip to Austin.

Traveling to Austin

I was so excited about my upcoming trip to Austin that I made sure I planned my activities in advance so as not to miss anything. I wanted to really take in the city. I would be spending time in downtown Austin, but I was also going to have some free time to go on a hike or two. I found out there was an amazing trail called the Barton Creek Greenbelt, which stretched many miles across the outskirts of the city. I planned my routes so I could hike all of it during the three days while I was there.

Even as I boarded the plane, I still couldn't believe I was finally traveling to Austin, the town I had wanted to visit for five years. When I got off the plane at the Austin airport, I could feel Mark's presence around me. I knew he would have been so happy that I finally made it to Austin, and I had no doubt that he was accompanying me on the journey.

Making my way toward the rental-car pickup, I got on a long escalator that took me down to the lower level. The escalators were surrounded by ten-foot-high replicas of guitars – the center point of the airport. I felt goosebumps pop up on my arms that told me Mark was still around. The guitars made me think about the musical influence this town must have had on him. I imagined how it would be if you traveled for a living and were constantly at the airport, where your hometown featured giant guitars to send you off and welcome you back home each time.

After standing in line to get my rental car, I was ready to begin my journey. But before leaving the building to retrieve the car, I decided I had better use the ladies room first. On my way, I heard a song playing through the speakers overhead – it was the song "*Never Be the Same*"! I was stunned to hear *that* song playing, as it was not a commonly played

Signs Surround You

song and it held such significance for me. The words from the song's title *"Never be the Same..."* hit me and I started to cry. This was the very song I had heard while driving in my car after learning I would be going to Austin, and it had brought tears to me then too. I just stood there and listened as the song played out.

When it finished, I walked into the ladies' room as a country song came on over the speakers. I was in Austin, after all, and country was more like what I would have expected to be playing in Texas. I washed my hands and then headed towards the bathroom exit as another country song began playing.

As I was leaving the ladies room, I saw a giant framed poster with a beautiful scenic picture labeled "Barton Creek Greenbelt Trail." It was interesting that there had not been framed posters anywhere else as I walked through the airport – and with any luck I would be on that very trail within the hour.

I hiked the Barton Creek Greenbelt trail every day for the next three days. As I did, I imagined Mark had been on these trails with his mountain bike. I also made a trip to see where he had lived during the time he was in my life. A next-door neighbor walked out her front door while I was standing there, but I resisted the urge to talk to her. She smiled at me and said hi as she passed by, and I wondered if she had liked Mark. He played his guitar almost constantly when he was off the road and may not have been the most popular neighbor. But he did turn off his amp at night so as not to disturb anyone – and since he was a very skilled professional guitarist, they may very well have loved being able to hear him make his music.

Farewell Austin, Until We Meet Again...

During the time I was in Austin, I documented all my activities in a little notebook. On the plane home, while waiting for it to be cleared for takeoff, I wrote about my last day there. The plane took off just as I finished.

I then took out the book I was currently reading, *Inside the Other Side* by medium Concetta Bertoldi, and I began reading. As I turned the

Signs Surround You

page to a new chapter, titled "Music," all about musical signs our loved ones in Heaven send us, the man sitting next to me noticed the title of the book. Gesturing toward it, he asked, "Did you just lose someone?"

I took out one of my ear buds and explained that I had just lost a friend seven weeks before and that he was from Austin. I confessed to him that this trip had been hard for me, and as I said those words tears came to my eyes. The man expressed that he was sorry for my loss. I thanked him and quickly put my ear bud back in, turning my face away to hide the tears.

The song *"Miracles"* was now playing, and when I looked at my screen I saw that it had begun only 15 seconds before. Incredible – my music on shuffle for the entire 1,100 song collection! I removed one ear bud again and excitedly said to the same man, while showing him my phone screen, "I just read in this book that our loved ones send us music – and when I put my ear bud back in, the song *'Miracles'* was playing. *'Miracles'* has been my favorite song for 25 years, and it's the whole reason my friend and I met." I followed that with the information that Mark had been the guitarist for the band *Starship* – and, in case he didn't know, *"Miracles"* was *Jefferson Starship*'s song that was playing. I added, "I'm leaving Austin now, and I feel this is Mark's way of acknowledging my trip and his part in bringing me *to* Austin!" The man seemed genuinely impressed.

When I could no longer hold back the tears, I turned my attention back to the song *"Miracles"* and my book. I silently thanked Mark for sending me such a beautiful sign at the end of my trip to Austin, and kiddingly admonished him for making me cry on the airplane.

Chapter 5

Dreams…with New Information

Dreams are another common sign. Everyone dreams, but not everyone remembers their dreams. I saw a statistic that we forget 60% of a dream within five minutes of waking, and 80% within 10 minutes. Dreams from your loved one, however, will probably feel more real than a regular dream, and often the details can be vividly recalled even years later. These dreams will generally not have the nonsensical feel that many dreams do.

People also report that in dreams their loved ones look vibrant, glowing, happy, and the most beautiful they have ever seen them look, no matter the age they present themselves as. Spirits have the ability to appear to you as a different age than they were when you last saw them or when they left this Earth. If your loved one died at 45, they may appear 25, possibly because that was when they felt the best about themselves. I have even heard of passed-away children showing younger versions of themselves; perhaps that was the time in their lives when they felt most happy.

Spirits seem to retain the same personality they had when they were here on this Earth. Whether they were funny, serious or a total smartass, it doesn't matter; they will make sure you recognize them in your dreams.

Connections Brought About from the Other Side

Shortly before Mark died was when I spoke with "Mark the Medium" about my situation at the time. After the reading with him, I decided it was time to schedule a more general medium reading, as it had been

Signs Surround You

several years since I'd had one. I was curious to hear what messages my passed-away loved ones would have for me.

Mark the Medium is a cousin to Allison DuBois. I found him on a recommendations list on her website. (I had never had a medium reading with Allison herself because, at the time, she only did readings for people who had attended one of her shows, which I had never done.) When I went to Allison's website again, I clicked on a link that led me to Dr. Gary Schwartz, who is known for his research and ratings of the credibility of mediums.

After reading an article written by Dr. Schwartz, I intended to close out of the computer's browser but was instead taken to a link for the website of a medium I'll call "Cindy." I was not familiar with Cindy, so I read about her and looked at her testimonials. Dr. Schwartz gave Cindy his highest recommendation, which was very impressive. I decided to book an appointment with her, based on all the credible recommendations I saw. I also felt it wasn't an accident that I had clicked on her site "by mistake." I sent an email to Cindy's assistant, requesting more information, and asked to schedule a reading. A week later, after not hearing back from anyone, I called again – again requesting info. Nothing.

Two months after Mark died, Cindy's assistant called me out of the blue, apologizing for not having contacted me sooner. She scheduled an appointment with Cindy for November 13. This whole process had begun two weeks before Mark's death, and now I would be able to connect with Mark through Cindy. I felt sure of that, and I marveled at the timing of it all.

I had been looking forward to the reading with Cindy, but two days before the scheduled appointment a "blocked" call came through on my cell phone. It was Cindy, apologizing that she needed to cancel our appointment as there had been a death in the family and she now needed to go out of town. I was disappointed, of course, but I understood and rescheduled the reading for November 30.

In the meantime, I scheduled an appointment with Moriah; a medium I had been having readings with over the past several years. Moriah is an excellent medium and I trusted her ability and skills. I

Signs Surround You

Dream Reading

I woke up on the morning of my appointment with Cindy, after having had a very vivid dream that included her. In the dream I was in a room high up in a skyscraper that had floor-to-ceiling windows with a view all the way around. It was dusk and the lights from the city were already shining brightly outside. I was standing in the middle of the room by myself, on a very squishy floor, when Cindy walked in through the door. I recognized her from her YouTube videos.

She walked up to me and began giving me my reading. She was talking but wasn't really giving me information; it was more like talking in circles. Impatiently, I kept waiting for her to connect with Mark, but she didn't. She then directed my attention to a large video screen and began showing me a commercial about herself. I was pissed at the thought that she was wasting my precious time when she could be connecting with Mark instead. AND I was paying for this rather expensive session.

When the commercial finished playing, Cindy returned to giving me a reading – again without really giving me any information. The whole time she talked, I had an overall feeling of agitation. I didn't interrupt her because I didn't want to be rude, and she might actually start to give me some good information at any moment. About 40 minutes had passed when she told me she needed to leave, explaining that the two men who were now walking into the room would be taking over my reading.

I blurted out, "Answer one question before you go: Do I have medium abilities?"

"No," Cindy replied, then turned and walked out the door.

Two tall, slender men now stood before me. They looked very much alike, and I had the feeling they were brothers and sons of Cindy. They appeared to be in their early to mid-twenties. They were dressed conservatively in black dress pants and long-sleeved, flowing white shirts. Both had very pale, porcelain skin, straight dark-brown hair

Signs Surround You

that fell just below their ears, and the most striking blue eyes I had ever seen on a person – a very pale blue that reminded me of the contact lenses people wear with Halloween costumes to make themselves look freaky. I couldn't stop staring at them.

Finally, I asked the older man, "Who is around me?"

He stepped forward and said, "A man, and his name is Mark." As he said those words, I could see he was holding two pieces of paper in his hands that measured approximately 10x15 inches in size. He took each piece of paper and flung it up onto the wall, where they stuck like clinging posters, side by side. The one on the right was a picture of a maroon El Camino, exactly like the only car Mark had ever owned. The other was a close-up of a car engine. Pointing to the picture of the engine, on the left, the man said, "Before Mark died, he had oil issues..." and, now pointing to the picture on the right, he added "...with his car."

Perplexed as to why he was telling me this, I looked at him and in exasperation replied, "I have no way of knowing anything like that; I haven't talked to him for the last three years!" I was pretty mad that these men had wasted the last 15 minutes of my reading. The man just stood there looking at me.

I then noticed the other man struggling with the middle section of a very large sushi fish, grayish white in color with lots of layers. The man who had spoken to me walked over to his "brother" to help him hold this rather large, awkward piece of fish. Ignoring me, they began to "read" the layers of the fish. I did not understand what they were doing and thought it was very odd.

Then I woke up. The dream was so extremely vivid that I could see it in its entirety even when I was fully awake. I got out of bed and went to my daughter's room to tell her all about the strange dream I just had. I wondered out loud if the dream was going to have something to do with my reading with Cindy later that day. Then I left to go on my walk and listen to music, to prepare myself for the reading. The first song I heard was *"Telephone Line"* by *ELO*:

"Hello, how are you?

...I'd tell you everything

If you'd pick up that telephone...

Signs Surround You

Telephone line, give me a sign

I'm living in twilight...

For real, not a dream..."

I thought about my dream for the entire walk...

You Have Got to Be Kidding Me

I showered and was getting dressed when my phone rang and the screen showed it was a "blocked" call. I had a bad feeling, knowing who "blocked call" was going to be. I knew it was going to be Cindy, but I was hoping she might be calling just to confirm my appointment for later that day. She wasn't; she was calling to cancel me for a *second time*. She apologized and said that this time a doctor's appointment had been moved and she wouldn't be able to do my reading that day.

I told her I knew her schedule included appointments for later that afternoon and asked if she could do my reading at a later time, as I had taken the full day off to prepare for it. She replied that I shouldn't have done that. I then asked her to cancel someone else's appointment, since I had taken the day off and she had already cancelled me once before. In her harsh Boston accent, Cindy said "No, I can't do that." But she felt bad about it and offered to do my reading the following Wednesday. I took the appointment and said "I have to believe everything happens for a reason." Cindy agreed.

On my way to lunch with Dawn, I called my mom and told her about the dream, and later at lunch I told Dawn. Mark's mom, Marilyn, was expecting me to call her later that afternoon with my news from the reading, so I called to tell her I had been canceled yet again. She too was disappointed. While I had her on the phone I told her about my dream from that morning. She agreed it was amazing.

Marilyn then told me about a conversation she had had with Mark's dad a few days before. He had shown her the final correspondence he got from Mark, a piece of paper that Mark had faxed to him. On the paper was a drawing of some problem Mark was having with his car engine, which his dad had been helping him with. Marilyn said she hadn't absorbed the details of the car problem but that she would talk to Mark's dad and ask him what they had been working on.

Signs Surround You

While we were on the subject of Mark's car, I shared with Marilyn that I wondered if he had ever put air conditioning in it. Mark lived in Austin, Texas, with its hot summer weather, and he had talked about putting air conditioning in his vintage car. When I last spoke with him, he was planning on installing it after the band's busy season ended. My guess was that he had never spent the money to do it, and I reflected on what a shame it would have been if he hadn't spent some of his hard-earned money on something that would make his life more comfortable...

Information from the Other Side

Later that evening, with just my son Ryan and I at home, I offered to take him out to dinner and let him choose the restaurant. He picked his favorite – sushi – which he seldom does because he knows it's expensive. I thought it was ironic that in my dream the men had been "reading" a piece of sushi fish and that Ryan picked a sushi restaurant out of all the choices he might have made for dinner that night.

While waiting for Ryan to get out of the car at the sushi restaurant, I noticed an email come through on my phone. It was from Mark's mom and it was about a new conversation she had had with Mark's dad:

"I just talked to Al and asked him what the problem was with Mark's car that he had been in the middle of helping him with. He said it was two things: putting in air-conditioning and fixing an oil leak on the top of the engine! Looks like that dream of yours wasn't just random."

As I read Marilyn's email, I got goosebumps all over my body. I marveled at the information that had been presented to me in my dream. Then it occurred to me that this may have been the reason my reading had been cancelled. If it hadn't been, I would have called Mark's mom to tell her about the reading instead of sharing my dream with her. In the

dream, I was given very specific information that I could not possibly have known – information that was validated when Marilyn talked to Mark's dad. I had also shared with her my thoughts about Mark not having air conditioning in his car, which led to her uncovering the information that Mark and his dad were working on installing it, just before Mark died. What remarkable evidential information I was given to confirm what I could not have known on my own. I also chuckled at the

Signs Surround You

information being delivered precisely upon arriving at the sushi restaurant – since the men in my dream were "reading a large piece of raw fish"; it finalized tying together every piece of the dream.

Angels

The next day, I called my sister to tell her the entire dream and medium story. When I got to the part about the tall men with the pale-blue eyes, she said, "Those men were Angels!" My sister should know – all our lives she has been seeing Angels, and she also has medium abilities. When she told me the two men were Angels, it was not something I had previously considered, but I immediately knew she was right. I strongly felt Angels were helping me from the Other Side, showing me my connection to it.

Everything Happens for a Reason

The appointment I had scheduled with Moriah was now going to be the day after Cindy's appointment, due to all the rescheduling. On the Sunday before the two appointments, I noticed a missed "blocked" call on my phone. The only one who ever called me from a blocked number was Cindy, and I had a feeling the news was not going to be good. I was right. Sounding terribly sick, she left me a message explaining that she had a horrible cold and sinus infection that would affect her ability to connect clearly to the Other Side. She would be cancelling all of her appointments for the next week to let her illness run its course before she continued any readings.

Again feeling very frustrated, but understanding because she sounded so sick, I reconciled the fact that I was not going to be connecting with Mark through her anytime soon. Wow – cancelled three times –

what terrible luck! But I was glad to know that Cindy only wanted to do a quality reading, and for that I was willing to wait. In the message, she asked me to call her back to reschedule. However, I was now contemplating not doing a reading with her at all, feeling that the cancellations were telling me I was not supposed to connect to Mark through her. At least I wasn't as upset as I had been with the previous cancellations, since Moriah's appointment was still scheduled for Thursday.

Signs Surround You

Kelly called me the morning of the scheduled reading with Cindy to wish me luck. When I told her about the latest cancellation and the upcoming reading with Moriah, Kelly said I must have been meant to talk to Moriah all along. She reminded me how evidential Moriah had been in the past and how much I had always connected to her readings. I hung up the phone satisfied that my reading with Moriah was all I had ever really needed. Kelly had made me feel so much better about the cancellations that it erased the stress from the last few weeks and restored my enthusiasm.

The rest of the morning moved along quickly, and I was filled with anticipation for my reading the next day with Moriah. But with all the previous cancellations from Cindy, I decided not to get my hopes up too much and not take a day off from work. I was working in my home office when I got an instant message on my computer from Melissa, the friend who had been there the day the Austin trip got scheduled. She was asking how the reading with Cindy had gone. Before I could reply, my phone vibrated and I noticed a "missed call" from Moriah's assistant – the phone had never even rung. On the voicemail, Moriah's assistant informed me that my reading with Moriah for the next day would need to be postponed indefinitely. Moriah had to leave town to be with her father, who lay on his death bed.

I was sorry for Moriah about her father, but completely frustrated at the same time. I answered Melissa's message, telling her that both of my readings had been canceled. She replied with a suggestion that I talk to an "energy healer" that her friend used. Melissa had never gone to this energy healer herself but said that the friend raved about her. I wasn't sure what an energy healer did, but at Melissa's insistence I agreed to give her a call.

Dede Hart, Energy Healer, didn't answer her phone, so I left her a message. I sat there thinking about the whole situation and decided I had better try now to reschedule Cindy's cancelled appointment. But as I listened to Cindy's voice on her answering machine, I couldn't help feeling discouraged about all the cancellations. When the other line rang through with Dede returning my call, I decided to abort the call to Cindy and take Dede's call instead. I would worry about rescheduling Cindy later...

Chapter 6

Energy Healing

Dede Hart sounded upbeat and sweet-natured as she explained her role as an energy healer: to help clear a person's energy by identifying dense energy stored in the person's body and field, and opening that space to light, love and clearing. She said she was guided by Angels and by God. I was intrigued but told her what I thought I really wanted and needed was a medium, and I explained my rotten string of luck with making appointments stick. Dede's reply was that we should schedule an appointment as soon as possible because, as she put it, "There is a man stuck inside your auric field who needs to be released." That caught my attention! I had never heard anything like it. Dede offered me an appointment with her in person at her house the next day – at the exact same time Moriah's reading had originally been scheduled. I decided that too many things had led me to Dede to ignore the coincidences. With a certain amount of apprehension, I took the appointment...

Let the Healing Begin

I drove to Dede's house the next day, still not knowing exactly what to expect. When I walked into her waiting room, I saw the message she had left for me to wait there while she finished up with the client before me. Her dog was there to greet me, and I filled the time petting him. I believe dogs are pure love and this one had a calming effect on me.

Dede greeted me warmly with a hug. Seeing my phone still in my hand, she assumed I wanted to record our session and encouraged it. Since this was not to be a medium appointment, I had not actually considered recording it; but, figuring I had nothing to lose, I did so.

Signs Surround You

Auric Fields

The scheduled one-hour appointment with Dede ran over by 20 minutes. During the session she talked about how I should be grounding myself, to protect myself in this physical world. She cleared and moved my energy around, addressing each of my chakras individually. She also connected to my Spirit Guides, my Angels and – most importantly – to Mark. I had not expected that Dede would bring Mark through, so I was taken aback when she relayed several messages from him.

Dede was about 45 minutes into our session when she got around to what she had alerted me to on the phone. She said that Mark had connected to me and was attached to my auric field (the energy field around the physical body). As this connection was affecting my energy, she suggested we release him – with my permission. I still didn't understand *why* he would be in my aura. Dede explained that I had been sending out the signal to Mark that I wouldn't be ok without him. She said I was keeping him around as a reminder of the love I once had with him, and this had caused him to bond tighter to me than he should. She explained that he wanted to stick around to provide me with more comfort, but that his attachment to my energy field was not good for either of us, and it didn't free my Soul up to create the love that I needed here on this physical plane.

She then asked that I allow her to release him. I had never read about or heard of anything like this before, but I reasoned if this connection wasn't good then I should let him go. As Dede released Mark, she said "He says he loves you, and he's always loved you, and he always will love you – and you can bank on that!" She also said that it was important for me to acknowledge and thank him for that experience. I whispered, "Thank you" to Mark. Dede further explained that by releasing him, I was allowing Mark to keep all of his energy and take it all to the Other Side.

I hugged Dede goodbye, thanking her for the wonderful session. When I left her house and got into my car, I sat there for a moment absorbing all I had just experienced. I realized that all the sadness I had been carrying around had been literally lifted off of me, and I felt physically lighter and happier. I had not expected any of this and would not have described myself as feeling heavy before the session, but the

Signs Surround You

difference was very discernible. My close friends later remarked that they could see a difference in me; they said I seemed happier and more like myself again.

The energy clearing seemed to be *exactly* what I needed, even though I was not aware that I needed it! Little did I know at the time that the *real* benefit and gift of this session would be revealed later. It would have a part in helping me discover what I believe is my life's purpose...

The Birth of Soul Heart Art

During the next few weeks I spent many of my daily walks listening to the recorded session with Dede. Listening to it again and again really helped me *hear* the messages and dig a little deeper into them, since it is difficult to receive so many messages and absorb them in one session.

About three weeks after the session with Dede, I was on my daily walk, listening again to the recording of it. I got to the part where Dede talked about my heart and said to me: "Your heart is affirming that you need to hold the love. It says: 'I am going to hold the space for the love. I allow myself to be loved. I am love; I am nothing but pure love."

As I listened to those words, I suddenly saw a picture in my mind of two flying hearts. Each had banners that said all of these affirmations and were attached to the hearts, flowing behind them as they flew through outer space. I felt VERY compelled to paint this picture, even though I had only painted two paintings in my life! The following week, over the New Year's holiday, I spent two days creating that painting.

Throughout the next few days and weeks, my mind was flooded with flying-winged-heart painting ideas that I would rush home to draw on paper. Feeling very inspired to create the paintings, I embarked on a mission to paint forty paintings in forty days. I don't know how or why I decided to do that, and I don't know what compelled me to pick *forty* paintings in *forty* days. Somehow, fifty sounded like too many and thirty didn't sound like enough.

I began by painting small, 3x5 inch paintings, but I was finding it hard to fit all I wanted to onto a canvas that small, so I decided to upgrade the size to 8x10. I really enjoyed making each painting different and

Signs Surround You

playing with various color combinations. Every night, I would take a picture of my newly created painting and text or email it to my friends and family members, who would wake up to a new creation each morning. Some paintings turned out better than others, but I would always look forward to creating something new each night. A couple days before I reached my paintings goal of forty, I realized the last painting would land on Mark's forty-seventh birthday. That served as a confirmation that Mark was helping me on my new journey.

After creating the fortieth painting, and with the encouragement of my friends and family, I decided to create a WordPress website that included a portfolio to launch my *Soul Heart Art*. The purpose of my art was to remind people that they were powerful beings who had the ability to create their heart's desire. I created the website over a one-week period by watching YouTube videos. On April 1, 2013, I launched the website www.SoulHeartArt.com/. It has been a labor of love that has expanded and changed over time to include my Daily Soul Whispers – messages introducing original paintings along with inspirational thoughts – posted and sent out by email. www.facebook.com/SoulHeartArtXO/

On my website, I also created a blog that expands on the "why" behind the paintings. The Daily Soul Whispers were a huge time commitment, requiring me to paint four original paintings each week to keep up with it. (One day a week, "Retro Wednesday," I take a look back at an earlier Soul Whisper.) I spent over twenty-five hours a week on these creations, in addition to my day job. Regardless of that, the ripple effect cannot be known nor discounted, and I knew I would continue creating my Daily Soul Whispers as long as I felt drawn to create the paintings. I eventually discontinued painting in the summer of 2018 after creating over 400 paintings. Spirit later confirmed that as I had healed the paintings no longer felt authentic to the loss and left me for something new to come in.

Follow-up Energy Clearing

Eight months after my original session with Dede in December, I received a message from her about a special summer promotion. I didn't feel I needed another energy-clearing session yet, but I made an appointment

Signs Surround You

anyway for the following Monday. When the day arrived, I realized it was Monday, August 12th – the six-year anniversary of the day I met Mark. Talk about confirmation!

The second session with Dede was extremely gratifying, and I could not have been happier with my messages from The Beyond that I could listen to over and over again. I am sure they will continue to bring me even more inspiration. As a thank-you to Dede for her incredible impact on my life, I painted her a flying-heart picture and called it "Highest and Greatest Good." The writings on the banners are all from my December session with her. Without that session, I would not have had my energy cleared, allowing what I now considered the next part of my life's purpose to manifest: To inspire and stimulate forward movement for women by showing them they can create their heart's desires. Thank you, Dede! I find it delightfully ironic that your last name is "Hart."

Signs Surround You

Chapter 7

Mark's Point of View from the Other Side

In order to hear Mark's point of view, I needed a translator – someone who could hear him in spirit form. Specifically, I wanted to connect with a medium.

A medium is a person who is able to connect with Spirits on the Other Side and pass messages from them to the living. Mediums connect with the Spirit World in different ways. Some are able to put pen to paper and let the messages flow out through the pen. Others see pictures in their mind that they translate the meanings of; this is called *clairvoyance*, also referred to as "seeing" with the third-eye. Others are skilled in hearing Spirit, which is known as *clairaudience*.

Some mediums see symbols they themselves have created, which those in Spirit can use to get a message to you. For example, a medium might see a picture in his or her mind of a dove while connecting with your loved one; for that medium, the symbol of the dove means your loved one is at peace.

Some mediums can even experience the feelings, emotions and sensations that Spirits are communicating to them, including being able to feel their pain and the cause of death – even the location of the pain, by feeling it in their own body, known as *clairsentience*.

Many spiritual teachers say that we *all* possess the ability to connect to the Other Side, and that it is just a matter of practice and recognition. I believe our loved ones on the Other Side do everything in their power to connect with us. Just because we don't think they have sent us signs doesn't mean they haven't – we might not be "picking up what they are putting down."

Signs Surround You

I have read a number of books written by mediums, and they all say our loved ones are at peace – that they transitioned easily out of their body and feel no pain now. They are with you every time you think of them. They know what is happening and has been happening in your life since they left the Earth. And, most importantly – they love you! Because love never dies...

In my quest to reach Mark on the Other Side, it made sense that I seek out people who have a great track record of connecting with the deceased. The messages I got from Mark though various mediums were both evidential and informational, and many of his messages included signs I could look for to help me connect with him on my own. It has been wonderful to find mediums who connected with Mark, and even more rewarding finding ways to understand how to receive messages on my own.

Medium Amanda

After Mark died, the first medium I was able to have a phone reading with was Amanda. I found her after the first medium I contacted had rescheduled me for the third time, when I was desperate to connect with a medium. I had never talked to Amanda before and this reading wasn't just for me: I prayed that morning that Marilyn and Mark's brother Jeff would also get a message from Mark.

When Amanda first connected with the Other Side, a woman who had recently passed away hijacked my reading to get a message to her sister – my mom. Amanda was having a difficult time getting around my "pushy" aunt, but she finally stepped aside to allow a connection with Mark.

The first evidential information Amanda received was a physical description of Mark including mention of some small scars on his face which, unbeknownst to her, had been acquired when he had chicken pox as a child. She was also able to identify his name as "Mark." That was pretty remarkable when you consider that she had to first determine that I wanted to connect with a man, and then discern his name out of the huge number of male names that exist – proving that she was indeed hearing and connecting to Mark himself. Amanda also knew nothing of

Signs Surround You

my relationship with Mark; she only knew my phone number and my first name – allowing no option for her to "google" me before our call.

I asked Amanda if she could determine when Mark had died. She said that, in response to this question, Mark was busy showing her a radio and radio stations and songs from the '80s. She then remarked, "But I feel like he was still around in the '80s." I didn't let on to her the significance behind what Mark was showing her, as I didn't want to "feed the medium" until after she had given me any and all evidential information.

Amanda went on to say that Mark played an instrument. When I asked her which one, she hesitated a moment, then said, "He plays a very, very long instrument." I had to laugh because, knowing Mark, I knew that by a "very long instrument" he was communicating that he played many instruments. Mark had studied at a music school and he was a very accomplished musician. One time he named all the instruments he was able to play, and there were several I had never even heard of.

Amanda then began describing how Mark was showing himself becoming engaged. She asked me if *I* had gotten engaged, which of course I had not. She said Mark was showing himself to be down on one knee and that it was Valentine's Day. She then understood this to be something that had occurred in the past. I knew nothing of Mark's engagement, other than the fact that he *was* engaged. Later, after the reading, I asked his mom Marilyn what she knew about Mark's engagement. She didn't know exactly when and where he had become engaged, nor did anyone else in the family. Later, we were later able to confirm with Mark's former fiancée that Mark had in fact gotten down on one knee to propose...on Valentine's Day.

Amanda next shared that Mark kept showing her a star. She kept repeating, "It's a star...a star." I didn't, at that point, give away his identity, but I thought to myself: *"He was with the band STARship, he called himself 'RockSTAH,' and he was a STAR in his profession."* I am sure the star she was seeing stood for all of these.

Amanda also relayed that Mark had made six home-studio recordings and three of them were songs with a message. He explained that although they were made for someone else, if I listened to the words, I would get a message and it would bring me comfort and healing. It was

Signs Surround You

significant that only one week before, Marilyn had gone to the trouble of emailing me six original songs Mark had recorded. Some of the lyrics and messages from those songs are these:

Ain't no sunshine. (I actually wondered when I first heard this song if it might have been recorded with *me* in mind.)

All I want to do is spend my time with you...

"You are my special girl...

I would do anything for you...

You are my girl – you are my world...

When you smile, you are amazing...

Every day, I need your love...

I can't stand to be away from you...

You are my baby...

I love you..." (This was the message I had longed to hear the most, and it was prominent in two songs.)

I asked Amanda if Mark had any messages for anyone else. She said he had messages for two people, and she remarked, "That's weird...is his mom still alive?" She was probably assuming his mom would have died before him. When I said she was still alive, Amanda responded, "She's one."

She then asked if Mark had a little brother. I said "No." But after a moment's hesitation, I realized that, yes; he did have a little brother! (His brother was 44 years old at the time of the reading – not exactly what I thought of as a "little brother.") It seemed to me that Mark had answered my direct prayer from earlier that morning, about sending a message to his mom and brother.

At the end of the reading, I shared with Amanda how each of her messages related to Mark, and even she was blown away by all the remarkable information he had been able to get across to me.

Later that night, my friend Kelly and I went out. At the end of the evening, we sat in her driveway while I shared with her the incredible

Signs Surround You

messages Amanda was able to give me from Mark. As I was relaying them, the song *"We Built This City"* by *Starship* began playing softly on the turned-down radio – that one put Kelly "over the edge."

Medium Moriah

The phone reading I had with Moriah was extremely evidential. Mark had a lot of messages for me. I recorded the session and used the recording to listen to Mark's messages whenever I felt I needed to connect to him.

At the beginning of the reading, Moriah explained to me that Mark was coming through to her sitting in a car. She said that in all her years of doing readings, she had never before had anyone come through to her while sitting in a car. I told her I had a photo in front of me of Mark in his vintage car. She said, "That explains it!" She added that he would occasionally be interrupted by a flight attendant waiting on him at his window. I was amused by the thought that his VIP status had followed him into Heaven.

Moriah then explained that Mark didn't remember his death very well. He simply said, "You know when you get an ice cream headache?" That was how he felt – and the next thing he knew he was not here anymore.

Moriah went on to say "He wants you to know you're stuck with him giving you guidance, and you should feel like you've got the A #1 guardian angel – who's not on a smoke break!" I loved how Moriah brought through Mark's sassy personality and how Mark threw in so many little things, like this smoking reference, to let me know I was really connecting to him. Moriah added that Mark was laughing and saying he'll be telegraphing his beliefs every day, and he showed himself putting his finger to my forehead and beaming information directly to me. "That's what he'll be doing to you," Moriah said.

Mark also relayed that he and I will always have this profound connection with one another. He wanted to talk about the day I discovered he had died: "When I died, you knew it on some level but couldn't put your finger on it – you just had this disbelieving sense." He wanted me to know that it was because he had come to visit me and I had felt him and "all the dimensions." He assured me that it WAS him, trying to connect with my heart and Soul. I explained to Moriah the thoughts I

Signs Surround You

had the morning I found out Mark had died. Mark responded with "Yes!" Moriah added, "He wants you to know you were right – that it was him."

Mark also referenced his long hair, and joked about having a pet monkey in his heaven. It was true about Mark having had long hair, but I didn't know anything about a monkey. Later on, I talked to Marilyn, who told me that when Mark was younger, he talked about wanting to have a pet monkey. These are the kinds of evidential pieces of information given during a reading that let you know you really are connecting with your loved one.

Mark also wanted me to know that from a "productiveness" on my part, I could open my own business, and that I had more support than I thought I did. He said that if I did open my own business, even though I downplay myself, in three to five years I could walk away and own my own company. At the time, I thought this was crazy because I didn't have any ideas or aspirations to own my own company. Little did I know what lay ahead for me. But Mark did...

Moriah then confirmed that Mark was indeed communicating with me through music. She asked me about a touch screen that Mark had indicated he liked to "screw around with." I immediately knew he was referring to my car screen, which had frozen-with several messages on it many times since his death but not once before his death.

Mark also wanted me to know he wouldn't be sending me any "cheesy" signs like doves. Moriah said, "He grinned this awful grin and asked, 'How about a beaver?'" She repeated it, incredulously: "He's like, 'How about a beaver?'" and then added, "That's rotten and wrong, but it's funny!" Shortly after this reading I had my first beaver sighting – and they haven't stopped. I don't know if Mark's comments were meant to be tongue-in-cheek or literal, but I don't know anyone else who sees beavers on a regular basis!

Moriah next asked, "Did you guys talk three months before he crossed?" I explained that it had been three *years*. She replied, "Mark said he wants to apologize about that time; he thinks you are still mad about it. He says if you can just forgive him...he was projecting on you...his own fears. And if you stop to reflect about everything, you won't be so upset...because he thinks his own judgments kind of separated the two of you. He felt like he had all these perceived things he thought you

Signs Surround You

were going to think were shortcomings." I agreed – knowing what he meant.

Moriah continued at some length: "Mark felt when the three-year period of no contact was happening, you weren't allowed to verbalize how you felt – you couldn't get it out. That's what he wants to apologize for the most. He feels like this has all vanished now, and he just wants you to forgive him. He wants you to have this acceptance, this love and this peacefulness...because it's ok, and he's sorry."

"And he knows that you were so much more unselfish then he was. He also felt like he killed your innocence, and that he made you feel like you needed to be embarrassed or shameful, and for that he is also sorry. He's not trying to be cliché or an ass – but it had nothing to do with you."

"Mark feels he can help you have a better life from his detached perspective now – in dream time, that is, because he thinks there aren't so many boundaries there. It's kind of like where your "self" dissolves into another kind of thinking. He says he'll meet you there!"

Mark explained through Moriah that when I have dreams it will be a window into his heaven and his absolute reality. He wants me to pay attention because he's going to be with me and he's going to do his best to help me. He thinks I just have to not panic about it, because the time thing is weird – when he says "soon", for those on the Other Side it's hard to be more specific.

Moriah then asked me if Mark had been gone since September. I said "Yes," at first, then corrected myself and said, "Since August."

"He keeps showing the number nine, and he seems to think it was September," she replied.

Somehow I got confused during the reading – he actually did die in September, on the 2nd. But I loved the added confirmation I got by disputing what Moriah said Mark was saying – while Moriah was still insisting that he was saying it. I kept toggling back and forth, not being able to get my mind around whether Mark had died in August or September. Moriah said again, "He seems to think it was September." A good medium will do just that – hold their ground and keep repeating the message your loved one is giving.

Signs Surround You

Moriah went on: "He doesn't know how to help you have a comfort zone again with another person; he thinks you get in a rut comparing everybody to him. He wants you to stop that – he just wants you to stop that." I said, "It's kind of a hard habit to break," and Mark jokingly agreed.

But for me now, time truly does have a way of healing. And through my artwork and this book, I have been able to let go of the feelings that had such a strong hold on me. Am I still in love with Mark? The answer feels like a "Yes." But people are "in love" with a lot of things in their lifetime. The heart seems to have unlimited space for more love – there are no limits where love is concerned!

In Mark's final message to me through Moriah, he wanted me to know that he is flying high – that there's "no dust on his wings." And he doesn't want me to have any pain; he wants me to have a rich life. I said to Moriah, "It's nice to know he'll be with me." And sassy Mark replied. "It should be..." Lastly, Moriah instructed me to keep an eye out for tiny white feathers that Mark would be sending me.

I am so incredibly grateful for Moriah's ability to bring Mark through the Veil – and to hear from him and know that his personality is still intact. Our departure from this realm to the next is merely an energy exchange.

Later that night, I went out to dinner with the same three friends I'd gone to Florida with, when I slept with my phone because I didn't want to risk missing a call from Mark. I told them all about the messages I had received from Mark through Moriah. When dinner was over, we left the restaurant to drive back and meet at one of the friends' house. As soon as I started my car, the screen said: *??? Starship* – but a non-*Starship* song played. I believe it was Mark, confirming the messages he had given me earlier from Moriah. I remembered she had warned me: "He messes with your computer – it's a touch screen." When I arrived at my friend's house I called everyone over to my car to show them the car's screen. This was the second time I received a sign directly after a medium reading.

Signs Surround You

Mac the Medium

Mac's medium reading on the phone was much different from his mom Moriah's reading. I had let Moriah "ramble away," as she called it, and interpret all the messages Mark wanted to share with me. With Mac, it seemed that Mark wanted to leave things open so I could ask him specific questions. I had never had a medium reading conducted like that, and in a way things didn't seem as objective or evidential, because I felt like I was asking him leading questions. But Mac gave me enough evidential information for me to understand, without a doubt, that he truly was connecting with Mark.

I began by asking Mark how he felt about me. Through Mac, he said that he was in love with me – and if he had known better, he would've done better, but now he gets to be with me all the time. I responded with, "Now he can see what he missed." Mark replied, "I do – every day. At least I get to be with you every day now." He indicated that he liked being around me and especially liked it when I talked out loud to him.

I explained to Mac that because of the three years Mark and I were apart, I wanted to know from Mark if during that time he thought about me every day; the way I had thought about him every day. Mark's answer was, "Every day – and it never stopped!"

Mark also shared that he had not known how to start things with me again and that he had gotten involved in another relationship, but that I had still been his "first thought" – he just didn't know how to act on it. I told Mac that Mark's answer made my year! Mark got indignant and kiddingly said, "Why did he make your year? I'm the one telling you this!" I also wanted to know how Mark felt about my new relationship with his mom, Marilyn; he indicated that he was very happy about our relationship.

Then, referencing information I got from Amanda's reading, I asked for Mark to elaborate about his songs and which ones had messages for me. Mark replied, "You know exactly which ones were for you – they were easy on the ears and romantic," and he added, "Those were the ones I wrote for you." Mac concluded the reading with this message from Mark: "He's very happy he gets to be around you forever and that you can't get rid of him!" How lucky am I?!

Signs Surround You

My Sister, the Medium

Almost two years after Mark's death, my sister Stephanie – who has medium and other psychic abilities – connected me to Mark. I had several questions I wanted to ask him through her. I wanted her to find out how he felt about me now. His response was admonishing: "How can you even ask that!" Then he said, "My love for you is indescribable. It is big and deep and has been so strong for so long that there are no words for it. All words fail to describe the depth of it."

Mark showed my sister a picture in her mind of him and me in a very large "space" where nothing else existed but love, and he showed her how our love filled up the whole space. He then assured me that he would still send the same signs and animals he had been sending me, and that I would know it was him.

Finally, I asked about the recent feathers I had received. He showed my sister, in her mind, a giant human eye. After a bit of contemplation, she figured out the eye meant "I" – as in "Yes! *I* sent you the feathers." The next day the first song that played on my phone during my walk had an album cover with a giant eye on it. Mark really does do a great job with his confirmations.

Chapter 8

Receiving Information Intuitively

You are Intuitive!

The medium Moriah, in addition to conducting medium sessions, teaches classes that help you develop your intuitive ability. Several years ago, I drove to another state to take one of her half-day classes. Moriah believes that everyone is intuitive and with practice can develop their intuition, including the ability to connect with the Other Side.

To demonstrate her theory, Moriah asked everyone in the class to partner with someone they didn't already know. That was easy – I didn't know anyone. I partnered with a woman in her thirties. We were asked to exchange a personal item with each other. I gave her my necklace, and she handed me her ring. We were instructed by Moriah to hold the item in our hand. She then asked us to close our eyes while she walked us through a guided meditation. Next, we were asked to clear our mind and let thoughts come to us about the person whose item we were holding, and then write the thoughts down on paper.

Some of my thoughts were very specific. I saw in my mind the image of a crown, but instead of writing the word "crown," I drew a picture of it on the paper. I "colored" it in with my pen and drew an arrow pointing to it with the words "yellow gold." Something else I saw in my mind was a white house with a white fence around it and railroad tracks and a train.

When it was my turn to share with my partner the thoughts I had received while holding her ring, I read everything I had written down. She said her house matched my description and that a train ran by the house. Then I showed her the picture of the crown. With that, her eyes grew wide and her mouth dropped open. She didn't say anything but bent down and

Signs Surround You

began rolling up her pant leg, revealing a yellowish gold crown tattoo on the calf of her leg. I was speechless – her tattoo wasn't where I could have seen it before that moment. Moriah seemed to be right that all of us have the ability to "see" things through our intuition.

Signs Surround You

Chapter 9

Animals and Insects as Messengers

Animals and insects, such as butterflies or dragonflies, are common signs. They either show up unexpectedly or act uncharacteristically. It seems to be easy for Spirit to use a butterfly or a dragonfly as a messenger to get your attention. Birds also seem to be special messengers. I have heard stories about hawks, doves, cardinals, blue jays – there is probably no limit. When any of these special creatures try to get our attention, it may be a reminder from our loved ones that they are thinking of us too.

Deer in the Woods...Or Was It?

Six weeks after Mark's death, I was staying at a beautiful hotel in northern New York. This hotel is in a secluded, wooded area with a great walking path that I took full advantage of while I was there. One day, I got out of my meeting early and had extra time to do a longer walk in the magnificent hotel property. I knew I could get in three circuits of the three-mile loop that I had created, for a total of nine miles. Walking nine miles at a fast pace would take me a little under two hours. We had finished the meeting before 5 p.m., but I knew it was going to be pushing darkness when I finished.

It started getting dark by the last two miles, and I was using the flashlight app on my phone to help see the path. As I was approaching an open space with tennis courts, I saw off to the right in the heavily wooded area what looked like a man walking in the woods. I thought it must have been a deer, since I had seen several in the area over the past few days, but I had not seen the white tail as I usually do when they run away. I continued along the path and had a quarter mile left of the walk when

Signs Surround You

once again my circuit had me approaching the tennis courts but this time from the opposite direction from where I had seen what looked like a figure.

I began to feel a little uneasy. After all, I was in the "big" State of New York. I started looking intently behind every tree I passed and even took out one of my ear buds to listen for noises. I was feeling a little scared now, thinking to myself, *"Crap, if someone jumped out to chase me, I wouldn't have much energy to outrun him after just completing almost nine miles."* Then I started to feel mad, knowing that Mark was probably with me and could send me a song for comfort, but hadn't done so.

Just as I was berating him in my mind, a deer jumped out of the woods, right in front of me! I hadn't seen it or heard it before it jumped out of nowhere – and at that very instant, the *Starship* song *"It's Not Enough"* began playing. Of course, I instantly *knew* that I was safe and that Mark really was with me. When I recovered from the deer-induced adrenalin rush, I felt elated that Mark had answered me. I cried at my own foolish thoughts, especially for admonishing him, and wondered if the male figure I had "thought" I saw was actually him...This new relationship between me and Mark on the Other Side was going to take some getting used to!

Butterflies in November

It was now November 18 and we had had several hard frosts already. But today was going to be unseasonably warm, hitting 50 degrees. A gorgeous fall day with crystal-clear, blue skies – it was a perfect day for a ten-mile walk. About seven miles into the walk I decided to play the song *"Could It Be I'm Falling in Love"* by *The Spinners*. This is a song I used to play a lot when Mark was alive, and it had been on my mind the day before. I pressed play and was intently listening to the words when I noticed a small yellow butterfly fluttering alongside me, almost like it was trying to get my attention. I was shocked to see it there, as the current temperature was in the 40's. I had read that because butterflies are cold-blooded and cannot regulate their own temperature, it is difficult for them to even fly in temperatures below 55 degrees. I hadn't seen a butterfly in weeks. How could this little guy have survived?

Signs Surround You

207

While I was noticing the tiny butterfly, the lyrics that played referenced heaven. I smiled at both the lyrics and the butterfly as I watched it leave my side and begin to fly off into the field of high golden grasses next to me. I watched it until I couldn't see it anymore and then continued on my walk.

The next song that played was by the group *Poco*. I liked the song, but after seeing the butterfly I wanted to hear *"Could it Be I'm Falling in Love"* again. I pulled out my phone and noticed in glancing that one of the band members in *Poco* reminded me of Mark. I pressed "previous song" and continued walking, wondering again what the chances were of seeing a butterfly after all our hard frosts that year. About halfway through the song, I saw *another* yellow butterfly, on my left. This could not have been the same butterfly, because I was still walking in the opposite direction of where the first one had flown away, and I had walked about a half mile.

The *Poco* song came on again. As I was listening to it, I looked at the picture once more, thinking of the resemblance one of the band members had to Mark. A very tiny orange butterfly was suddenly on my left side, fluttering around a tree. It was only there for a moment; then it was gone. The song finished, and as I walked I kept thinking about the butterflies. When I saw the first one, I had been in a large area surrounded by fields. Now I was in a densely wooded area. I let the song *"Could it Be I'm Falling in Love"* play one more time, and at the very end, a small yellow butterfly crossed the path right in front of me.

I was still shocked about all these butterflies and began to think to myself, *"It's going to be a warm day; maybe it's not that unusual that the butterflies are out."* I decided to walk in silence, listening only to nature's song for the last twenty-five minutes of my walk. I didn't see any other butterflies for the rest of the walk, even though I was on "butterfly watch" the entire time.

At the end of the walk, my skeptic left brain showed up to keep the jumping-up-and-down right side of my brain in check. In the parking lot, I asked a couple who were riding bikes if they had seen any butterflies that day. The question was met with a sideways glance and a look of "What you talkin' 'bout, Willis?" *No*, they had not. After polling a few other people, with the same results, the skeptic left brain took its walls down a little bit.

Signs Surround You

Later that night, while recording the butterfly story in my Mark journal of signs, I played the song *"Could It Be I'm Falling in Love"* one more time, to make sure I was copying the lyrics correctly. When it ended, the song *"Count on Me"* by *Starship* began playing – confirming for me all the thoughts and feelings I had had about the butterflies that day.

Beavers, Beavers, Everywhere.

From the time Moriah told me Mark would be showing beavers to me, I had been seeing them quite often at the ponds.

On Valentine's Day, I went to get a pedicure and took my own book to read. But when I walked by the stack of magazines, one of them caught my attention. Instead of reading what I'd brought, I started thumbing through the magazine. I turned the page and noticed an advertisement featuring a beaver. When I saw it, the first thing I thought about was what Mark had told Moriah: "He won't be sending you any 'cheesy' signs like doves. 'How about a beaver?'" It felt like a Happy Valentine's Day wish from Mark to me.

The Thank-You Beaver

The two-year anniversary of Mark's death was approaching. I had spent some time creating the Daily Soul Whisper that would be published on that date, September 2, 2014. It read:

Two years ago today, a piece of my Soul left this Earth along with Mark's Soul. The Soul that remained was so inspired that it created all of these thoughts and this artwork. Thank you, Mark, for your constant whispers...

What have you done for love...what would you do for love?? Sometimes finding love calls for extremes! If your Heart is calling, then search 'til your Heart is content...love is ALWAYS worth the effort...xo Laurie

After I wrote the above, I headed out to walk at the ponds. I had planned on walking much earlier in the day, but the time had slipped away from me and it was now after 7 p.m. As I rounded the first pond, I noticed something swimming in the water far off in the distance. I immediately recognized it as a beaver. I crept down to the edge of the water and continued watching it swim my way. I stood very still, as

Signs Surround You

beavers are very skittish, and watched it swim to the shore, a mere two feet from where I stood. He was a good-sized beaver, weighing at least 35 pounds. He sat there for a few minutes, never noticing me, before swimming away and diving under the water.

Remembering Moriah's words from Mark about animal signs – "How about a beaver?" – I thanked Mark for sending me the sign. The song *"Higher Love"* by *Steve Winwood* then began to play. All this must have been the reason I was off my walk schedule that day. And, of course, Mark was acknowledging my *Soul Heart Art* post to him, recognizing the anniversary of his passing.

The Beauty of Your Face

It was an overcast fall day, over two years since Mark had gone. I only half felt like going on my walk. It was also very late in the day, so I decided to do a short version of only two miles. As I began, I was lamenting to Mark about how I missed the way he made me feel about myself. He really made me feel beautiful. I asked him if he could send me a song telling me I was beautiful. I let him know it was going to be a quick walk and he only had twenty-five minutes to work with.

I decided not to press shuffle on my songs but instead just let them play. The song *"Hold on to the Nights"* by *Richard Marx* came on first. As it began, I noticed a beaver swimming in the middle of the pond. He dove under the water and came back up just as this line of the song played: *"I saw you smile and my mind could not erase the beauty of your face."* It felt to me like Mark delivered the line through the beaver, the next best thing to him being there in person.

Signs Surround You

Signs Surround You

Chapter 10

Feathers

Feathers are one of the most common signs. I was told my loved one Mark would send me white feathers, and I have a bagful of them that I have collected. Feathers can show up in very strange places. They can also be used with another sign, such as a song, to help you understand that it really is a message for you.

Before I was told through my medium reading with Moriah that I would be watching for little white feathers from Mark, I had never really noticed feathers. That would soon change for me.

Feathers seem to be associated with words of love when I find them. I didn't connect them that way until I saw the stories I had written down while writing this book. Perspective can change the meaning of your signs, making them even more significant than you first thought.

Feather on the Path

On my walk one day, I was listening to the recording of Moriah's reading where she brought Mark through. I got to the part where she said I'd be looking for little white feathers. Just as I did, I noticed a tiny white feather in front of me, sitting in the middle of the gravel path I was walking on. It was a very windy day and I was surprised it hadn't been carried away by the wind. There were no other feathers for the rest of my walk.

Signs Surround You

Moriah and More Feathers

It had been nine months since Mark died and six months since Moriah's reading. I had listened to the recording many times, but it had been a few months since I last played it. On my walk this day, I decided to listen to it again. While listening, I encountered a person I sometimes see on my walks but hadn't seen in some time. I forgot to pause the recording, so it continued playing while we chatted for a few minutes. After the conversation, I realized the recording was still playing, so I randomly moved it back a few minutes and continued walking and listening.

As I rounded a corner, I got to the part where Moriah was saying I'd be "looking for little white feathers from him, too." At that moment, I saw that on both the right and the left, there were numerous little white feathers strewn alongside the path for about 15 feet. It looked like a bird massacre must have occurred, but I only saw feathers, no other bird remnants. I couldn't have planned that kind of timing. It was a beautiful confirmation!

Always

On another walk one day, I thought of the song *"Always"* by *Bon Jovi*. The lyrics had caught my attention after Mark died and had inspired a painting two months before this day. The song was about someone dying and telling their loved one, *"When I die, you'll be on my mind, and I will love you always."*

Listening to it while walking along the bridge on my walk route, I couldn't help but think of Mark and wonder if he still loved me from the Other Side. When I stepped off the bridge back onto the path, I noticed little white feathers on both the right and left side of the path. Feathers do seem to send me a message of love.

I Saw the Sign

On one of my daily walks around the ponds, almost a year after Mark's death, the song *"Show and Tell"* by *Al Wilson* started playing. When the lyrics *"...show and tell, just a game I play when I want to say I love you"* played, my attention moved to a small white feather floating on my right

Signs Surround You

side at eye level. It followed me for a few feet, then rose higher and higher towards the east, continued up into the trees, and was gone. I did not see any other white feathers that day. But I did notice the coincidence of the lyrics "*I love you*" playing as I saw the feather. I felt I was given a beautiful message that day.

A couple months later, as I was driving to work the song "*Show and Tell*" by *Al Wilson* came on again. I thought about the tiny feather that had appeared the last time I heard that song. As it was playing, I exited the highway in a double left-turn lane, with a big truck in the lane in front of me. Normally, I would have changed lanes to race around a slower vehicle, so as not to miss the green light up ahead. But on that day, I was in no hurry and I could see I would easily make the light anyway. I also had to turn right at the next light, so I stayed where I was, in the right lane. From that position, I saw a car passing me on the left with a bumper sticker that caught my eye. I then noticed the next car passing me on the left had a license plate that said "MUZC MN". I knew immediately that it was a confirmation and I got the goosebumps! I felt like Mark was saying "Yes! It was me sending you the message of love the other time, and here I am again."

If I had been in the left lane, I would have been in front of the car with the "MUCZ MN" license plate, and because my office was the next right turn, that car would not have had time to pass me and make it possible for me to see the "message." The timing was incredible for all these pieces to come together – the song playing, the thought of the feather and its message of love, and the license plate sign. Spirit's ability to coordinate signs continued to astound me!

And in case I still hadn't gotten the message loud and clear from Mark, as I was parking my car, another song – "*The Sign*" by *Ace of Base* – began playing: "*I saw the sign, and it opened up my mind – I saw the sign!*"

I Love You

It was the one-year anniversary of the day I learned of Mark's death. By a sorrowful irony, I had to attend a wake later that day for friends whose 18-year-old son had died tragically; making this day especially painful for me. I took the day off and spent the morning reading old emails from

Signs Surround You

Mark that I had not had the courage to look at in four years. After a while, running an errand was a welcome distraction.

When I pulled into a parking lot, there was one space available in the front row. I parked my car and left it running so I could finish listening to the song that was playing on the radio. Right as I heard the lyrics "*I loooooove youuuuu,*" I looked down and saw six white feathers on the ground. I collected them all and scanned the parking lot, looking for a plethora of birds that must have been around for that many feathers to be sitting there in one spot. But I did not see any birds. I then walked up and down my row of parked cars, examining all the spaces, looking for more feathers, but I found none. I concluded it must have been a message from Mark – and I really needed a message on that difficult day. I especially loved the timing.

Chapter 11

Multiple Signs Woven Together

Sometimes a person will get a string of signs that seem unrelated. The person should eventually notice that the signs weave themselves together in a story that can only be understood in hindsight, when the full picture has revealed itself after some time has passed. Pay attention to those stories and document them for you to be able to revisit later. Our human memory can be affected over time, and it is comforting to reread descriptions of signs we have received, with full detail of how they happened and when they happened. You may think you will never forget some amazing sign, but you probably won't remember it exactly as it happened if you haven't written it down right away.

Do You Hear Me Talking to You?

My friend PJ and I became acquainted with one another through my *Soul Heart Art*. We both have lost guitar guys, and both of us receive signs from them regularly, which we frequently share with one another.

One time, PJ had been reading a book called *Never Say Goodbye* by Patrick Matthews, when she stopped to send me a text message about a dream she had had the night before. The dream had her guitar guy in it and someone else she thought was Mark. PJ connects with the numbers 5-13, a special date when she was given a really big sign. (Coincidentally, that date is also my birthday.) After she texted me, she noticed that she had "randomly" stopped reading on page 153. She went back to reading on the same page – where the author shared a story about someone named Mark. PJ sent me a second text message telling me about these cool interconnections.

Signs Surround You

Later in the day, I was on my walk and was thinking about my reading with Moriah, where she told me: "Mark says he will see you in your dreams. He wants to show you his absolute reality." I thought about how much PJ connected with dreams and how I myself hadn't had many dreams of Mark over the two years since he had been gone. I then had a conversation with God and asked that He allow Mark to come into my dreams. I also told Mark that I wanted him to visit me in my dreams, as he had promised through Moriah.

Just as I was having these thoughts, I passed my old foreclosure house- that I had since sold- and the song *"Lucky,"* a duet with *Jason Mraz* and *Colbie Caillat*, came on my music. I felt the words were an answer to my previous conversation with Mark and God. In the song, Jason sings: *"Do you hear me talking to you, across the water, across the deep-blue ocean, under the open sky? Baby, I'm trying."* Colbie then sings: *"Boy, I hear you in my dreams, feel your whisper across the sea, keep you with me in my heart. You make it easier when life gets hard."* It felt like the lyrics was a pretty direct answer to my request.

I also found it fascinating that this song came *immediately* after I had the conversation in my head – and that at the same time that I was in front of my old foreclosure house, the words *"I hear your whispers"* were sung, and then the word *"heart"* came up. With regard to "whispers," I have always felt that my Daily Soul *Whispers* are whispered to me from the Other Side.

While recording this story into my notebook later that night, I played the *Jason Mraz* and *Colbie Caillat* song. As soon as the song finished, *"We Built This City"* began playing, followed by one of Mark's very own original songs. I don't think I have to say that once again Mark found a way to confirm my signs from him from the Other Side. Altogether, it was a pretty nice string of "coincidences" that day.

Mark has yet to show me, through my dreams, his "absolute reality," as communicated through Moriah. But I certainly have had many visits from him in dreams over these years – including the dream that started this whole book.

Signs Surround You

Questions 67 and 68

Shortly after meeting PJ through my *Soul Heart Art*, she told me in an email that her loved one on the Other Side would be letting me know what band he had played guitar for. I had absolutely no knowledge of what band he had been with or any idea of how he would let me know, but I had been very curious about him and I knew he would find a way.

Several days after PJ sent me that email, I was blueberry picking near our cabin in the upper peninsula of Michigan. I began talking out loud to Terry, PJ's loved one. His first name and the length of time he had been dead was all I knew. I told him I was going to set the music on my phone to shuffle, and I asked him to play a song for me if his group had any songs in my collection. I pressed shuffle, and just as a song from the group *The Police* began playing, I got stung by a bee. I noted the humor in getting stung – with the lead singer of that group being a guy named Sting. I didn't think Terry played with that band, but I got the distinct feeling that the bee sting was designed to get my attention. It happens that I am highly allergic to bee stings and swell up terribly, and a sting usually hurts for several days. So while I was at it, I asked Terry to take the pain and swelling away if it had been designed to get my attention.

The next song that played was by the group *Chicago*, one of my all-time favorite groups, and I *knew* as I heard the song "*Questions 67 and 68*" that this was it! I had no doubt in my mind that this was the band Terry was with. At the time, the only name I knew from the band *Chicago* was the lead singer, which is the usual case for me with most of the bands I am familiar with. I quickly sent PJ an email telling her my theory. She was on line when my email came through and was able to quickly send me the confirmation that, yes, her Terry had been the lead guitarist for the band *Chicago*!

I went back to blueberry picking. After a while, I got in the car to drive to where I wanted to hike. Another *Chicago* song – "*Feelin' Stronger Every Day*" – was playing on the radio. I drove to a hiking trailhead and embarked on a 45-minute hike. When I returned and started my car, I heard the familiar first notes of the song "*Feelin' Stronger Every Day*." I thought my alarm must be going off on my phone, as that song is the alarm tune. But it wasn't my phone; the song had just begun playing on the same radio station again – within 90 minutes of

Signs Surround You

when it had last played. That is a very unusual thing for a radio station to do, and I felt that Terry was pulling out all the stops with his confirmations to me. The other amazing thing was that my bee sting was no longer visible, and any pain I had earlier was gone.

I returned to the cabin and got my book of signs out to document the Terry story, but first I told my son all about what had happened. While I was writing about it in the journal, a *Chicago* song began to play – in the background of the movie my son was watching. There is no doubt that Terry and Mark are working in tandem on the Other Side. I am sure they connected me to PJ, since what we are each creating in this world is very similar. Our relationship has been one of the most important in helping me to recognize the signs from the Other Side. PJ is a hospice nurse. Her job exposes her to death through her patients and therefore allows her to witness signs in far greater numbers than anyone I know. Her work and acknowledgement of signs, coupled with her personal experiences with the Other Side, have been invaluable as I continue my own work.

Manifest Your Reality

My sister recommended a book by Pam Grout called *E-Squared* (E^2). It is a book of nine do-it-yourself energy experiments designed to prove that your thoughts create your reality, either helping or hindering you to manifest what you want to have in your life – that is, to manifest your reality. It isn't necessarily about manifesting material things; it is more about learning how YOU shape your own reality.

Each chapter includes an experiment that you can do to practice manifesting specific results within 48 hours. The second chapter I read was about manifesting a certain color car into your field of reality. (I know it sounds funny, but stay with me.) The author suggests that you "ask" to see green cars, since green is not the most common car color. The idea behind these manifesting experiments is to pull what you intend into your reality and to do so within 48 hours.

The next day, while running a string of errands, I tried the green car experiment... Nothing! On a busy Saturday morning, in the suburbs of Chicago, driving 15 miles and making two stops – I did not see a *single green car*. It didn't seem possible – how could I have created the exact

Signs Surround You

opposite of what I was trying to create? Up to that point, I thought I was pretty good at manifesting and creating my reality. I knew green cars were not common, but I certainly expected to see at least a few. The main "errand" I had tried to run was a bust – and I had to go back on the exact same route the following day to complete it.

As I left my driveway Sunday morning, I was still feeling discouraged about the failed green-car experiment from the previous morning – but before I even left my short, one-lane street, I saw my first green car. Hmmm...curious. After that, they practically came in droves – by the time I arrived at my destination, I had counted 20 green cars! This abundance of green cars was repeated on the way home, and when I pulled into my driveway, I had counted 52 green cars – whereas the day before I counted zero. Unbelievable! I even counted three more green cars driving by when I was out on my walk.

The conclusion I came to was that The Universe was showing me the difference from day to day in what you can draw to yourself – first proving on day one that green cars aren't that common, then showing me the real power of my own mind on day two. I continued to see green cars for months and eventually even bought one!

A couple other experiments had similar results, but the fourth experiment was about to blow my mind...

San Francisco

The next chapter I read, titled "The Abracadabra Principle," talked about picking one thing you most wanted to manifest into your life and focusing your attention on manifesting it within 48 hours. At first, I thought about my newly created *Soul Heart Art* business and how I wanted to get my art work licensed. Then another, better, thought crept in: I wanted to meet Mark's mom by the end of the year. Marilyn and I had gotten to know each other pretty well over the last year via email and phone, but we had not yet met in person. It was a lofty goal, as she lived 2,100 miles from me and the end of the year was only 50 days away – and I didn't have any business trips that ever took me to that area of the country, especially moving into the holiday season. So I wasn't sure how this was going to work.

Signs Surround You

The idea in the book was to manifest the goal of each exercise *within 48 hours* – by not focusing on the how, just focusing on the idea and letting The Universe take care of the rest. Of course, I could have just bought myself a plane ticket and flown there, but I really didn't want to have to explain that to Jason. So I followed the exercise instructions and just concentrated on the end result, not on the "how it would happen."

When I arrived at my client's office the next morning, I pulled out my phone to check emails before heading in. There was a curious one with the subject line: *Great event for your clients: Announcing a Sales Force convention.* The email had been forwarded to me by one of my colleagues. When I looked closer at it, I realized the convention's location was to be in Mark's old stomping ground, San Francisco, which was about 35 minutes from where Marilyn lived. Remembering my previous night's "ask," this convention prospect raised my hopes – but not too much, as these conferences didn't usually pan out. And if I were to go, I would first need to find a customer who was planning to go.

I called my colleague to get more details. He said he didn't think any of my clients were attending, but he told me to ask around that day when I was on site. When I hung up the phone, the *Journey* song *"Lights"* was playing on the radio – which references San Francisco. I smiled at the sign, thinking to myself, *"This is gonna happen."* And with that thought, I walked into my client's building.

I was at the client's office all day, but I was so busy I didn't have a chance to ask anyone about the conference. I left their office a few hours later than I ever do. About half a mile from my house, I was thinking about the conference and noticed the license plate on the car ahead of me – it said "MARK 47". Mark would have been 47 years old if he had still been here on this Earth. I knew it was a sign from him and confirmation that I *would* be going to San Francisco. I have not seen that license plate since, even though I had seen it very near to my house in a small suburb of Chicago.

The next morning I got an email from my colleague. He had looked into the Sales Force Conference and found out that none of my clients were registered to attend – which made me wonder about the signs from the previous day. It was now over 30 hours into my experiment and things started looking less hopeful.

Signs Surround You

I headed to my client's office again, where I would be working for half the day. I shared an office there with a co-worker from my company, who often has our clients stopping by the office to ask questions and make requests. On that particular day, a guy stopped in who had never done so before. I asked him about the conference; he said he thought his boss Jim might be attending. Jim wasn't in that day, so I printed an informational flier about some events we were sponsoring at the conference and handwrote a note to leave in his office. Later, on my way out, I ran into Jim's boss – who confirmed that Jim was indeed going to the Sales Force Conference. I called my boss on the ride home, who gave me his blessing to attend. I couldn't believe how things had turned out; this trip was really happening. I was really going to San Francisco to meet Mark's mom!

When I got home, I spent some time researching the conference and saw that Deepak Chopra and Dr. Wayne Dyer were to be two of the free keynote speakers. I signed up to attend their sessions, then booked my flight by 8 p.m. – just making the 48-hour goal for making this trip a reality. I would be in San Francisco for four days total and would be leaving for it in six days – fulfilling my before-the-end-of-the-year "ask" with more than a month to spare. When I called Marilyn to share the news, she was thrilled. I told her about the conference I would be attending and shared that I had registered to see Deepak Chopra speak. Marilyn asked, "Did you know that Mark really liked Deepak?" Actually, I didn't...

The following Monday afternoon I was on a plane to San Francisco. I was able to drive directly to Marilyn's house, where we had dinner and spent hours talking and laughing and catching up. At one point, I excused myself to use the bathroom, and when I returned Marilyn had placed the book *The Seven Spiritual Laws of Success* by Deepak Chopra at my place setting. It was a small hardcover book that had belonged to Mark, and Marilyn wanted me to have it. As soon as I saw it, I set the intention to have it signed by Deepak Chopra himself. Why not? "Only" 25,000 people would be in attendance at the conference – how hard could it be to have him sign a book?

Kidding aside, I knew it would be a longshot getting Deepak to sign my book. On the other hand, I doubted that many others would have thought to bring a book with them to have signed, so I figured I would at least have that advantage. When you set an intention to manifest

Signs Surround You

something into your life, it doesn't mean you think it once, then set that thought free to just let things happen around you; I believe you still have to play your part in manifesting what you want. For me, that means taking action.

As "luck" would have it, at the first session I attended, a guy sat next to me who worked for the company hosting the conference. I explained what I was trying to do with my Deepak Chopra book and asked him if he could help me in getting Deepak to sign it. We exchanged information, and he said he would see what he could do.

Later that day, I drove back to Marilyn's house for a second visit. She had arranged for us to drive a short distance to Mark's childhood home, where we would visit Mark's dad and brother. When we arrived at the house, Mark's dad was standing outside waiting for us. After the introductions, he told us that five minutes before, the power had gone out in the house, although we could see that the houses across the street still had power. Fortunately, it was the middle of the day, so there was enough light for us to go back inside the house to visit.

We talked with Mark's dad and brother for a few minutes in the family room. Then Mark's dad took us into the formal living room where they had created a memorial for Mark. There was a large picture of Mark, and a beautiful box holding his ashes sat on a table over to the side of the room. Mark's dad was talking about Mark's amp and guitar sitting on the floor next to the table – when the power flickered. We all felt it was Mark making his presence known, and everyone got goosebumps. Marilyn had previously told me that the same thing had occurred a few hours after they got the news of Mark's death – the lights flickered in a way they never had before.

We all visited for a while in the living room before heading back into the family room. Mark's cousin Lizzy then arrived. She, Marilyn and I had planned to leave at 6 p.m. for dinner, but we were having such a great time visiting that we had to force ourselves to leave at 7 p.m. The three of us had a lovely dinner at a nearby steakhouse that was supposed to close at 10 p.m. When we settled our bill about that time, our waitress said we were welcome to stay. By 11:30 the restaurant seemed completely deserted, and we let ourselves out without seeing another soul. I hugged Lizzy and Marilyn goodbye, all of us sad that our visit had to come to an end.

Signs Surround You

We Built This City

On the forty-five-minute drive back to San Francisco, I had to switch radio stations a couple of times because each eventually turned to static. About twenty minutes from my hotel, I lost the radio station signal again and turned the station to 98.7 FM, which came through crystal clear. Shortly after I switched, the radio screen said *"We Built This City"* by *Starship*, and the song began playing. I couldn't believe I was hearing *that* song – it was always the last song *Starship* played in concert. It felt like Mark was saying this is the end of the show.

As the song was playing, I started the drive across the 4.5-mile Bay Bridge. In the middle of the song, there were several references to San Francisco: *"I'm looking out over that Golden Gate Bridge* [which, at that very moment, was visible across the Bay] *on another gorgeous sunny Saturday, not seein' that bumper to bumper traffic....the city by the Bay, the city that rocks, the city that never sleeps..."*

It brought me to tears! I marveled at how this song, with its San Francisco references, just so happened to play. As I neared the end of the bridge, the song ended but the radio screen still said *"Starship"* – even though a song by the *Stray Cats* had begun playing. When that song ended the next song to come on returned the radio screen to the correct display and the screen was normal for the rest of the drive.

Deepak Chopra

I was never able to connect with my customer while I was in San Francisco as he had a family emergency and had to fly back – which made me feel like the purpose of my trip was solely to meet Marilyn. Dr. Wayne Dyer and Deepak Chopra gave wonderful keynote speeches. Unfortunately for me, Deepak was promoting his twenty-eighth book and everyone in the audience got one – which meant there would be many people trying to get their book signed after the show. However, the guy I had met the day before found someone who could take my book behind the scenes to get it signed. We made plans for me to text him when the speech was over, and he would retrieve my book and take it backstage to be signed. I wouldn't get to meet Deepak, but I would at least be able to get my book signed. But it didn't turn out that way...

Signs Surround You

When Deepak's talk ended, he stepped off the circular stage only one section over from me, but people quickly crowded around him, all holding books up to be signed. I was back at least six people deep around Deepak. He signed about ten books, and then the security guards started moving him along toward the exit. I am not even sure how it happened, but I suddenly found myself by Deepak's side. I explained to him that I had this book from my deceased friend that I wanted him to sign. He glanced at me, smiled, and – while continuing to walk – signed my book as I was thanking him. After that, only one other person succeeded in getting his signature. I felt incredibly lucky to have been successful in having Deepak sign Mark's book. The conference room held over one thousand people, all with books, yet I had somehow manifested my intention.

I was looking forward to reading Mark's copy of Deepak's book on the plane ride home. Before we even took off, I opened the book and began reading. The words seemed so familiar...I felt like I had read this book before. But that was impossible because I didn't own any of Deepak's books...but I did have one of his books on tape that I had downloaded shortly after Mark died, to listen to on my walks. Sure enough, it turned out that I had received from Mark's Deepak collection the one and only book I had already read. Considering the volume of books Deepak had written, it was an amazing coincidence that Mark and I owned the same Deepak book.

My trip to San Francisco exceeded my expectations in every way. To start with, I had an amazing visit with Mark's family. I was also introduced to Muir Woods, just north of San Francisco, with its forest of huge redwood trees – which I would eventually visit again and it would become one of my all-time favorite hiking areas. Add to that my meeting Deepak Chopra, whom I had so admired from the time he was on Oprah's Super Soul Sunday show. On top of it all, I now had a precious book that once belonged to Mark. But more importantly, I had precious connections with people who meant the world to him.

The Monday after I returned home, I was exhausted and slept in later than normal. When I woke up, the kids had just left for school and the house was empty except for the dog and me. I walked into the living room, which was flooded with sunlight; a spot of white caught my attention and I turned for a closer look: A three-inch-long white feather

Signs Surround You

225

sat mysteriously in the middle of my gray leather couch. I don't have feather pillows or blankets in the house, nor do I own a white bird. I was stumped as to how a feather could have found its way to my couch. The only logical explanation, when you consider the workings of Spirit, was that I had received a final gift from Mark in acknowledgement of my trip to San Francisco. It appeared to be Mark's stamp of approval.

Random Happening

On the two-year anniversary of his death, Mark's family planned a get-together in his honor. I purchased gift cards for Marilyn, Mark's Dad, brother, aunt, his two cousins, and sent them to California. I wrote each of them a note inviting them to enjoy a Pumpkin Spice Latte in honor of Mark. Mark loved Starbucks coffee, and the Pumpkin Spice Latte was his favorite flavor. This is a seasonal drink that you can only get in the fall, and normally, the pumpkin lattés don't come out until *the end* of September. But this year they were released on – you guessed it, September 2, the two-year anniversary of Mark's death.

Miracles Painting

This might be my best story yet! During my Energy Clearing session with Dede Hart, about a year after Mark's death, she told me I would have some amazing things happen to me that would come from Mark and that I would know *without a shadow of a doubt* had happened because of him.

The second painting I ever created was a tribute to the song "*Miracles*." I painted a beautiful heart in various shades of blue, with wings and five banners, each representing a favorite lyric from the song. The heart was depicted as flying in outer space, surrounded by stars, because this song "*Miracles*" seems otherworldly to me as it represents such a big purpose in my life. I hung the painting in the kitchen, where I could see it every day.

One day, I was working on my computer and listening to music on the Pandora app through my phone. The song "*Miracles*" came on – first in the original radio version, then again later in the live-recorded

Signs Surround You

version. I didn't know why but at that moment I felt compelled to search for Marty Balin's concert schedule. Marty Balin had been part of *Jefferson Airplane/Jefferson Starship*, and he wrote the song *"Miracles."* He was now in his 70's and last I checked, several years before, he wasn't doing concerts anymore. I did a concert search for Marty Balin on my computer anyway and was shocked to see that he would be performing in Springfield, Illinois – three hours from my house, and in just three weeks!

I instantly decided I would attend the concert. I then searched for tickets, which were only available from scalping sites and were going for $250-$350 for "great seats." I was fine on spending that much money for my ticket, but Jason wanted to go with me and I didn't want us to spend that much for his ticket, as I knew his interest in attending was just to be with me, not to see the concert. I decided to wait to buy a ticket, thinking I might just go by myself.

Three days before the concert, I went back on line to purchase a ticket but could not find a single ticket for ANY price! I called the concert venue, Sangamon Auditorium, and asked if they had any tickets available. The man on the phone said the concert was sold out, but he asked me if I wouldn't mind holding as he had six tickets that management had just released that he might be able to sell. I actually got a front row ticket for $43!

I should have purchased a ticket for Jason too, knowing that he wanted to go, but I really wanted to attend Marty's show alone. The songs held so much emotion and meaning for me that this was one of the rare times I just wanted to be alone. Besides, there were no tickets left to purchase that were seated together – a good excuse for why I didn't buy Jason one. I explained the situation to him after the fact, but he insisted he still wanted to go, even if it meant sitting separately. In any case, the concert would be ending late and he felt it would be best for me to have some company for the long, three-hour drive home.

Later that night, I wrote an email to Marty, explaining how his song *"Miracles"* had changed my life, and told him about the *"Miracles"* painting I had created. I was hoping I could show the painting to him at the concert and thank him in person for his incredible influence on my

Signs Surround You

ife. I had no idea whether he would even get my email, but I called my friend Dawn and told her the whole story. When I hung up, the song *"Somebody to Love"* by *Jefferson Starship* began playing on the radio. I took that as a sign from Mark that he had things under control. Nevertheless, I am a control freak and, not wanting to leave anything to chance, I continued to "work it" from my end.

Friday morning, the day before the concert, I noticed that Marty Balin had posted a comment on Facebook about his excitement for the upcoming performance in Springfield. I posted a response to his post with a link to the *"Miracles"* story on my website, for him to read. Either he or someone working for him deleted the comment (probably thinking the link was spam). I decided my chances to meet Marty were pretty slim.

Saturday, September 21, 2013 – Concert Day! I took my *"Miracles"* painting with me to the concert along with a couple of sharpie pens for Marty to sign with – just in case. We decided to leave early enough to have a nice dinner before the concert. But as we arrived in Springfield I could no longer see the map I had been following, with directions to the restaurant. I had lost the internet connection on my computer that I was navigating with. I implored Jason to "Pull over!" He usually doesn't listen to that sort of "demand," but this time he abruptly turned into a shopping plaza. There we sat in our car – facing Starship Billiard Parlor. I CAN"T MAKE THIS STUFF UP!! That was it – my *"without any doubt"* sign from Mark!

After that, we made it to the restaurant, ate dinner, and drove to the concert. When we arrived at the venue, I opened the trunk and took out my *"Miracles"* painting. Jason asked what I had in the bag. I opened it to show him and declared my intention of getting Marty to sign the painting. Jason chuckled and said he doubted I could get Marty to sign it. (Doubter! LOL)

Seated in the intimate concert hall, ironically on opposite sides of the venue from each other, we watched Marty perform twenty-four songs in a little over two hours – including *"Hearts"* and *"Miracles."* It was surreal for me – really a dream come true. When the concert ended, Marty and the band thanked everyone and then walked backstage. The lights in the auditorium came back on, and I walked over to Jason's seat

Signs Surround You

to tell him that I wanted to wait to see if I could get Marty to sign my painting.

Thirty seconds later, Marty came out to greet his fans. I happened to be the first one he made eye contact with, and he walked directly to me. I handed him my *Soul Heart Art* card with a note on the back giving him a link to the thank-you letter I'd written to him, and then showed him my painting. Being an artist himself, he loved it and was shocked that I would want him to sign *the front* of the painting.

He asked, "...Are you sure...right here on the front of the canvas?!" I was sure. He wrote: *'Miracles'* and signed it *Love, Marty Balin*. I told him his song *"Miracles"* was my all-time favorite, and I thanked him for the impact he had had on my life. His reply was *"Miracles* has been very good to me!"

Now, I ask you – what are the chances of all THAT happening?! My Miracles Story come true. Thank you, Mark!! In hindsight Jason's attendance was meant to be because of the part he played in the Starship Billiard Parlor sign. He was no help on the drive home however, but I had plenty of alone time to reflect on my day as I drove through the darkness with Jason sound asleep beside me.

Letter to Marty Balin

A couple of days before the concert, I posted the following open letter on my website:

Dear Marty,

We don't always get a chance to hear how we influence others, so I wanted to share a quick story with you about how dramatically you have impacted my life. I grew up listening to Jefferson Airplane *and* Jefferson Starship *and* Starship. *As I got older, I became more attached to songs with lyrics that resonated with me. I can remember being in college, driving in rural Iowa late at night, and hearing your song "Miracles." I mean, really hearing it. That was over twenty-five years ago, but that night "Miracles" became my all-time favorite song,*

Signs Surround You

because the lyrics, the music and your voice touched me deeply. I purchased every CD I could find with every version of that song that you recorded!

Fast forward to August 2007... Our city, Addison, Illinois was having a summer festival and I saw that Mickey Thomas' Starship *would be performing. Hoping to hear "Miracles," I wanted to see that concert so much that I skipped going to a family reunion so I could go. I was not disappointed – Mickey Thomas sang "Miracles." His version wasn't quite the same as your version, but **that song** drew me to **that show**!*

My son had just started playing guitar and he wanted to get a guitar pick signed – which he was able to do when we were lucky enough to meet the band after the show. Mark Abrahamian was the lead guitarist. Mark and I started corresponding and that lead to an amazing emotional connection that lasted for two years. Our relationship changed so many things in my life, and I grew more – spiritually and emotionally – in that time than I had in all my previous forty years combined!

*Mark's life and my life moved in different directions, but I connected to him every time I heard a Starship song, especially when I heard "Miracles." As you say, "Love is a magic word." Mark and I were not in communication for three years after we parted ways, but during that time, in my heart I always felt that we would find each other again in the future and rekindle our emotional connection. Tragically, before I had the chance, Mark died of a heart attack after performing at a concert in Nebraska on September 2, 2012 (you may have heard this news). I have never felt so devastated in my life. Music is a funny thing for me, and the song "Miracles" has followed me and come up in so many ways over the last year that it is **CRAZY**. It has brought me to sobbing tears – and made me smile from my head to my toes!*

This song "Miracles" now connects me to Mark in the deepest way! I still feel about Mark: "Can't even believe it with you, it's like having every dream I ever wanted come true." (BEST lyric ever!!!) And, "I picked up your vibes, you know it opened my eyes –but I'm still dreamin'...still dreamin'."

Signs Surround You

*So, Marty Balin, I write today to **THANK YOU** from the bottom of my heart for your song "Miracles." It impacted my life in the biggest way –*

without it there would not have been a catalyst for me to meet the greatest teacher and love of my life! Ironically, I was going to send Mark an email three weeks before he died, asking him to listen to your song "Hearts," because that song said everything I wanted to say to him during the three-year lapse we had. But I was afraid it would start things again, so I never sent it...

I started painting after Mark died. The "Miracles" painting was the second painting I created and my painting has improved over time, but I wanted to share it with you anyway, as I know you paint too and knew you would understand.

Two weeks ago, I was listening to Pandora and your song "Miracles" came up twice. I felt compelled to search for your concert schedule and, wouldn't you know, here you are! I will be at your concert in Springfield, Illinois this Saturday, September 21. If it is possible, I would love to bring the painting to show you in person, but most of all I would like to be able to tell you "Thank you" in person for the amazing impact you have had on my life...

Sincerely,

Laurie Majka

The day after Marty's concert, I was writing a post for my website, and I included the above letter to Marty. Five songs that Mark played in concerts came up on my Pandora app, including the *Toto* song *"Africa"* that Mark played with *Toto* – THAT IS CRAZY – and three of those songs were ones that Marty had played at his concert the night before. It seemed that the Other Side had worked overtime to pull all this together.

Signs Surround You

231

Chapter 12

Signs I Received While Writing This Book

I have over one thousand one hundred songs on my phone, and I often let them play on shuffle mode so that they play in a random fashion. It defies mathematical odds that when working on this book, almost without exception a *Starship* song would play while I was writing, including at some point during business trips.

One time, I was proofreading a difficult part of the book, and there was Mark with *"Nothing's Gonna Stop Us Now."* I remembered that two days before, the same song had played on the radio of my rental car after I had just been working on the book on the airplane. I had parked the car and was ready to turn the engine off when *"Nothing's Gonna Stop Us Now"* was played by special request from a radio show caller. It blows my mind and humbles me to know that Mark finds a way to let me know he is around...

Feed Your Head

My connection with Mark had been so deeply fulfilling, especially the deep conversations we had which I had been emotionally craving. Despite the chaos the relationship was causing in my life, our connection fulfilled me emotionally, spiritually, and intellectually. Chapter 6, Part 1, Guitar Man, is the chapter where I talk about Mark kissing me for the first time, and about how our connection had caught me off guard – and how it was so unlike me to be caught up in this kind of situation. Just as I finished dictating that chapter, the song *"White Rabbit"* by *Jefferson Airplane* began playing from the music on my phone. *"White Rabbit"* was a song played at every *Starship* concert I had attended, and I thought the lyrics were quite apropos:

Signs Surround You

"When logic and proportion have fallen slowly dead

And the White Knight is talking backwards

And the Red Queen's off with her head

Remember what the dormouse said

Feed your head, feed your head "

Listen

Chapter 21 You're Still Here was the story about the thoughts I had that Mark had died, before I learned he was indeed gone. I had just finished dictating it and was walking the same forest preserve trail I had been walking that September morning. I passed the very spot on the path where I had had the first thought of Mark dying. The song *"Get Together"* by *The Youngbloods* started playing on my phone, and the lyrics caught my attention:

"We are but a moment's sunlight fading in the grass...

If you hear the song I sing, you will understand (listen!)

You hold the key to love and fear, all in your trembling hand

Just one key unlocks them both – it's there at your command..."

As the impact of the lyrics hit me, I got goosebumps over my entire body. I glanced to my left just in time to see a beaver that was swimming in the pond dive under the water.

Who Would Believe It

On a hike at Red Rock Canyon in Nevada, I was walking the three miles back to my car when the scene of Mark's death came into my head in its complete form, as written in Chapter 22. I didn't have to think about trying to remember it – it was just there, waiting for me to offload. My day had been rushed and when I got back to the car, I felt hurried to get on the road for my thirty-minute drive back to the hotel, and to get ready

Signs Surround You

233

for a client dinner that night. But I felt very strongly about needing to first write down what was stuck in my head. I sat in my car writing the chapter on a tiny pad of paper.

As I wrote, the radio station switched suddenly to a new station – causing me to jump. The song "*Miracles*" was playing on the new station, satellite XM's "The Bridge." I was moved and brought to tears, realizing the unlikelihood of this happening. But it was happy tears, as it was almost the beginning of the song and I knew Mark was there dictating to me what had transpired in his last hours. I had previously been listening to the station "80s on 8" and actually had the thought, moments before, to change the station to "The Bridge," my favorite station. But I was so deep into the writing that I didn't listen to the thought. Instead, Mark changed the station for me.

When I think about the complexity of this having happened, it blows my mind. To start out with, when I arrived at the rental car location at 12:30 a.m. to retrieve my car, they did not have the car I had requested ready for me – and as I had arrived so late, the "Preferred" counter was closed, forcing me to walk back into the airport to exchange the car. To my surprise, there was a line at 12:30 in the morning, and I thought to myself how crazy I would be not to just take the car that was already reserved for me – but I didn't. I waited in line to get the car I had requested – only to find there were none. Thus, a car different from what I normally rent was given to me – through no choice of my own.

Secondly, when I turned on the radio in my newly assigned car, I was surprised to see the satellite stations activated. It was a rental car, and only once, out of all the dozens of cars I have rented, have I had a car where the satellite radio was activated. That would be expected, since activation has to be requested and is an extra charge. I thought back about it and remembered that when this happened the one other time, "*Miracles*" was also playing on "The Bridge."

Thirdly, while resting mid-hike, I spent longer than planned writing a chapter of my book. On the walk back to the car I had very specific thoughts about originating this chapter; and even though I really didn't have the time to stop and document it at that moment, I felt compelled to do so. I had just gotten into my car about three minutes before and had begun writing when the radio station switched. The

Signs Surround You

timing had to be just right for me to be in my car when the song "*Miracles*" played. I have absolutely no doubt that Mark was behind the whole thing!!

Two Days Later

I got into my car at 3:27 a.m. to head for the airport for an early flight. When I started the car, the *Starship* song "*We Built This City*" had just begun playing on the satellite station "80s on 8." Ten minutes later, as I was driving along, a message appeared on the screen of my car: *Sirius subscription not active. [Please call to activate].* I was returning the rental car seven hours early, too early for the activation to have been turned back off in conjunction with the rental – and I had not activated this feature in the first place. I felt sure Mark had orchestrated the use of satellite radio to get his messages across to me – and was now making sure I wouldn't get charged for it.

Obsession

I was at the cabin and had spent ten hours the night before working on editing Part 1 of my book, ending the session at 4 a.m. I was now on my hike, with my music playing, when the song "*Obsession*" by *Animotion* came on. I listened to the lyrics, and after hearing several good lines, chuckled to myself, thinking, "*It's too bad I have all the chapters written and named with song titles; this would be a great song to use for a chapter!*" I liked the play around the word "obsession," because at times that was certainly how I viewed my connection to Mark.

When the song ended, a song that Mark had made a home-studio recording of, his own rendition of "*Hallelujah*," began playing. I only have six of Mark's personal recordings in my 1,100-plus music collection, and they rarely play. The timing of Mark's "*Hallelujah*" made me feel he was agreeing with my thoughts about the song "*Obsession*."

Later that night, I was working on editing Part 1, continuing from where I had left off the night before. I was on Chapter 18, and I realized that I had not created a separate chapter where I should have. I had to

Signs Surround You

create a new Chapter 19, and ironically the title and lyrics for the song *"Obsession"* fit perfectly. I felt it had been divinely decided by Mark.

Rock your Faces Off – Again

On the ride home from the cabin I was not driving but was editing my book. I had just reread all the anecdotes about signs in the "Music" section in Part 2 when we stopped for ice cream in a tiny town in northern Michigan. Just as we walked inside the store, the radio announcer said "Radio XYZ – where we rock your faces off!" I had not heard anyone use that saying since I heard it on a radio station on my drive to the cabin three years before! Yet another confirmation while writing my book.

Eight-Year Anniversary of Meeting Mark

I was in Texas on a business trip and was working in the hotel room late at night, trying to finish Part 2 of my book. I had set this day – August 12, 2015, the eight-year anniversary of meeting Mark – as my deadline for completing the book. While documenting the chapter sections Butterflies in November and Beavers, Beavers Everywhere, I was listening to the songs related to those stories. As I wrote the last words that finished Part 2, the song *"Rosanna"* by *Toto* began playing. This was the guitar-solo song Mark had performed for me several years before. What timing! It further confirmed for me the feeling I had that this song was uniquely special and that my epiphany several years later, when I was in Japan, was correct.

Moments before I finished writing the story, I had turned the page in my notebook of signs from Mark and read this line from the medium reading with Mac: *"Mark was in love with you. He thought of you every day and it never stopped..."* Thank you, Mark. I needed that special message from you today!

Back Again to Austin (Written on the Airplane)

I only had one other opportunity to travel to Austin after the trip in

Signs Surround You

October 2012. A business trip came up that would have me traveling to Austin for a one-day meeting – on my birthday, May 13, 2015. I was in awe of the timing and excited to go, but my manager wanted me to attend an internal meeting in Dallas, instead of the customer meeting in Austin. That was so close! I was disappointed about not being in Austin for my birthday, but I appreciated coming close, knowing that Mark was behind the gesture as a "Happy Birthday" to me from him.

In late August of 2015, I was still working on my book, with a new deadline of completing it by the three-year anniversary of Mark's death on September 2. I had finally finished writing the contents of the book on a Monday at 5 a.m., with only the editing by the copy editor left to complete the project. I had essentially beat my self-imposed deadline by nine days.

The next day I was invited to attend a customer meeting to be held the following week – in Austin! I would be in Austin for three days of meetings, with the last day of the trip landing on the three-year anniversary of Mark's death. Again, the timing was unbelievable.

Two days before the trip to Austin, medium Allison Dubois was in my area, and my daughter and I attended her show. Since everyone going to this VIP session would be meeting Allison, there were copies of her books available to purchase that she would sign. There was only one book of Allison's that I had not read and I wanted to purchase that one, but they had run out of copies. About fifteen minutes before the show started, Allison's assistant approached me to ask if I still wanted to buy the book *Talk to Me: What the Dead Whisper in Your Ear* – one copy had "turned up." I excitedly purchased it and Allison signed it: *"To Laurie – Love, Allison."* It was a thrill to meet Allison in person and watch her conduct meaningful readings for people

On Sunday, travel day to Austin, I brought Allison's book with me to read on the plane during takeoff and landing. I would be working on my book edits for the majority of the flight, but during those times computers had to be shut off and stowed. I got situated in my seat and began reading as we headed toward the runway, ready to take off for Austin.

After take-off I was eager to open my computer and resume working on my book edits, but there were only three pages left of the chapter of Allison's book I was on, so I decided to finish it. The chapter

Signs Surround You

was titled "How Spirits Talk to Me," and I was reading a section of it called "Signs." I turned the page and the "Signs" section continued with "Mark's Story." Wow, what are the chances I would be reading a book with a section referencing signs – the subject of my book – and that it would refer to someone named Mark!

My mouth dropped open as I read on and realized the "Mark" Allison was referring to was her cousin Mark. "Mark the Medium" was the one who had given me a phone reading before my Mark died – when I was trying to decide whether I should send the five-year anniversary email to him. My jaw was on the floor as I read the line at the bottom of the page that began: "As we were driving from Austin to San Antonio…"

I finished the chapter and sat there reflecting on what had just occurred. I thought about how Allison's book had come into my possession and how I had tried to read it the night I got it, but only got through the first chapter before falling asleep. I had been exhausted from lack of sleep over the previous few days while trying to complete my own book. All of that allowed the timing for the second chapter to be read on the airplane on the way to Austin. The signs had come full circle all the way back to the beginning of my own book and the story of Mark the Medium that was highlighted in Chapter 3 of Part 1.

I thought about all that had transpired over the last seven days: I had finished writing my book and, the night before, had painted the painting that was the book's namesake and would be featured in the book; on the night I finished writing, I heard three songs on the radio that were titles of chapters; I had booked a business trip to Austin that had suddenly and inexplicably come up; lastly, I had connected to one of the most evidential and scientifically studied mediums in the world, and she was to be a part of the last amazing sign that would finish my book – which had occurred during the trip to Austin, no less!

I began documenting that story on the airplane right after it happened so as not to lose any of the details. In order to drown out the people having a loud conversation behind me, I turned on my music from my phone. While I was writing, the *Chicago* song *"(I've Been) Searchin' So Long"* started playing. This song is the title of a chapter in my book as well. Thank you, Mark, for showing me you still care about me.

Signs Surround You

According to Allison Dubois, in her book *Talk to Me, What the Dead Whisper in Your Ear*, our loved ones on the Other Side are "emotionally based beings, so their messages are motivated by *their* feelings for you, not always your feelings for them." The medium Moriah told me, "He [Mark] will be projecting his thoughts to you telepathically every day." I have been paying attention and have been listening to my intuition, so that I can connect with what he is sending...

Signs Surround You

Chapter 13

The Story of This Book
"Love is All Around You"

"So you think that it's over

That your love has finally reached the end

Anytime you call, night or day

I'll be right there for you…

Love is all around you…"

~Love Song by Tesla

https://open.spotify.com/track/0vJUdlefT5caKla9H8b1q4?si=3mius1wVQni8TrYTsII2Pg

(This song played as I finished writing this last chapter.)

I had been chugging along with the *Soul Heart Art* paintings for over two years, and the first anniversary of the Daily Soul Whispers was now approaching. On April 22, 2015, I had a dream that began with me standing around a campfire with several other people at dusk. Mark was there. He didn't look like himself, but I still knew it was him. I walked over to him, held out my hand, and said "Can we walk for a bit?" He didn't reply but took my hand and we began walking in silence.

The trail I chose for our walk was steeply climbing. I glanced his way – it WAS Mark, now in the form that I recognized, still holding my hand. I said to him, "I can't believe you've been gone for two and a half years and I still feel like I'm in love with you – as if you had never died." After letting that thought sink in for a minute, I continued, "If you were still here, I would want to marry you."

Signs Surround You

He stopped our climb, smiled, and looking directly into my eyes while still holding my hand, he replied, "You know, I'm most proud of Our Story..." He let the words hang in the air...

Before I could reply, I was awake. Instantly, I remembered the dream and the feelings I had in it. Wow – he was proud of "Our Story"! I believe it really was Mark in the dream, not just something I would make up in my imagination – mostly because of how he phrased what he said to me. Mark was articulate and always chose his words carefully, and he had a very specific way of phrasing his thoughts. His wording, "I'm most proud of..." is not the way I would have phrased a thought like that. I would have said something like "I'm very proud..." It would not even have occurred to me to phrase it the way Mark did.

I documented the dream immediately, so as not to lose the memory of any part of it – but I never will, because I had already deeply committed it to memory. My belief is that when a dream feels real to you, it is. You will probably wake up from the dream and remember every bit of it vividly and be able to recall the details flawlessly even years later.

Later that afternoon, I was feeling exhausted and decided to take a nap, something I almost never did. As I lay there preparing to fall asleep, my mind was busy turning thoughts into words, words into sentences, sentences into paragraphs, and soon a chapter had formed. It was so clear in my mind that I felt the urge to grab a notebook and begin committing it to writing. Within forty-five minutes, I had the chapter transferred from my mind to the notebook.

I had never had a writing experience like that. Many times I will have an idea form in my mind, but when I try to capture it on paper, I can only grab bits and pieces. Then I sit there, trying to remember exactly what I had thought only minutes before. The information from my dream state was different; it sat in my head as a whole body of work, only requiring me to be the transcriber.

The ideas kept coming, and I continued to write and write over the next few days. Two days after I had written the original chapter, I needed to document a saved text message for a new chapter that I was working on, a message that Mark had sent me years before. When I found

Signs Surround You

the text, what I read made me smile: "I'm most excited that..." There it was – Mark's particular style of phrasing in his very own words.

It has been over three years now since Mark passed, but I can still remember everything about him, which keeps him alive in my Heart. I can see him standing before me, flashing a smile and mouthing "You are beautiful." I can feel the strength of his hand as he holds mine tightly. I can feel the bounce of his curls as he leans over to kiss me softly on the lips. I feel his curiosity as he murmurs into my hair "What was that thought?" in reaction to a sigh I made while he was holding me close. I can still feel him as I watch him play the guitar in a video on YouTube – feel the vibrations of his energy. He is pure energy now, but he is still here. Only his form has changed.

When Mark left this Earth he took a piece of my Heart with him. Slowly over time, he has been giving it back to me – through my experiences with others, through my paintings and Soul Whispers, and with this book. And now my heart overflows with LOVE! Thank you Mark, for wanting to show me that you were around. I will love you for all of Eternity!

THE END

(Until we meet again…)

Signs Surround You

A New Beginning

From the Book: ~~Once~~ A Cheater

Mark has never left me. Not that I get signs every day, but his songs continue to play beyond any kind of statistical norm. As well, he has been gone for seven years now, yet his sign activity has greatly increased in recent months (or else I've gotten much better at picking up what he is putting down!) – at the same time that a new project has been looming large. In 2014, two years after Mark's death, I got a "download" one day while taking a shower. I saw it all at once as a fully formed idea. It was presented to me as the Tic Tac Challenge. Now, maybe Spirit wasn't worried about being sued by Tic Tac, but I was. I eventually renamed it Super Power Challenge, because I also understood in that moment that I was meant to send this special message into the world – but *I* wasn't quite ready.

Since that day back in 2014 my life experiences have changed in countless ways. I accelerated my spiritual development through a lot of reading books and working on myself. I finished writing this book, *Signs Surround You,* got divorced, moved to Arizona, began my hiking obsession, changed jobs, met the greatest love I have ever known – and maybe most importantly, through my spiritual work I fell in love with every part of my life. I learned to accept myself at the deepest level and to truly understand the power of my Soul, the brightness of my light, and the love we are meant to have for ourselves.

Mark recently made it known through the medium Thomas John Flannigan that he had a new project he had begun working on with me. It was at a large group reading (attended by over one hundred people) hosted by Thomas that Mark came through with his message for me. I was surprised because I had just had a private twenty-minute reading with Thomas one week before – Mark had made his presence known and sent me messages that day as well. In the middle of a reading for my mom, Thomas abruptly said...

Signs Surround You

[Thomas] *I'm hearing a song – Spirit has been doing this more and more and I'm not a singer so I'm not going to sing the song – but it's a song from the 80s.* [He paused for a bit, listening, then said...] *"Nothin's Gonna Stop Us Now."*

[Me] *That's Mark!*

[Thomas] *How in the world is that song connected to Mark?*

[Me] *Mark was the lead guitarist for the band* Starship. *He probably played that song five hundred times in the 14 years he was with the band.*

[Thomas] *Wow.* [Even Thomas seemed impressed.] *Well, Mark is stepping forward, and he is showing me that he's getting ready to do something very big in the world with you. He says you have been anxious about it, but he's telling me he doesn't want you to be anxious – he wants you to be* **excited!**

Ironically, I had recently been playing with the revival of the Tic Tac Challenge idea presented to me by Mark five years before, and I felt a great pressure to figure out how to bring this new idea into the world. I had already had several conversations about it with family and friends. I had even mentioned it to Thomas the week before, when Mark made a similar comment during my phone reading.

The very next day, a series of signs began weaving themselves together over a twelve-week period. The signs left me utterly flabbergasted at their complexity and Mark's ability to get my attention from the Other Side. The following is that series.

Signs to Hold the Line

https://open.spotify.com/track/4aVuWgvDOX63hcOCnZtNFA?si=wCfZjfQPTp2i2t9ZKmhs_A

How do you move on after touching a love like Mark and I shared. He still continued to touch my life, even after he had been gone for many years. I had accumulated a lot a knowledge about love, but since love is our greatest lesson to learn, Spirit still had more in store for me to learn where love was concerned. How do you attract someone with

Signs Surround You

enough strength to understand and embrace the relationship I still had with Mark without feeling like they couldn't compete with it. It wasn't a competition, but we are taking about guys here. It was going to take a man as strong as steel to handle not only me, but everything that came with loving me. After a five year search, I found him – at the bottom of the Grand Canyon. And he had "heart" in his name, that was surely a sign, and more signs followed...

In June of 2019 Wylie Heartly, the new love in my life and I did a CrossFit workout and got smoothies afterwards This was the day after the Thomas John show my mom and I saw in person. I told him about it while we drank our smoothies. I described how Mark had communicated through Thomas that he would be helping me with this new project I was bringing into the world. We left the smoothie shop to sit in my Jeep and finish our conversation. When I started the Jeep, the *Toto* song "*Hold the Line*" was playing. The radio screen, however, indicated it was *Bread* "Make it with You" – except it wasn't. When "*Hold the Line*" ended, the screen updated and played *England Dan & John Ford Coley, "Nights Are Forever Without You.*" I took pictures of both screens. Wylie was pretty amazed at what happened. He had heard a lot of "hype" around my signs over the previous two years that we had been together but had never experienced it for himself. I too was amazed, as it had been several years since Mark froze my screen like that.

I took a vacation to the cabin I had once owned with my ex-husband in the Upper Peninsula of Michigan (UP). I rented a car in Chicago and began the six-hour drive. I was looking forward to listening to my two favorite FM radio stations once I got close to the cabin. The radio itself worked fine in Chicago and all the way to the cabin, but once I got there the only station that would pick up was 102.5, a country station. I was able to scan through all the stations, but that was the only one that would connect. Even when I manually typed my stations into the radio they wouldn't stay tuned in. I reluctantly listened to the country station – not that I don't like country music, but I was looking forward to listening to the music on the FM stations. On Sunday, they didn't play music at all but broadcast the NASCAR race instead. I decided I was going to have to play my own music. As I pulled up the options to connect my phone music to the car, I saw the XM radio options. I should point out that XM is a $13.99-per-day option, which I had not activated, and only two times in all my years of renting cars has the XM option ever even worked. I pushed the button anyway and to my amazement the XM stations came to life! I set up my favorite stations – The Bridge, 80's on 8

Signs Surround You

and Yacht Rock. I was getting my "fix" of the FM radio stations inside the cabin, and now I at least had music I liked in the car.

I went on one of my favorite hikes near the cabin. I hung my hammock by Fish Lake to read a book and take a nap. When I woke up, I was staring at the lake. At that moment, I felt compelled to pray about Wylie and me. It had only been one week since I left our relationship, and I was having a difficult time with the situation and the complexities around the break. I needed guidance and prayed out loud to God, and asked my Spirit team to gather to help me get through this time. I played some songs I had previously included on a new Spotify playlist called *Twin Flame Choices* and loudly sang each of them, especially the song "*I Still Believe*" by *Mariah Carey*. I then packed up to leave.

When I started the car, I heard the song "*Hold the Line*" by *Toto*. I thanked Mark for listening to me pray and responding so quickly. My last contact with Mark before he died was at a concert where they played three *Toto* songs along with the usual *Starship* lineup. "*Hold the Line*" was one of the three *Toto* songs. I looked at the screen and noticed it indicated: XM Yacht Rock, *Looking Glass* "*Brandy (You're a Fine Girl)*" – except the *Toto* song was playing instead. The entire song played and when it finished, the screen flashed and updated to "*Diamond Girl*" by *Seals and Crofts*. I have long said this is God's song to me, and it felt like this was a double message from both Mark *and* God, answering my prayer. But only when the lyrics "*Hold the line, love isn't always on time...*" really sank in, did I FREAK OUT! I thought the message was that love *wasn't* on time and *wasn't* going to work out. I felt sad. I felt let down because usually when Mark communicated to me he was sharing something good. I had never really pondered this song's lyrics before.

I–drove for a while and then changed the station to 80s on 8. "*Africa*" by *Toto* was playing – another one of the three *Toto* songs from the concert long ago. This song prompted me to begin talking to Mark in my head, asking if what I had just heard was true and proposing that if Wylie and I were *not* going to work out, to please move Wylie to email me and give me an answer. Let him verbalize whether we were or were not going to work out – have him answer this question.

Later, I Googled the dictionary meaning and song meaning of "*Hold the Line*," and I saw it also had a military term meaning: Do NOT give up – hold the line – maintain your current position – stand firm and

Signs Surround You

do not retreat. I also viewed a website where people were commenting on the lyrics. Many of them were saying that when love wasn't on time, if you were patient and gave it time it would eventually work out. With this new understanding, I began to have hope again.

The next day I spent three hours in the car with Ryan and decided to tell him what was going on with Wylie and me. Ryan was super supportive. I also told him about what had happened a couple days before, when the song "*Hold the Line*" had been playing while the screen indicated a completely different song. I was still talking to him about it as we approached a tiny town. I wanted to stop at a store there, so I pulled over to go into the store but noticed a sign in the window that said they close at 5:00. I glanced at the clock in the car and realized they were already closed, as it was 5:30. In a lull in the conversation, I noticed the song "*Hold the Line*" was quietly playing in the background, although the screen said "*Make It with You*" by *Bread* – but once again that song was not the song playing. This time Ryan was my witness. He could not believe it! To top it off, when we got back to the cabin I had an email reply from Wylie in my inbox, saying he did not want our relationship to be over. The time of the email: 5:30 – the exact time my screen froze.

Stacy and Sal had driven their RV from Arizona to the UP to spend part of my vacation with me. On their first full day there, Stacy and I were supposed to meet at the cabin to pick blueberries at 7:30 am, but her phone was on Central time and mine was on Eastern, and she showed up an hour later than I expected her. Having extra time, I sat down to respond to Wylie's email from the previous day. The response just flowed out of me. I quickly sent the email to him.

Ryan was there at the cabin too and we all left for our kayak trip. When we got there, I had to wait for Sal and Stacy to unload their kayak. I sat in the car re-reading the email I had sent Wylie, now panicking that my response had been too hasty. While reviewing it, I heard the song "*Hold the Line*" begin to play on the radio. The screen said Yacht Rock: *England Dan & John Ford Coley* "*Nights Are Forever Without You*" – again a repeat song from earlier, and again it was not the song playing. Stacy and Ryan both walked over to the car in time to hear the song and see the car screen as well. Double witness! They were both shocked. I was shocked too, because each time this has happened I felt Mark was telling me to stop worrying about all this – Spirit had me covered.

On my last day at the cabin. I was running out of time to hike Bruno's Run, a ten mile trail, so I had to run it. When I finished, I only had twenty minutes to relax in the hammock next to the lake. I decided to use my time playing four songs from my *Twin Flame Choices* playlist:

Signs Surround You

"Lessons in Love," "With a Little Luck," "Truly Madly Deeply," and *"I Still Believe."* I sang each of them passionately, sobbing the whole time. I then packed up my hammock and headed to the car. When I started the engine, the music didn't begin playing right away, and I thought to myself; "Hey Mark, what do you have to say to me now?" The XM station The Bridge then came to life and began playing a song I didn't like, so I switched the station to Yacht Rock. The screen indicated *Doobie Brothers "Minute by Minute"* was playing – only it wasn't. The last verse of *"Hold the Line"* was streaming from the speakers. This time I was truly dumbfounded, because never before had these incidents happened with such frequency – and this, once again, was on the heels of a very intense time for me with Wylie. I snapped a picture of the screen and later wished I had taken a video instead. The crazy thing was that as I drove back to Chicago I remembered the radio-freezing episode with Wylie back in June after telling him about the reading I had received at Thomas's show, and I was able to connect the final dots that tied all the *"Hold the Line"* songs together. For confirmation I had taken pictures of the screen that day, and luckily they were still on my phone.

A few weeks after my vacation my sister Stephanie was in town for our Dad's 70th birthday. My parents got us all tickets to see *Chris Isaak* in concert. Stephanie and I decided to drive separately and meet my parents at the venue. On the drive home, we talked about the concert and how musicians are spiritually open. I mentioned Mark and then started talking about Wylie – and at that exact moment *"Hold the Line"* began playing on the radio. The screen said *Boz Scaggs "Jojo"*– was playing but it was not. This time I didn't miss the opportunity to videotape the screen with my phone.

Watch video on YouTube: www.youtube.com/watch?v=BvTnrw3T4Jo

My Sister had previously heard the stories of *"Hold the Line"* and was now a new witness to the phenomenon. When the song ended, the screen updated and started playing *Michael McDonald "I've Gotta Try."* This time I was in my own vehicle and *my* radio has a feature called Replay. Replay allows me to press a button and rewind back through songs that had played over the previous hour of listening. Just out of curiosity, I hit the Replay button and scrolled back to the beginning of where the screen said *"Jojo"* and let it play. This time the entire song *"Jojo"* did play – not *"Hold the Line,"* which had played moments before – just as it would have if the radio had not been taken over by Mark. It was a neat confirmation! And for the record, *"Hold the Line"* is not a Yacht Rocky song – that is, not a song they play on that XM station. Yet it was played over and over again – just for me.

Signs Surround You

My friend Melinda had already been a witness to my songs as signs phenomena when we attended a concert together, and I was anxious to share my new *Hold the Line* signs with her. It had been several weeks since she helped me on the night I discovered *Bumble-Gate*. We made plans to catch up at a local movie theater bar. I shared some of the email correspondence Wylie and I had shared since our separation. Melinda and her husband had gotten to know Wylie on our Hiking Adventure trip to Havasupai a few months earlier. In an effort to protect my feelings she had kept one piece of information to herself that she decided to disclose now. Three of the couples had gotten together after that trip. Melinda hadn't given them any information about Wylie and my separation, and their conversation had naturally flowed to the trip. She wanted me to know that all three of the husbands felt Wylie had not been nice enough to me on that trip. They felt he had over-shared information about me that made them feel uncomfortable, and they felt it wasn't presented in a loving way. And while they liked him, they (all six husbands and wives) had felt that I deserved someone who treated me better. I felt a twinge of embarrassment at hearing the feedback, because Wylie's behavior felt like a direct reflection on me. I knew the exact comments they were referring to, and I had allowed the treatment from him. While we can't control what people say, we do teach others how to treat us by what we accept from them. Melinda's comments were shared with me out of love and caring, and I didn't want to make excuses for Wylie, but in hindsight he had already been talking to the women on Bumble by that trip. When you have other women stroking your ego, it becomes easier to treat the person you are with disrespectfully in an effort to subconsciously push them away. Perhaps he cared less about me and my feelings and my reactions because he knew he had someone new he could run to. Melinda hugged me and I could feel the sting of tears in my eyes as she did. The tears were part embarrassment, part sadness in hearing that other people had noticed Wylie was not on his best behavior with me, and part gratitude that she was a good enough friend to not withhold information that could potentially help me. Perhaps it was time to "Hold the Line"... for myself.

The mysteries of the Universe continue to astound me to this day, and I am well on my way in this new life purpose. I do hope you will come along with me on this journey to see where it takes us. I promise it will not be a boring ride. To be continued....

Signs Surround You

Appendix

Summary of Sign Types

Animals, Birds and Insects

Animals and insects, such as butterflies or dragonflies, are common signs too. They either show up unexpectedly or act uncharacteristically. It seems to be easy for Spirit to use a butterfly or a dragonfly as a messenger to get your attention. Birds also seem to be special messengers. I have heard stories about hawks, doves, cardinals, blue jays – there are probably no limits. When any of these special creatures try to get our attention, it may be a reminder from our loved ones that they are thinking of us too.

Brought Together by the Other Side

The creation of new relationships can also be facilitated by the Other Side. Sometimes we need assistance in meeting a Soul Mate, or creating the circumstances perfect for "bumping into" one. We can't forget that we were all connected before we came to this Earth, and when the timing is right, the Soul from the Other Side will move Heaven and Earth to make a needed connection happen.

Coins

Some people find coins, usually pennies or dimes. One person I know has collected a jarful of dimes sent from his passed-away dad. I myself rarely find money, but my son has amusingly promised that when he passes he will send us hundred-dollar bills.

Signs Surround You

Dreams

Dreams are another common sign. Everyone dreams, but not everyone remembers their dreams. I saw a statistic that we forget 60% of a dream within five minutes of waking, and 80% within ten minutes. Dreams from your loved one, however, will feel more real than a regular dream, and often the details can be vividly recalled even years later. These dreams will generally not have the nonsensical feel that many dreams do.

People also report that in dreams their loved ones look vibrant, glowing, happy, and the most beautiful they had ever seen them look, no matter the age they present themselves as. Spirits have the ability to appear to you as a different age than they were when you last saw them or when they left this Earth. If your loved one died at forty-five, they may appear twenty-five, possibly because that was when they felt the best about themselves. I have even heard of passed-away children showing younger versions of themselves; perhaps that was the time in their lives when they felt most happy.

Spirits seem to retain the same personality they had when they were here on this Earth. Whether they were funny, serious or a total smartass – it doesn't matter – they will make sure you recognize them in your dreams.

Electricity and Electronics

We are surrounded by electronics, and loved ones in Spirit seem to like to play with electricity and electronics. After all, our loved ones are pure energy now. They are capable of turning the lights on and off, making the phone ring, even changing your computer screen or freezing it with a special message. Electronics can also be used to send us a double sign, such as changing the radio station to a different one while playing a particular song just for you. Signs that seem to be favored by many in Spirit include lights flashing in the room, the power going on and off or just staying off

Signs Surround You

Feathers

Feathers are one of the most common signs. I was told my loved one Mark would send me white feathers, and I have a bagful of them that I have collected. Feathers can show up in very strange places. They can also be used with another sign, such as a song, to help you understand that it really is a message for you.

Feeling Our Loved Ones Around Us

This one is probably the most common sign of all. People often report *feeling* their loved one around them; feeling their spirit. Sometimes the feeling produces goosebumps on the arms or over the entire body. Similarly, I have a friend who can feel heat on her back as she lies on the bed watching the favorite sport of her passed-away loved one. She feels it is a sign that he is there watching with her.

Some people report feeling the temperature of the room drop, like what was portrayed in the movie *The Sixth Sense*. Our loved ones don't want to frighten us; they are just using whatever means are available to them to get our attention.

Sometimes the feeling of our loved ones around us includes a physical effect within the body, such as a ringing in the ears. When that happens, pay special attention – they may be sending you a message and using the ringing, for example, to get your attention. Virtually any sensation is possible, even your stomach "hurting" (in a good way).

Goosebumps or Hair Standing on End

We have all experienced a cold chill that caused goosebumps or your hair to stand on end. Now that your loved ones are in spirit form, they have merely transformed from a physical body to an energy existence. Many people report a drop in the air temperature when a spirit is near them. This can cause goosebumps or your hair to stand on end. Or, we may feel our loved ones around us energetically causing our hair to stand on end in response to the new energy.

Signs Surround You

I have often heard mediums ask a client if they just got goosebumps, then explain that the Soul of their passed-away loved one moved through their physical existence at that moment. I personally experience the sensation of the hairs inside my left ear standing on end when Spirit communicates with me. You may even feel a sensation of physical touch when your loved one tries to let you know they are still around you.

Mediums and Energy Healers

A medium is a person who is able to connect with Spirits on the Other Side and pass messages to the living. Mediums connect with the Spirit World in different ways. Some are able to put pen to paper and let the messages flow out through the pen. Others see pictures in their mind that they translate the meanings of; this is called *clairvoyance*, also referred to as "seeing" with the third-eye. Others are skilled in hearing Spirit, which is known as *clairaudience*.

Some mediums see symbols they themselves have created, which those in Spirit can use to get a message to you. For example, a medium might see a picture in his or her head of a dove while connecting with your loved one; the symbol of the dove for the medium means your loved one is at peace.

Some mediums can even experience the feelings, emotions and sensations that Spirits are communicating to them, including being able to feel their pain and the cause of death – even the location of the pain, by feeling it in their own body, which is known as *clairsentience*.

Many spiritual teachers say that we *all* possess the ability to connect to the Other Side, and that it is just a matter of practice and recognition. I believe our loved ones on the Other Side do everything in their power to connect with us. Just because we don't think they have sent us signs doesn't mean they haven't – we might not be "picking up what they are putting down."

I have read quite a few books written by mediums, and they all say our loved ones are at peace, that they transitioned easily out of their body and feel no pain now. They are with you every time you think of them. They know what is happening and has been happening in your life since

Signs Surround You

they left the Earth. And, most importantly – they love you! Because love never dies...

Multiple Signs Woven Together to Tell a Story

Sometimes a person will get a string of signs that seem unrelated. The person should eventually notice that the signs weave themselves together in a story that can only be understood in hindsight, when the full picture has revealed itself after some time has passed. Pay attention to those stories and document them for you to be able to revisit later. Our human memory can be affected over time, and it is comforting to reread descriptions of signs we have received, with full detail of how they happened and when they happened. You may think you will never forget some amazing sign, but you probably won't remember it exactly as it happened if you haven't written it down right away.

Numbers

Many people see special number combinations that remind them of their loved ones. Numbers are visible everywhere in our world, but they can feel special when presented in a certain combination, or when received at a certain time. A couple of friends of mine see their late son's football jersey number everywhere they go. Another friend sees numbers in the combination of a date that is significant to her.

Number patterns like 111, 1111, 222, 333, 444, 555 etc. carry a lot of spiritual significance. Many of these number are believed to be signs from Angels. You may notice them especially when associated with times and dates. Often, the same number sequence will often be noticed by you. As an example, you may find you wake from a sound sleep only to notice the clock says 2:22. You may "catch" the numbers 111 or 1111 frequently throughout the day, on a clock, a license plate, a store receipt, or they can randomly stop in combination – such as on a gas-station pump. Now, if only they could show up in a winning lottery ticket! But I'm sure if I researched it, I would find this has happened!

Signs Surround You

Physical Manifestation

Less commonly, your loved ones may physically manifest in your presence, perhaps in a hazy or filmy way, or completely clear and solid looking. They can appear as any age and may choose the age when they were happiest here on Earth, but you will always recognize them.

You may see them sitting at the end of your bed, or see their reflection in the mirror, or just catch a brief glimpse of something you swear was them. Rest assured, they are not trying to scare you, and there is nothing to be frightened of. They only want to communicate. People who have had this experience hold it as one of their most precious gifts from the Other Side. Many report that their loved ones look vibrant, beautiful and have a glow about them, showing they are happy and at peace.

Scents

Some people are very connected by means of scents. They may smell their loved one's perfume or cologne. It doesn't have to be a particularly good smell, though. My Mom used to smell cigar smoke all the time after we moved into our new house – which was odd, because no one in our family smoked. The previous owner, who had built the house as his dream retirement home, had died, and his wife told us he loved to smoke cigars.

My mom would only smell cigar smoke in the basement, and it always gave her a peaceful, good feeling. Perhaps his wife had only let him smoke in the basement and he knew he couldn't smoke around her, so he would visit us sometimes and have a stogie in his old house. Addictions apparently cross over to the Other Side – or maybe they aren't allowed to smoke in heaven, so they have to come back here! This type of ability to smell what may not be physically there is called *clairalience*.

Signs Designed to Give You a Message

There are times when our loved ones in Spirit want to get a specific message to us. It might come through a dream or through a communication from a person here on Earth. Sometimes, it is an actual

Signs Surround You

physical sign that you see, with an idea in writing that has been trying to "hit you over the head" to get across to you.

Signs can come to you in any way, in any form, at any time. When you are given the gift of information, don't ignore it. There are no accidents. By following the suggestion of a sign from the Other Side, you may even avoid a problem or a hassle.

Songs and Music

Music has the ability to bring out emotions we might not otherwise tap into. So much of what we enjoy about music is how it makes us feel – whether it's a soft, smoky beat that calms your nerves and puts you in a Zen moment, or an upbeat techno rhythm that makes your blood pump. Whatever it is, music seems to speak directly to our Soul.

To our human mind, it seems impossible to think that something outside our physical reality could determine *what*, *when*, and *where* music shows up in our lives. But we have to remember that Spirit is not limited by the laws of the physical world. And since music is created purely from vibration, it is something the Other Side can easily use to communicate with us. People commonly report hearing songs that remind them of their loved one. Songs can show up and catch your attention at home or when you are out somewhere – when you are thinking of the person or not thinking of that person, either way. You may even hear lyrics that feels like you have been given a special message or an answer to something you were thinking about. Music is a wonderful gift from the Other Side.

Telepathic Communication of Thoughts

Your passed-away loved ones don't have a body or a physical voice anymore, but they can communicate with you telepathically. You may not hear their voice, but you could have a thought that you feel did not originate in your own mind, and it could be your loved one's thought. It takes practice to recognize the subtle differences, but these thoughts are real and can bring you peace and valuable information. One thing that

Signs Surround You

can help is to remember what you were thinking about at the time the new

thought entered your mind. If you can trace it back to see how it was triggered, then it was probably your own thought. If you can't, and you feel strongly that it was from the Other Side, then it probably was!

Signs Surround You

Resources

Connecting with People in this book

- **Dede Hart – Energy Healer**

DeeDee, your words set me on a journey I could not have conceived of in my wildest dreams. You are a true healer and I am forever grateful for your energy healing! http://www.DedeHart.com

- **Moriah Rhame – Medium**

Moriah, your abilities blow me away. Thank you for connecting with Mark many times over the years. Your readings have brought me comfort, insight and closure. What a beautiful gift you are to the World! http://www.MoriahTheMedium.com

- **Stephanie Cochran – Medium, Intuitive Reader**

Stephanie has been an exceptional source of confirmation for me over the years. Her greatest strength is her ability to connect with Spirit as they guide her to uncover the hidden emotions that keep people stuck. Stephanie's abilities are enhanced by her own NDE. www.IntuitiveReadingsbyStephanie.com

- **Thomas John Flannigan – Psychic Medium, Intuitive**

Thomas, no one has been able to bring Mark back to life the way you have. Your skills are second to none! I am so grateful to have spent an entire day with you, you have blessed me more than you will know. I think your life review and the ripple affects you have caused in this world will astound you. https://www.MediumThomas.com

- **Allison Dubois – Medium**

    https://www.AllisonDubois.com

Signs Surround You

Song Lyrics Copyright Permissions

Always

Words and Music by Jon Bon Jovi

Copyright © 1994 UNIVERSAL - POLYGRAM INTERNATIONAL PUBLISHING, INC. and BON JOVI PUBLISHING

All Rights Controlled and Administered by UNIVERSAL - POLYGRAM INTERNATIONAL PUBLISHING, INC.

All Rights Reserved Used by Permission Reprinted by Permission of Hal Leonard LLC

Be Near Me

Words and Music by Martin Fry and Mark White

Copyright © 1985 Neutron Music Limited

All Rights Administered by Sony/ATV Music Publishing LLC, 424 Church Street, Suite 1200, Nashville, TN 37219 International Copyright Secured

All Rights Reserved Reprinted by Permission of Hal Leonard LLC

Get Together

Words and Music by Chet Powers

Copyright © 1963 IRVING MUSIC, INC. Copyright Renewed

All Rights Reserved Used by Permission Reprinted by Permission of Hal Leonard LLC

Hearts

Words and Music by Jesse Barish

Copyright © 1980 Great Pyramid Music and Painted Desert Music Corp.

All Rights Administered by Figs. D Music c/o Bicycle Music Company

All Rights Reserved Used by Permission Reprinted by Permission of Hal Leonard LLC

HEAT OF THE MOMENT

Words and Music by JOHN WETTON and GEOFFREY DOWNES

Copyright © 1982 WC MUSIC CORP., ALMOND LEGG MUSIC CORP and NOSEBAG MUSIC, INC. MUSIC

All Rights on Behalf of ALMOND LEGG MUSIC CORP Administered by WC MUSIC CORP.

All Rights on behalf of NOSEBAG MUSIC, INC. Administered by UNIVERSAL-POLYGRAM INTERNATIONAL PUBLISHING, INC.

All Rights Reserved / Used By Permission of ALFRED MUSIC

Heat Of The Moment

Words and Music by Geoffrey Downes and John Wetton

Copyright © 1982 Palan Music Publishing Ltd., WC Music Corp. and Almond Legg Music Corp

All Rights for Palan Music Publishing Ltd. Administered by BMG Rights Management (US) LLC

All Rights for Almond Legg Music Corp. Administered by WC Music Corp. International Copyright Secured

All Rights Reserved Reprinted by Permission of Hal Leonard LLC

Hello, It's Me

Words and Music by Todd Rundgren

Copyright © 1968, 1969 Screen Gems-EMI Music Inc. Copyright Renewed

All Rights Administered by Sony/ATV Music Publishing LLC, 424 Church Street, Suite 1200, Nashville, TN 37219 International Copyright Secured

All Rights Reserved Reprinted by Permission of Hal Leonard LLC

HELP ME

Words and Music by JONI MITCHELL

Copyright © 1973 (Renewed) CRAZY CROW MUSIC

All Rights Administered by SONY/ATV MUSIC PUBLISHING, 8 Music Square West, Nashville, TN 37203

All Rights Reserved / Used By Permission of ALFRED MUSIC

Signs Surround You

261

Hold On To The Nights

Words and Music by Richard Marx

Copyright © 1987 BMG Monarch All Rights Administered by BMG Rights Management (US) LLC

All Rights Reserved Used by Permission Reprinted by Permission of Hal Leonard LLC

Hold the Line

Words and Music by David Paich

Copyright © 1978 Hudmar Publishing Company Incorporated, USA.

All Rights Administered by Sony/ATV Music Publishing LLC, 424 Church Street, Suite 1200, Nashville, TN 37219 International Copyright Secured

All Rights Reserved Used by Permission Reprinted by Permission of Hal Leonard LLC

If You Leave Me Now

Words and Music by Peter Cetera

Copyright © 1976 BMG Songs, Inc./Big Elk Music

All Rights Reserved Used by Permission Reprinted by Permission of Hal Leonard LLC

I'll Be Over You

Words and Music by Steve Lukather and Randy Goodrum

Copyright © 1986 by Universal Music Publishing MGB Ltd. and Randy Goodrum Inc.

All Rights for Universal Music Publishing MGB Ltd. Administered by Universal Music - MGB Songs International Copyright Secured

All Rights Reserved Reprinted by Permission of Hal Leonard LLC

(I've Been) Searchin' So Long

Words and Music by James Pankow

Copyright © 1974 Make Me Smile Music and Big Elk Music Copyright Renewed

All Rights Reserved Used by Permission Reprinted by Permission of Hal Leonard LLC

Just Remember I Love You

Words and Music by Rick Roberts

Copyright © 1976 Stephen Stills Music Copyright Renewed International Copyright Secured

All Rights Reserved Reprinted by Permission of Hal Leonard LLC

LOVE SONG

Words and Music by FRANK HANNON and JEFFREY KEITH

Copyright © 1988 City Kidd Music ASCAP

All Rights Reserved / Used by Permission of ROUND HILL SONGS (ASCAP)

Lucky

Words and Music by Jason Mraz, Colbie Caillat and Timothy Fagan

Copyright © 2008 Sony/ATV Music Publishing LLC, Cocomarie Music, Wrunch Time Music and Goo Eyed Music

All Rights on behalf of Sony/ATV Music Publishing LLC, Cocomarie Music and Wrunch Time Music Administered by Sony/ATV Music Publishing LLC, 424 Church Street, Suite 1200, Nashville, TN 37219 International Copyright Secured

All Rights Reserved Reprinted by Permission of Hal Leonard LLC

Miracles

Words and Music by Marty Balin

Copyright © 1975 by Figs. D Music o/b/o Diamondback Music Copyright Renewed

All Rights Administered by Figs. D Music c/o The Bicycle Music Company

All Rights Reserved Used by Permission Reprinted by Permission of Hal Leonard LLC

Rosanna

Words and Music by David Paich

Copyright © 1982 HUDMAR PUBLISHING CO., INC.

All Rights Reserved Used by Permission Reprinted by Permission of Hal Leonard LLC

Signs Surround You

262

Sara

Music by Peter Wolf and Ina Wolf Words by Ina Wolf

Copyright © 1985 Universal Music - Careers and Universal Music - MGB Songs

All Rights Reserved Used by Permission Reprinted by Permission of Hal Leonard LLC

Should've Known Better

Words and Music by Richard Marx

Copyright © 1987 BMG Monarch

All Rights Administered by BMG Rights Management (US) LLC

All Rights Reserved Used by Permission Reprinted by Permission of Hal Leonard LLC

Show And Tell

Words and Music by Jerry Fuller

Copyright © 1973, 1981 EMI Blackwood Music Inc. and Fullness Music Co. Copyright Renewed

All Rights Administered by Sony/ATV Music Publishing LLC, 424 Church Street, Suite 1200, Nashville, TN 37219 International Copyright Secured

All Rights Reserved Reprinted by Permission of Hal Leonard LLC 7 P

Telephone Line

Words and Music by Jeff Lynne

Copyright © 1976, 1977 EMI Blackwood Music Inc. Copyright Renewed

All Rights Administered by Sony/ATV Music Publishing LLC, 424 Church Street, Suite 1200, Nashville, TN 37219 International Copyright Secured

All Rights Reserved Reprinted by Permission of Hal Leonard LLC

THE SIGN

Words and Music by BUDDA, MALIN BERGGREN, JENNY BERGGREN and JOKER

Copyright © 1993 MEGASONG PUBLSIHING (KODA)

All Rights in the U.S. and Canada Administered by WARNER-TAMERLANE PUBLISHING CORP.

All Rights Reserved / Used By Permission of ALFRED MUSIC

The Voice

Words and Music by Justin Hayward

Copyright © 1981 NIGHTSWOOD LTD./WB MUSIC CORP.

All Rights Reserved / Used By Permission of ALFRED MUSIC

We Built This City featured in ROCK OF AGES

Words and Music by Bernie Taupin, Martin Page, Dennis Lambert and Peter Wolf

Copyright © 1985 LITTLE MOLE MUSIC, UNIVERSAL MUSIC - CAREERS, UNIVERSAL MUSIC - MGB SONGS and IMAGEM LONDON LTD.

All Rights for LITTLE MOLE MUSIC in the U.S. and Canada Controlled and Administered by UNIVERSAL MUSIC CORP.

All Rights for IMAGEM LONDON LTD. in the U.S. and Canada Controlled and Administered by UNIVERSAL MUSIC - Z TUNES LLC

All Rights Reserved Used by Permission Reprinted by Permission of Hal Leonard LLC

When It's Over

Words and Music by Paul Dean and Duke Reno

Copyright © 1981, 1982 EMI April Music (Canada) Ltd. and EMI Blackwood Music (Canada) Ltd.

All Rights Administered by Sony/ATV Music Publishing LLC, 424 Church Street, Suite 1200, Nashville, TN 37219 International Copyright Secured

All Rights Reserved Reprinted by Permission of Hal Leonard LLC

White Rabbit

Words and Music by Grace Slick

Copyright © 1966 IRVING MUSIC, INC. Copyright Renewed

All Rights Reserved Used by Permission Reprinted by Permission of Hal Leonard LLC

Signs Surround You

Acknowledgments

Thank you seems like such a small word when reflecting back on everyone who has supported me on this journey. No matter your role, big or small, I am so very grateful for the support system surrounding me!

To my parents, Chuck & Ivy: you have loved me unconditionally and I am who I am today in large part because of your love, care and nurturing. I am so blessed & lucky to have you both. I'm patting myself on the back for picking you.

Ryan and Rachel: you have both blessed me beyond anything I could have imagined. I am so proud of you both and I love the friendship that has developed between us as you have come into your own. Rachel you are such an advanced Soul for your age, and I value your wisdom and am in awe of the way you see the world. The World is a better place because of you! Ryan thank you so much for your help with this book. You worked tirelessly to get the web site just right and the front cover of this book is incredible because of you! I am beyond blessed to have had this extra time with you before you start your new life. I know you are meant to protect the World. Of all the boys in the World, how do you think I got lucky enough to get the very best one?!

To my sister Stephanie, wow what a journey! I wouldn't want any other sister but you. Thank you for your love, support, wisdom and guidance. Remember the first time you told me you saw Angels? I was 8 and you were 5. For a long time I had a hard time accepting that concept, but now I have absolutely no doubt!! Thank you Trey for being the wind beneath her wings.

Dawn, you are so much more my sister than my friend, as that word seems too small for you. I would not have survived my journey with Mark without you by my side every step of the way. Our Friday morning calls & long lunches got me through those trying times. Our love of music is such an incredible bond. I cherish our friendship more than I can ever express. I love you! Dale, thank you for being my friend and for loving Dawn the way you do!

Signs Surround You

Paul, don't ever doubt our deep Soul Mate connection. We grew in so many ways together, I am grateful for it ALL. I will always love you no matter what.

Kelly, we will always be twins separated at birth – no matter where our lives take us. You were my Jiminy Cricket and I cannot imagine my life without you in it. Thank you my beautiful friend.

Gina, you are my little sister and I am so grateful for our connection. You lived so much of this book with me day in and day out. I am so grateful for that time and how we have been able to love and support each other and grow together. I love you!

Mar, Mark once told me you were his closest Soul Mate on Earth, and knowing you as well as I do now, I can see why. Your strength astounds me. Thank you for bringing such a beautiful Soul into this World. Through this book Mark lives on forever and it would not be the amazing creation it is without your insightful editing. Thank you for spending countless hours with me on the phone and off. I treasure our connection. I love you! Lizzy, Jeff and Al thank you all! xo

Kim, you were a true friend in every sense of the word during this journey. I am sorry for the stress it caused you. You are one the the the most thoughtful and kind people I have ever met. Your friendship means the world to me and I am grateful to have you in my life. Love you!

Karen, you were behind the scenes guiding me and supporting me through my Mark journey. You are one of the most beautiful Souls I have met and I am grateful for our friendship. I love you.

Phyllis, your signs validate my signs! I'm sure our guitar guys are smiling down on us for bringing us together. Never doubt that! xoxo

Lisa, meeting you has been such a blessing! Thank you for your manuscript review and for wanting to help get this book out to help as many people as we can. I am so grateful our paths have crossed.

Raymond, you are an inspiration & true pioneer! Thank you for being a part of my journey to help reach more people.

Stacy, thank you for your support, love, council, comedy relief, & hiking adventures. You have listened tirelessly as I shared my hopes, dreams, and fears with you. You are one of the most AMAZING friends I have ever had. I love you.

Signs Surround You

Leeann you were not with me during my Mark journey but I wanted you to know how much your friendship means to me. You are a special part of my life. Thank you for your guidance and for always being willing to listen. I love you.

Mark T., thank you for your part in this story. Drive safe always.

Will, Mark said he went back for the love of William and I have no doubt you are my Twin Flame. The love that burns between us is Eternal. You are free!

To my friends who are supporting me as I launch this book: Angela; Chris Ford; Matt; Melissa; Denise; Gary & Bonnie. Your friendship means the world to me! I love you all xo!

To my KC spiritual tribe: Jami, I treasure our life-long friendship – friends forever! John thank you for loving Jami. Shannon, you are truly my spiritual Soul sister! Jami & Fred you are two of the most generous people I have ever met. You are true connectors. Nate & Steven you bring joy to everyone and everything you do. I am so blessed to have you ALL in my life, I love you guys!

About the Author

Laurie Majka is an *Inspirational Artist* – which means she receives the ideas for her artwork and writing in powerful "downloads" or fully formed ideas she "sees" in her mind. She believes these concepts are inspired from her Higher Self, Universal Consciousness, God and her Spirit Team. Laurie began receiving communications from the Other Side in 2012 when her Soul Mate Mark passed away, confirming her belief that love never dies. Now, with this book, she hopes through her story you will understand her signs in a way that lets you recognize signs from *your* loved ones. Laurie also believes her life's purpose is to send positive energy into the world. She created *Soul Heart Art* as a way to help do that by encouraging people to harness the power of their Soul. Her Daily Soul Whispers have inspired millions of people worldwide. Laurie grew up in Lawrence, Kansas and has a degree in Business Administration with a minor in Communication Studies from the University of Kansas. She built her career working for several Fortune 50 companies including Pfizer, IBM and Hewlett Packard. She has been a part of strategic teams selling multi-million dollar deals. Laurie lives in Arizona with her dog Storm. They enjoy hiking mountains and spending time connecting with nature. Laurie has two grown children, Ryan, a pilot for the United States Air Force and Rachel who is working toward becoming a Clinical Psychologist. You can connect to her YouTube channel: Laurie Majka, on her web site www.LaurieMajka.com and with her podcast Powerful Soul! She would love you to share stories of signs you have received from *your* loved ones...

More Books By Laurie Majka

More Books By Laurie Majka

Made in United States
Troutdale, OR
06/14/2024